LETTERS TO AMERICANS

KARL MARX AND FREDERICK ENGELS

Letters to Americans

1848-1895

A SELECTION

INTERNATIONAL PUBLISHERS, NEW YORK

Translated by Leonard E. Mins

CONTENTS

EDITOR'S PREFACE

THE LETTERS in this volume have been selected from the voluminous correspondence of Karl Marx and Frederick Engels with Americans. Most of the letters are to Americans of German origin, who came to play an important role in the labor and socialist movement of the United States. Covering a half century, from 1848 to 1895, the correspondence deals with many events and themes of great historic interest and with the views and activities of numerous personalities in Europe and the United States.

Marx and Engels have scarcely a peer as letter writers, either in the encyclopedic range of their interests, the sheer volume of their correspondence, or the influence they exerted through this medium. For nearly thirty years they had to rely on the mails for the continuous exchange of views between themselves, the working out of plans, and critiques of each other's literary projects. Except for visits at rare intervals, Engels was tied to his desk at his father's firm in Manchester, while Marx was working in London, in the British Museum or at home, on his analysis of capitalist society and as the inspirer and organizer of the proletarian movement all over Europe.

In their capacity as leaders of world socialism, Marx and (especially after Marx's death) Engels were in constant correspondence with the principal figures of the labor movements in France, Germany, Austria, Russia, Great Britain, Spain, Italy, and other European countries, as well as in the United States.[1]

In the mid-century, when the correspondence begins, the United States was a haven not only for European capital seeking profitable investment, but also for immigrants fleeing religious and political

[1] The correspondence between Marx and Engels, comprising 1569 letters from 1844 to 1883, when Marx died, was published in four large volumes by the Marx-Engels Verlag, Berlin, in 1929, under the title, Karl Marx und Friedrich Engels, Briefwechsel (Correspondence), as Part III of the Gesamtausgabe (Collected Works) of Marx and Engels. The volumes were prepared by the Marx-Engels, now the Marx-Engels-Lenin Institute in Moscow, which has published the Collected Works in Russian translation comprising 29 large volumes, including five volumes of correspondence of Marx and Engels with others, in addition to the four volume of letters between themselves. The collection of letters by Friedrich A. Sorge, Briefe und Auszuge aus Briefen an F.A. Sorge und Andere

persecution, and mainly seeking better economic opportunities. The stream of German, Scandinavian, Irish, English and other European immigrants provided the labor force and most often the skilled workers for nascent industry, soon to be spurred to rapid development by the Civil War. Many joined the stream of settlers from the East to the free lands toward the West. In the fifties the country was already reaching a level of capitalist development which made possible the overthrow of the slave system, the last major obstacle to the unification of the country and capture of the home market. This was followed toward the end of the century by the emergence of the United States as a great industrial power, ready to embark fully upon the imperialist stage.

The extensive and rich correspondence of Marx and Engels with their friends in the United States reflects their deep and lasting interest in the development of capitalism in the new country, which they viewed as a confirmation of their basic analysis of capitalist society. Their interest in the United States was also enlivened by the fact that the influx of political immigrants following the bourgeois-democratic revolutions of 1848 in Europe brought to the new country the ferment of socialist ideas. Earlier, the Utopian socialists—followers of Charles Fourier, Étienne Cabet, Robert Owen, and others—established short-lived model colonies of "socialism," but even more important was the influence of these ideas upon working class and progressive circles. The controversies which the founders of scientific socialism carried on with the Utopians, the "true" socialists, and the Proudhonists, and then with

(*Letters and Excerpts from Letters to F.A. Sorge and Others*), published by Dietz Verlag, Stuttgart, in 1906, contains 170 letters from Marx and Engels to others during the period 1868 to 1895, when Engels died. A volume of 185 letters to German and Austrian Socialist leaders was prepared by the Marx-Engels-Lenin Institute and published in 1933 in the Soviet Union, under the title, Karl Marx-Friedrich Engels, *Briefe an A. Bebel, W. Liebknecht, K. Kautsky und Andere, Teil I, 1870-1886* (Letters to August Bebel, Wilhelm Liebknecht, Karl Kautsky, and others, Part I, 1870-1886).

A Russian translation of 193 letters of Marx and Engels to Russians, covering the period from 1846 to 1895, was published by the Marx-Engels-Lenin Institute in Moscow in 1947, under the title, *Correspondence of Marx and Engels with Russian Political Leaders.*

A collection of 234 letters between Marx and Engels and between them and others in English translation appeared in New York and London in 1942 under the title, *The Selected Correspondence of Karl Marx and Frederick Engels, 1846-1895.* Another collection of 62 letters was published in the same cities in 1934: Karl Marx, *Letters to Dr. Kugelmann.* Sixty-one letters between Marx and Engels are included in Karl Marx and Frederick Engels, *The Civil War in the United States,* New York, 1937. Many letters are repeated in the various selections.

Michael Bakunin, Ferdinand Lassalle and their followers, as well as their later polemics against reformists and revisionists in Europe, were reflected in this country where followers of these conflicting trends were also to be found in the labor and socialist movements. The letters therefore abound in lively discussions of the various trends and ideas at conflict within working class circles in the period following the revolutions of 1848, then in the First International (1864-1876), and later in the socialist and labor parties which formed the Second International in 1889.

The chief correspondents of Marx and Engels on this side of the Atlantic played an important role in the American socialist and labor movement. From the fifties on, German-American workers were active participants in the struggle of the Negro people to free themselves from bondage, and their organizations in New York, Boston, Chicago and elsewhere were in many cases the precursors of the first nation-wide trade unions of the American workers as a whole. German-American followers of Marx organized the pioneer socialist groups and became the core of the First International in America and subsequently of the Socialist Labor Party.

Joseph Weydemeyer and Friedrich A. Sorge were the outstanding socialist leaders, the former during the fifties and sixties, and the latter in the period following the Civil War. Marx and Engels were thus in direct touch with the most active socialist forces then at work in the United States. Through these letters and in their numerous articles in the *New York Tribune,* which cover the same period as the correspondence with Weydemeyer, as well as in other publications, Marx and Engels made their influence felt during the formative period of the labor and socialist movement in the United States. In the letters to Hermann Schlüter, as well as to Florence Kelley and other non-German Americans, the direct Marxist influence was continued into the years of the great labor upsurge of the eighties and nineties. By this time also, some of the basic writings of Marx and Engels had become available to the American public.

The letters to Weydemeyer, which open the present collection, are of special interest, not only because he was a very close friend of Marx and Engels but also because he may be considered the first American Marxist leader. A Prussian artillery officer and engineer by profession, he left the military service to devote himself to the revolutionary-democratic movement of the forties in Germany. Associated with Marx and Engels from the time they first began their life-long collaboration, Weydemeyer participated actively in the German Revolution of 1848. He remained in Germany after the exile of Marx and Engels, in an attempt to reorganize the Communist League, but he was forced to flee to Switzerland in 1851. Unable to earn a living there, and with the reluctant agreement of Marx and Engels who had tried in vain to find work for him in London, Weydemeyer emigrated to America, landing in New York on November 7, 1851.

On his arrival, he received two letters from Marx written during his journey (the letters of October 16 and 31), which included suggestions for the publication in the United States of English and German editions of the *Communist Manifesto* and other writings of Marx and Engels. This was the beginning of a long trans-Atlantic collaboration, in which Weydemeyer acted as literary representative for Marx and Engels in the United States, placing their articles in various periodicals and arranging for the publication or sale of their larger works. For their part, Marx and Engels obtained the collaboration of their European associates as correspondents for the various papers in which Weydemeyer was interested. A similar relationship had been established when Weydemeyer was still in Germany and Marx and Engels in exile in England, and in the new country Weydemeyer eagerly resumed his role as an energetic promoter of the works of scientific socialism. In his short-lived journal, *Die Revolution,* which appeared in New York in 1852, he published for the first time Marx's *18th Brumaire of Louis Bonaparte,* which has since become a classic of historical writing. This important work was published in Europe only in 1869.

Weydemeyer himself soon began writing in the German-American press on current problems, and he was also active as an organizer, forming the Proletarian League in New York in 1852. From the beginning he fought against the sectarian tendency among the German-American workers and directed their attention to the organization of American labor as a whole. As co-editor in 1853 and 1854 of *Die Reform,* a New York weekly for which Engels was a London correspondent, and as a lecturer, Weydemeyer sought to develop and to encourage trade union unity between the German and native-born workers. Moving to Milwaukee in 1856, he continued these activities in the Middle West, becoming especially active in the anti-slavery struggle and participating in the first Republican campaign of that year. In his lectures and writings he called attention to the economic roots of slavery and its relationship to capitalist development. As editor of *Stimme des Volkes (People's Voice),* a daily labor paper published in Chicago, Weydemeyer helped win the support of the important German community for the nomination of Lincoln in 1860 and thus overcome the threatening split in the young Republican Party.

On the outbreak of the Civil War, Weydemeyer called upon the workers to enlist in the armed anti-slavery struggle. He was soon appointed by President Lincoln to serve as an artillery captain on the staff of General John C. Fremont, who had been named Commander-in-Chief of the Department of the West, with headquarters in St. Louis. He was promoted to lieutenant-colonel in command of a volunteer artillery regiment, and led successful warfare against Southern guerilla forces in Missouri. Mustered out at the expiration of his term in September 1863, Weydemeyer returned to public activity, supporting the Radical wing of the Republican Party and also urging unity behind Lincoln to assure victory—a position sustained by the Address of the International Workingmen's Association (First International), written by Marx, congratulating Lincoln on his re-election in 1864.[1]

On the eve of that critical election, Weydemeyer again entered the Union Army as colonel in command of the 41st Infantry Missouri Volunteers. After active service, he was mustered out as a major-general together with his regiment in July 1865. There is no record of correspondence with Marx and Engels during his first period of military service, but during the second period he received at least three letters from them. A letter from Marx enclosed the First International's Address to Lincoln, and the two letters from Engels were a detailed discussion of the military strategy of the Civil War, including the final campaign of 1865.[2]

Weydemeyer now turned his attention to the organization of the American sections of the First International. His work in Chicago, St. Louis, and Milwaukee led to the affiliation of the German-American labor bodies in these cities to the International Workingmen's Association and later to the National Labor Union as well. An indication of the high public esteem that Weydemeyer enjoyed was his election as County Auditor in St. Louis, taking office on January 1, 1866. But six months later, on August 20, at the age of 48, Weydemeyer died, a victim of the cholera epidemic of that year.[3]

After the death of Weydemeyer, Marx and Engels continued a sporadic correspondence, mostly with German-Americans active in the sections of the First International. However, the correspond-

[1] See pp. 65-66.
[2] For a detailed study of Weydemeyer's activities, see Karl Obermann, *Joseph Weydemeyer: Pioneer of American Socialism*, New York, 1947.
[3] See pp. 63, 65, and 67.

ence with Sorge, which began in 1870, continued until the death of Engels in 1895.

The son of a progressive Saxon pastor, Sorge was brought up as a radical democrat, and participated in the Revolution of 1848. Under sentence of death for his part in the military campaign against the Prussian counter-revolutionary troops in Baden, Sorge lived for a time in Switzerland and Belgium, and then came to London, intending to embark for Australia, but he was placed aboard the wrong ship and landed in New York on June 21, 1852. After trying his hand at various trades, he finally established himself as a music teacher.

Sorge's public activity in the United States began with the formation of the Communist Club in New York in 1857, the successor to the Marxist Proletarian Club organized five years before by Weydemeyer. Sorge played a leading role in the Communist Club, which made significant contributions to the fight against slavery, many of its members and followers enlisting in the Union Army. In the decade following the Civil War, this small but influential club played an important role in the upsurge of the labor movement, with which Sorge's name is closely linked. Like Weydemeyer, Sorge was aware of the sectarian dangers which beset the German workers organizations and of the Lassallean influences which simultaneously tended to divert them into reformist channels. As a result of the fight against these tendencies, Sorge and other followers of Marx became the leaders of the most important sections of the First International in the United States, which also affiliated to the National Labor Union, providing the link between the first nationwide organization of American labor and the international working class movement. It was largely as a result of Sorge's activities, and of Weydemeyer's earlier influence, that relations were established between the First International and William H. Sylvis, founder of the National Labor Union and advocate of affiliation to the I.W.A.

In the early seventies, Sorge became the leading figure in the American branch of the International. At the Hague Congress in 1872, to which he was a delegate, Sorge was elected general secretary of the I.W.A., which transferred its headquarters to New York. He held this post until 1876, when the International was dissolved. During these years, he corresponded with sections in many parts of the world, and continued these contacts for the rest of his life. In the American movement, after the organization of the Socialist Labor Party in 1877, he was active mostly as a publicist. He was also a contributor to the *Neue Zeit*, theoretical organ of the

Social-Democratic Party of Germany. His series of articles on the American labor movement in that journal, appearing in 1891-92 and written at Engels' suggestion and encouragement, still serves as a reference source for labor historians. Sorge lived for a time in Rochester, New York, and for many years in Hoboken, New Jersey, where Engels visited him during his short trip to the United States.

The correspondence of Engels with Hermann Schlüter belongs to the later period, that is, after the death of Marx. While both Weydemeyer and Sorge began their political activity during the formative period of the socialist movement in Europe, Schlüter came to this country in 1889, direct from work on the editorial board of the *Sozialdemokrat*. As the central organ of the German Social-Democratic Party during the period of Bismarck's Anti-Socialist Law, it was published abroad, first in Zurich and later in London. The correspondence between Engels and Schlüter began when the latter was still in Europe, and was continued when Schlüter became an editor of the New York *Volkszeitung*, the German daily organ of the Socialist Labor Party until 1900, and later of the Socialist Party, a post he retained until his death in 1919. The best-known book by Schlüter is his *Lincoln, Labor and Slavery*, a pioneer history of the labor movement during the Civil War era, and he was also the author of a history of the First International in America, a book on the Chartist movement (which he studied during his stay in England), and a history of the Brewery Workers' Union.

Some of the most trenchant criticism of the dogmatic and sectarian policies of the Socialist Labor Party is contained in Engels' letters to Florence Kelley. She was married to Dr. Louis Wischnewetzky, a New York physician whom she met while studying in Switzerland, where she made her first acquaintance with Marxism. Engels addressed her as "Mrs. Wischnewetzky"; after her marriage terminated in divorce, Florence Kelley resumed her maiden name, by which she was known in the socialist and labor movement. During the period of correspondence with Engels, she was a member of the Socialist Labor Party, and translated his *Condition of the Working Class in England in 1844*, arranging for its publication here in 1887. She also translated Marx's Brussels address on *Free Trade*, and supplied Engels with reports and other data on conditions of labor in the United States.

Florence Kelley became outstanding among social reformers of the late nineteenth and early twentieth centuries, especially in the campaigns for protective laws for women workers and effective child labor measures. An aggressive fighter against the sweatshop, she became the first chief factory inspector of Illinois. A member

of the Socialist Party, Florence Kelley was an energetic crusader for
labor and social legislation, always proclaiming her belief that only
socialism can guarantee full rights of labor.

Many of the letters in this volume appear for the first time in
English; others are printed here for the first time in any language.
The principal source of the present volume is the voluminous
correspondence with Sorge, and letters to others which he collected.
Shortly before his death in October 1906, Sorge turned these valuable files over to the New York Public Library, together with his
own library and his collection of labor papers. At the request of
the German Social-Democratic Party, he sent a transcript of selected letters from his collection to J.H.W. Dietz, the party's publishing house in Germany, which published them in 1906.[1] In his
introduction to this volume, dated August 1906, two months before
his death, Sorge thanks Karl Kautsky and Franz Mehring for their
advice and assistance in preparing the letters for publication.
    Comparison of the holograph letters in the Sorge collection
in the manuscript division of the New York Public Library with
the texts published in 1906 indicates a double censorship. Certain
passages were crossed out in red crayon in the manuscript, apparently by the hand of Sorge, in preparation for the transmission of
copies of the letters to the German publishing house. These deleted passages mostly refer to Sorge's own personal affairs or to
personal matters reflecting upon other Americans then still alive.
Sorge states in his preface that in making the selection from the
many hundreds of letters in his possession, he omitted those which
seemed to him unessential and unimportant.
    However, it appears that Sorge did not presume to exercise a
political censorship of the sometimes biting criticisms of German
and other European socialist leaders voiced by Marx and Engels.
The political censorship of the letters was done by the German
editors, who often failed to indicate in the published text where
such deletions had been made. Deleted passages which are pertinent
to the basic thought of Marx and Engels and to their criticisms of
the policies and tactics of various Socialist leaders have been restored in the letters included in this volume.
    A Russian translation of the *Letters to Sorge* was published in
St. Petersburg in 1907, with a preface by V.I. Lenin. Though Lenin

---

[1] *Briefe und Auszüge aus Briefen von Joh. Phil. Becker, Jos. Dietzgen, Friedrich
Engels, Karl Marx u.A. an F.A. Sorge und andere* (*Letters and Excerpts from
Letters by John Philipp Becker, Joseph Dietzgen, Frederick Engels, Karl Marx
and others to F.A. Sorge and others*), Dietz Verlag, Stuttgart, 1906.

at that time did not know of the political editing to which the
letters had been subjected, he considered this collection of such
importance in laying bare the sources of dogmatism and sectarianism in the labor movements of the United States and Britain and of
opportunism in the European Social-Democracy that his preface
turned into a full-length essay on the subject. Because of its political
as well as historical importance, Lenin's preface is printed as an
appendix in this volume.

In addition to 96 letters selected from the Sorge collection, the
present volume contains 69 letters which have since become available. Two of them, to John Swinton, exist in photostat form in the
New York Public Library, while excerpts from others were published by Franz Mehring in Vol. 25 of the *Neue Zeit* (1907). Most
of the new material in this volume, however, exists in the original
or in photostat form in the archives of the Marx-Engels-Lenin Institute in Moscow, which has graciously made them available. The
new material[1] includes the correspondence with Joseph Weydemeyer, as well as the letters to Adolph Cluss, Moncure D. Conway,
Theodore Cuno, Adolph Hepner, Isaac Hourwich, Henry Demarest Lloyd, Siegfried Meyer, Phillip Van Patten, and August Vogt.
Also included are seven additional letters to Sorge, four to Schlüter,
and three to Florence Kelley, which are not contained in *Letters to
Sorge.* Thanks to the new material, it is possible to present a more
rounded picture of the correspondence of Marx and Engels with
Americans than can be found in the Sorge volume, and also over a
longer period.

In the course of preparing these texts for publication, evidence
was found of many other letters written by Marx and Engels to
Americans which have not been located. The diaries and notebooks
of Marx and Engels indicate that many letters to Hermann Meyer,
Adolph Cluss, Karl Speyer, and others have been lost.

The numerous letters to Charles Anderson Dana, managing
editor of the *New York Tribune*[2] and later editor-in-chief of the

[1] Some of the recently uncovered letters have appeared in *Selected Correspondence of Marx and Engels,* referred to above.

[2] The *New York Tribune,* founded by Horace Greeley in 1842, was the most
influential newspaper in the United States at the time. During the early years
of the *Tribune,* Greeley was an advocate of Utopian socialism, especially of the
theories of Charles Fourier, the great French Utopian. Albert Brisbane, Fourier's
chief American disciple, popularized his theories in the *Tribune.* Brook Farm
in Massachusetts was the most famous of the two-score Fourier communities
founded during the forties in the United States. The outstanding intellectuals
of the day were associated with it, among them Ralph Waldo Emerson,
Nathaniel Hawthorne, John Greenleaf Whittier, Henry Thoreau, and Margaret
Fuller. As editor, Greeley gave the paper a pro-labor tone, himself having been

New York *Sun,* were negligently thrown away after his death in 1897. This correspondence dealt with the many articles written by Marx and Engels not only for the *Tribune,* for which Marx was European correspondent from 1851 to 1862, but also for *Putnam's Monthly,* a leading literary magazine, and for the *New American Encyclopedia,* of which Dana was an editor. The generally cordial relations which existed between Marx and Dana, although ideologically they were far apart, are indicated by a letter of March 8, 1860, from Dana to Marx, evidently written at the latter's request to be used in refutations of slanders current at the time. In his letter, Dana recalls that Marx had already written for the *Tribune* for almost nine years without a single week's interruption and refers to him as "one of the most highly valued" contributors to the paper. Dana also recalls that Marx had written some "very important articles" for the *Encyclopedia,* and adds: "In all your writings which have passed through my hands, you have always manifested the most cordial interest in the welfare and progress of the laboring classes; and . . . you have written much with direct reference to that end." Since, as this letter also reveals, Dana often differed with Marx on his interpretation of events, the correspondence between the two would have been of unusual interest.

As far as is known, every available letter that was addressed to an American by Marx and Engels has been scrutinized and considered for inclusion in this volume. However, this is not a definitive edition. Letters and portions of letters have been selected with a view to presenting a large cross-section of the vital, rich and extensive correspondence with Americans which, if published in full, would have filled a volume double the present size.

the first president of the Typographical Union of New York (now known as the "Big Six"). The *Tribune* also became one of the outstanding Abolitionist organs of the decade preceding the Civil War.

Dana, who was particularly interested in European affairs, first met Marx in Cologne during the Revolution of 1848. Considering him its outstanding leader, Dana asked Marx in 1851 to write a series of articles on the revolution in Germany. These were written by Engels at the request of Marx, who was busy at the time with his initial economic studies, culminating in his *Critique of Political Economy,* which was published in 1859. Marx also felt that he had not as yet attained fluency in English. Thus began the period of Marx's contributions to the *Tribune.* Though Marx wrote most of the articles during his decade of association with the newspaper, he frequently called upon Engels for aid in connection with articles dealing with military matters, in which he considered his great friend his superior. This was an example of the creative collaboration of the two men of genius which remained unbroken during the span of forty years.

In a correspondence of this scope carried on simultaneously with many individuals repetition is inevitable, and in making the present selection this has been avoided wherever possible. For the most part, the deletions and omissions deal with personal affairs, obscure personalities of the immigration, numerous requests for data and acknowledgment of their arrival, and arrangements for publication and distribution of periodicals and of the writings of Marx, Engels, and their associates. Omissions in letters are indicated in the usual manner.

In some cases, letters written by Marx and Engels to correspondents before their emigration to the United States have been included, notably to Weydemeyer and Schlüter, to indicate the nature of their continuing relationship over many years in Europe and in this country. Four letters from Mrs. Marx have also been included, since they were written at the request of Marx and are of intrinsic value. Written by Marx, the Addresses of the First International in this volume are correspondence in the broader sense, since they were directed to the American people or to American labor as a whole.

The letters are arranged chronologically, and most of them are translated from the original German. When writing to non-German Americans, Marx and Engels usually wrote in English, as in their correspondence with Moncure D. Conway, Isaac Hourwich, Florence Kelley, Henry Demarest Lloyd, John Swinton, and Phillip Van Patten. Foreign words and phrases, which abound in the prose style of both Marx and Engels, have been given in the original and translated into English [in brackets]. Footnotes are by the translator, Leonard E. Mins, who also drew upon the notes appearing in the Sorge volume to annotate the text and for the biographical index.

In addition to Lenin's preface, the Appendices include "American Travel Notes," an unfinished fragment by Engels which supplements his impressions as given in his correspondence about his short visit to the United States, and also Engels' article on "The Labor Movement in America," which summarizes for the American reader the same views which he expressed in numerous letters to his friends in the United States.

ALEXANDER TRACHTENBERG

January 1953.

LETTERS TO AMERICANS

MRS. MARX TO WEYDEMEYER

Paris, Thursday [March 17, 1848]

Dear Mr. Weydemeyer:

My husband is again so busy in this gigantic city, with a host of things to do, that he commissioned me to request you to publish the following notice in the *Westphälisches Dampfboot:* Several German societies have been formed here (Mr. Lüning has been informed of them in detail), but the *German* Workers Club, headed by the London Germans—Schapper, Bauer, Moll—and by the Germans from Brussels—Marx, Wolff, Engels, Wallau, and Born (also directly connected with the British Chartists through Harney and Jones) —have nothing in common with the German Democratic Society headed by Börnstein, Bornstedt, Herwegh, Volk, Decker, etc.—a society that has raised the black-red-and-gold banner (in this respect, moreover, the Federal Diet anticipated it), that talks about "Father Blücher," and that engages in military drill by section under the command of retired Prussian officers. It is absolutely necessary to repudiate this society before the public opinion of *France* and Germany, because it is a disgrace to the Germans. If the *Dampfboot* isn't appearing soon, place a brief article based on these facts in some German newspaper, with which you down in the South have closer contacts. Try to have this circulated as widely as possible in the German press.

I should like to write you much more about the interesting movement under way here, which is growing from minute to minute (400,000 workers marched past the City Hall tonight). The masses of demonstrators are growing and growing. But I am so overburdened with housework and caring for my three little ones that all I have left is time to send you and your dear wife cordial greetings from afar.

Salut et fraternité
Citoyenne et Vagabonde
Jenny Marx

MARX TO WEYDEMEYER

[Paris, *ca.* August 1, 1849]

Dear Weydemeyer:

. . . Now tell me how, in your opinion, pamphlets can be issued.

I should like to begin with the brochure on *wage labor,* the beginning of which was printed in the *Neue Rheinische Zeitung.* I would write a short political preface for this brochure on the present state of affairs. Do you think that Leske, for instance, would agree to this? But in any event he would have to pay, and pay well, immediately upon receipt of the manuscript, for I know that this pamphlet would sell and that even now there are very many who are ready to order it in advance. My present finances do not allow me to settle my past accounts with Leske.

If Leske finds that the booklet sells well, we can continue to operate in this fashion.

I received a letter from Engels yesterday. He is in Switzerland and participated in four battles as Willich's adjutant.

The sword of Damocles is still hanging over my head. My deportation has been neither revoked nor carried out.

No matter how grievous our personal situation and the general state of affairs, I still count myself among the contented. Matters are going very well, and the Waterloo suffered by official democracy must be looked upon as a victory. The governments by the grace of God are taking upon themselves the task of wreaking our vengeance upon the bourgeoisie and punishing it.

During the next few days I may send you a little article on the situation in England for your newspaper. At the moment I am sick and tired of this subject, since I have already dealt with it at length in various private letters.

Write me *directly* at *my* address: Rue de Lille, Monsieur Ramboz.

Regards to you and your wife from my wife and me. My wife doesn't feel too well—the natural result of her "interesting condition." Good-bye, dear friend, and write soon.

Yours,

K. M.

ENGELS TO WEYDEMEYER

Lausanne, August 25, 1849

Dear Weydemeyer:

After so many incidents, after so many delays in Hesse and the Palatinate, after three weeks of idling in Kaiserslautern, after a month of glorious campaigning, during which for the sake of diversity I strapped on a saber and became Willich's adjutant, after a month of tedious billeting in a camp in the canton of Vaud together with a detachment of refugees, I have at last managed to get here, to Lausanne, and am standing on my own feet. First of all, I am going to sit down and write the gay story of the whole comical Palatine-Baden venture. But as I have no contacts in Germany anymore and do not know which cities are under martial law and which are not, I don't know what publisher to turn to. I don't know any of them. On the spot, you have a clearer picture of what publishers would be inclined to begin negotiations for publishing such a history, which is completely harmless, of course, and involves no danger of confiscation or a lawsuit. It may be that a publisher of that sort can be found in Frankfurt. But he must have money. Be so good as to write me about this as soon as you can, so that I can take the necessary steps at once.[1] . . .

Sincere regards to your wife and all our friends from

Your

Engels

MARX TO WEYDEMEYER

London, December 19, 1849

Dear Weydemeyer:

. . . Here in England an extremely important movement is developing at the present time. On the one hand, we have the agitation carried on by the protectionists, based on the fanaticism of the rural population — the results of free trade in corn are beginning to be felt exactly as I predicted several years ago. On the other hand, the free-traders are drawing further political and economic conclusions from their system, playing the part of financial and parliamentary reformers in domestic politics, and acting as the party of peace—in foreign affairs. And, lastly, there are the Chartists, who are working together with the bourgeoisie against the aristocracy, but at the same time have resumed their own party movement against the bourgeoisie, with increased energy. If, as I hope—and this hope of mine is not without solid foundations—the Tories replace the Whigs in the Cabinet, the conflict between these two

---

[1] Engels later wrote this story as part of his *Die deutsche Reichverfassungskampagne* ["The Campaign for a Constitution for the German Reich"], published in the first three numbers of Marx's *Neue Rheinische Zeitung—Politisch-ökonomische Revue* in 1850.

parties will assume tremendous proportions, and the outward form of agitation will become stormier and more revolutionary. Another event, not yet noticed on the Continent, is the approach of a tremendous industrial, agricultural, and commercial crisis. If the Continent postpones its revolution until the crisis breaks out, England may turn out to be from the very start, even against its will, an ally of the revolutionary Continent. A premature outbreak of the revolution—provided it is not provoked directly by Russian intervention—would be, in my opinion, a misfortune, for at the present time, when trade is expanding more and more in France, Germany, etc., the laboring masses, as well as all the small shopkeepers, may be in a revolutionary mood in words, but not, of course, *en realité*.

You know that my wife has presented the world with a new citizen. She asks me to send you and your wife her warmest regards. Give your wife my cordial regards too. Write soon.

Yours,

K. Marx

ENGELS TO WEYDEMEYER

London, April 25, 1850

Dear Weydemeyer:

Your letter to Marx, together with £5 for the refugee fund and a note for me, arrived today. And you, in the meanwhile, most likely have received two letters with statements and appeals on behalf of the refugee committee. Print them as soon as possible, and do everything you can in your area to collect money for the emigrés. You will learn the rest from the enclosed letter to D[ronke]. Perhaps something can be collected in Franconia, in Nürnberg, Baireuth, etc. The *Neue Rheinische Zeitung* used to sell fairly well there. If you know of anyone to write to in Munich, let us know, too. You understand that now, when that jackass Struve and his partners are trying to get into the newspapers on the eve of the revolution, utilizing the refugees for this purpose, it is a matter of honor for us to continue to support at least our emigrés, thus keeping the best among the new arrivals from falling into the hands of these jackasses.

We thought that both of the subsequent issues of the *Revue*[1] had reached you: the second number five weeks ago, and the third,

[1] *Neue Rheinische Zeitung—Politisch-ökonomische Revue*, a monthly edited by Karl Marx and published in Hamburg from January to April, 1850.

a few days ago. It turns out that the jackass Naut didn't send them to you! We wrote him a sharp letter today, demanding that he send them to you at once. The third number will probably be in his hands within a week. Don't criticize until you get the third number, in which the first series of articles is concluded.

Good-bye,

Your
F. E.

We have just learned that the blackguards Struve, Tellering, Schramm, Bauer (of Stolp), and others are spreading the rumor in several German newspapers that our committee is allegedly eating up the refugee funds itself. This slander is also being repeated in private letters. You can't have read of this anywhere, for otherwise you would have taken a stand in our defense long ago. You know that all of us have laid out money for the revolution and that it hasn't brought us a single cent. Even the *Neue Preussische Zeitung* and other papers never dared to accuse us of such things. Only the rascally democrats, the impotent "great men" of the middle classes, were despicable enough to spread such infamous libels. Our committee has already issued three reports, and each time we have asked our contributors to appoint authorized representatives to audit our books and receipts. Has any other committee done that? We have a receipt for every cent. *Not a single* member of the committee has ever gotten a cent of the moneys received, nor has he ever asked for any, no matter how difficult a situation he might have been in. Not one of our closest friends has ever received more than any other emigré, and no one possessing any source of funds at all has ever gotten a sou.

If D[ronke] has already left, open the letter, read it, and forward it to him.

MARX TO WEYDEMEYER

London, July 27 [1850]

Dear Weydemeyer:

Send Naut money. The man is an honest jackass. I'll explain the whole thing to you some other time. You mustn't take offense at my wife's excited letters. She is nursing, and our situation here is so extremely miserable that the breaking of one's patience is pardonable. . . .

This is a day of great significance. It is possible that the Cabinet will fall today. Then a real revolutionary movement will commence here. It is quite likely that we ourselves will be the first victims of

the Tories. I dare say we have been marked out for deportation for
a long time now.

Yours,

K. Marx

ENGELS TO WEYDEMEYER

Manchester, June 19, 1851

Dear Hans:

Marx has just forwarded your letter, from which I at last learned
your precise address. I have been looking for it long enough, as I
want to ask you about the following:

Since I arrived in Manchester I have begun to bone up on military
affairs, on which I have found fairly good material here—for a beginning at any rate. The enormous importance that the *partie militaire*
[military aspect] will have in the next movement, an old inclination
of mine, my articles on the Hungarian War in the [*Neue Rheinische*]
Zeitung, and finally my glorious adventures in Baden have all
impelled me to this study, and I want to work in this field at least
enough to be able to express a theoretical opinion without disgracing myself too much.

The material available here—dealing with the Napoleonic and,
to some extent, with the Revolutionary campaigns—presupposes
the knowledge of a mass of detail, which I do not know at all or
know only very superficially, and about which one can obtain only
very superficial information, laboriously unearthed, or no information at all. Self-instruction is always nonsense, and unless one
follows up a thing systematically, one won't achieve anything worthwhile. You will get a better idea of what I really need if I remind
you that—aside from my promotion [to adjutant] in Baden—I never
got any further than a Royal Prussian Landwehr bombardier; thus,
to understand the campaigns I lack the intermediate schooling,
which is provided in Prussia by the examination for promotion to
lieutenant, in the various branches of the service.

What I mean are not the details of military drill, which are of
no use to me at all, as I am finally convinced by now that my
blindness[1] makes me unfit for active service. What I need is a
general survey of the elementary knowledge required in the various
branches of the service, with as much detail as is required for an
understanding and a correct evaluation of historical facts of a
military nature. Thus, for example: elementary tactics; theory of
fortifications, more or less historically, covering the various systems

---

[1] See pp. 201 fn., 262, *passim.*

from Vauban down to the modern system of *forts détachés* [detached forts], together with a study of field fortifications and other matters within the province of the engineers, such as the various types of bridges, etc.; as well as a general history of military science and the changes produced by the evolution and perfection of arms and of the methods of using them. Then something thorough on artillery, as I've forgotten a lot and many things I don't know at all, as well as other requirements that don't come to mind at the moment, but that you most certainly know.

Please give me the sources for all these elementary questions, and do so in such a way that I can procure the books at once. What I would like to have are works from which I could learn the contemporary general status of the various branches, on the one hand, and the existing differences between the various modern armies on the other. For example, differences in the design of field-gun carriages, etc., the varying tables of organization of divisions, army corps, etc. I should particulary like to study all the details of the organization of armies, the supply system for hospitals, and the matériel required for any army.

This will give you a general idea of what I need and what books you should recommend. I suspect that in handbooks of this sort German military literature has more serviceable works than the French or the English. It is a matter of course that I am interested in knowing practical matters, what actually exists, not the systems or hobbyhorses of unrecognized geniuses. As far as artillery is concerned, Bem's handbook is probably best.

Whatever I find here by way of books on the history of war in modern times—I am more or less uninterested in the military history of previous eras, and for that I have the old Montecucculi—is in French or English, of course. Outstanding among the latter is the history of the Peninsular War by Lieutenant General William Napier—by far the best military-historical writing I have read up to this time. If you don't know it and can get it over there, it is worth reading (*History of the War in the Peninsula and the South of France*, six volumes). I have no German books at all, but I must get some—the first to come to mind are Willisen and Clausewitz. What about them, which one is worth the trouble and which is not? Theoretically as well as historically? As soon as I have made some more progress, I shall study the campaigns of 1848-1849 thoroughly, especially the Italian and the Hungarian campaigns. Do you perhaps know of a more or less official, or at least fairly objective, report on the Baden affair as seen from the Prussian side?

Furthermore, I should like to have you recommend good special
maps of Germany, not too expensive, but good enough for the
study of the campaigns subsequent to 1792 (especially Württemberg,
Bavaria, Austria for 1801-1809, Saxony, Thuringia, Prussia for
1806-1807 and 1813, Northeastern France for 1814, Lombardy,
Hungary, Schleswig-Holstein, and Belgium). I have the big Stieler
atlas, but it is wholly inadequate. I have the plans of the battles
during the period from 1792 to 1814; they are included in the atlas
furnished with Alison's history of Europe from the time of the
French Revolution, but I have discovered that many of these battle
maps are incorrect. Isn't there a similar collection of maps available
in Germany, not too dear, but reliable?

Do you know Monsieur Jomini, about whom the French make
such a fuss? I know of him only through M. Thiers, who has
plagiarized him unscrupulously, as everyone knows. This little
Thiers is one of the most barefaced liars in existence—not in a single
battle are the figures he gives correct. But since M. Jomini later
went over to the Russians, it might be thought that he had reasons
for reducing the *exploits de la bravoure française* [exploits of French
valor] to less superhuman dimensions than M. Thiers, in whose
book one Frenchman always beats two enemies. . . .

F. E.

Address: Ermen and Engels, Manchester.

MARX TO WEYDEMEYER

[London] June 27, 1851

Dear Hans:

. . . If it is dangerous for you to remain in Germany, you ought
to come here. If you can live in Germany quietly, however, it is
better to stay there, of course. For manpower is needed there more
than here.

Yours,

K. M.

. . . England's foreign trade is at least one-third of its total
trade — even more after the abolition of the Corn Laws. But Herr
Christ's whole argument isn't worth anything.[1]

[1] A. Christ was the author of a pamphlet, *Ueber den gegenwärtigen Stand der
Frage der Schützzölle* [*On the Present Status of the Problem of Protective Tariffs*],
published in 1851; Weydemeyer wrote a pamphlet attacking Christ's position,
entitled *Ueber die Stellung des Proletariats zu den jetzigen Bewegungen der
Bourgeoisie* [*On the Attitude of the Proletariat to the Present Movements of the
Bourgeoisie*].

Even Pinto pointed out that if ten-tenths were required for certain objects, the last tenth was just as important as the previous nine-tenths. Even if we assume that England's foreign trade is only one-quarter (which isn't true), it is beyond doubt that without it the other three-quarters could not exist; so much the more so the four quarters which make up the digit 1.

The democrats have long been accustomed not to let an opportunity pass without compromising themselves, making laughing-stocks of themselves, and paying for it dearly. . . .

It might be well for this period of quiet to last a few years more; all this 1848 democracy must be given time to rot away. No matter how untalented our governments, they are still shining lights compared to these dozen vainglorious jackasses. Adieu!

I am usually at the British Museum from 9 o'clock in the morning to 7 o'clock at night. The material I am working on has so damned many ramifications that I won't be able to finish it for another six to eight weeks, in spite of all my efforts. Then there are always the practical interruptions, unavoidable in the miserable conditions under which one vegetates here. But despite it all the job is rapidly approaching completion. One must break off somewhere or other by main force. The democratic simpletons, to whom enlightenment comes "from above," naturally don't require such exertions. Why should they, these Sunday's children, trouble themselves with economic and historical material! . . .

MARX TO WEYDEMEYER

[London] August 2, 1851

Dear Weydemeyer:

I have just received your letter from Engels and hasten to reply. I should, of course, have very much liked to see you and talk with you before your departure—since it was impossible to keep you here.

But once you are going to America, you can't be doing so at a more opportune moment, both to find a means of existence over there as well as to be useful to our party.

For it is as good as certain that you will get a job as editor with the *New-Yorker Staatszeitung*. It was previously offered to Lupus [nickname of Wilhelm Wolff]. He is enclosing a letter to Reichhelm, who is one of the owners of the paper. That much for practical matters. But you mustn't lose any time.

Now, another point. Herr Heinzen, together with the worthy Ruge, is blowing his trumpet in the *New-Yorker Schnellpost* every week against the Communists, particularly against me, Engels, etc. All the democratic riffraff over here use this paper as a pit to dump their garbage, from which, to be sure, there grows neither fruit, nor seed, but a luxuriant crop of thistles. And, finally, Heinzen hates the *Staatszeitung,* and the latter is no match for even such an adversary.

Whatever the American politics of the *Staatszeitung,* in European politics you will have *la voix libre* [free speech]. Over there, Heinzen is strutting about everywhere as a great writer. The American press will be glad to have some one come over to rap this clumsy loud-mouth.

If you become an editor we shall give you all the support we can for your department. Unfortunately, the London correspondent of the *Staatszeitung* is the rogue and jackass Seiler. It is also necessary to shut up the member of the European government, Ruge.

Your article, aimed at Christ, is good. There is nothing I'd want to change in it; I observe merely that in factory regions workers actually marry in order to squeeze *money* out of their children. This is deplorable, but it is a fact.

You can imagine that my circumstances are distressing indeed. It will be the end of my wife if it goes on like this for long. The never-ending worries, the pettiest everyday struggle, are wearing her out. And then the infamies of my opponents, who have *never* even attempted to attack me objectively and try to take revenge for their impotence by impugning my reputation and spreading the most unspeakable infamies about me. Willich, Schapper, Ruge, and a number of other democratic rascals have specialized in this. Some one need only arrive from the Continent for them to start working on him at once, so that he in turn may get busy in this campaign.

A few days ago the "illustrious" young barrister Schramm met an acquaintance on the street and immediately began to whisper in his ear, "No matter where the revolution may lead, everybody agrees that Marx is *perdu* [through]. Rodbertus, who has the greatest prospect of success, will have him shot at once." And that's how they all behave. I, of course, would laugh at all this filth; I don't let that sort of thing disturb me in my work for a moment; but you can understand that my wife, who is ill and is involved in the most dismal bourgeois poverty from morning to night and whose nervous system is upset, is not helped by the fact that every day stupid go-betweens bring her the pestiferous vapors of the democratic cess-pools. The tactlessness of some people in this respect is often amazing.

Moreover, this is not a matter of parties. The great men, despite their *pretended* differences of opinion, are busy here doing nothing but confirming their own importance to one another. No revolution has ever brought to the surface such riffraff. When you are in New York, go to A. Dana [Charles Anderson Dana] of the *New York Tribune* and give him my regards and regards from Freiligrath. Perhaps he may be of some use to you. Write me as soon as you arrive, but always at Engels' address, since he can best bear the postal fees. . . . If you can stay in New York, you are not far from Europe, and with the total suppression of the press in Germany, it is only from over there that a battle can be waged in the press.

Yours,

K. Marx

ENGELS TO WEYDEMEYER

Manchester, August 7, 1851

Dear Weydemeyer:

Many thanks for your communication. I would be greatly obliged if you could send me more information from Hofstetter's book. But I thought you might have remembered the titles of some manuals and various military textbooks; what I particularly need are the simplest and most ordinary material: what is required for the ensign's and lieutenant's examinations and, for that very reason, is everywhere taken for granted. I obtained the book by Decker while I was in Switzerland, in a poor French translation and without maps, but Marx mislaid it and I doubt he will be able to find it. I shall get an atlas myself, but I still need a map of Hungary. I know that the Austrian General Staff issued some works on this subject. Let me know whether your map is good enough for this and how much it costs. At worst, it is probably better than Stieler's big atlas. As for Baden, especially the Baden-Swiss Rhine frontier, I kept good enough maps of that area from the time of our campaign. I shall find out the prices from Weerth, who is now living in Hamburg again, and shall then decide on what to buy. But, I repeat, I shall be very glad to have you get me some more material.

That you are going to America is bad, but I really don't know what other advice to give you if you can't find anything in Switzerland. There's nothing much doing in London, and Lupus still hasn't found a thing to do. He is looking for a job, and I am trying to get him one here, but without success up to now. The competition in the musical field over here is enormous. *Après tout* [after all], New York doesn't seem to be very far away from England and, especially, from here, when one sees the steamers regularly making the crossing from Wednesday of one week to Saturday of the next, and they hardly ever take the full ten days. In New York you will meet the little Red Becker. Up to recently he was in the mail department of the *Arbeiter Zeitung,* but I don't know whether he's still there, since I haven't heard from him for a long time. His last address was 24 North William Street, upstairs; if you don't know his present address, you can most likely get it from Lièvre, Shakespeare Hotel, or at the *Staatszeitung.* Moreover, there's a lot to be done in New York, and a regular representative of our party, who also has theoretical education, is needed there badly. You will find elements enough. Your greatest handicap, however, will be the fact that the useful Germans who are worth anything are easily Americanized and abandon all hope of returning home; and then there are the special American conditions: the ease with which the surplus population is drained off to the farms, the necessarily rapid and rapidly growing prosperity of the country, which makes bourgeois conditions look like a *beau idéal* to them, and so forth. The Germans over there who think of going back are mostly worthless fellows, revolution-exploiters *à la* Metternich and Heinzen; the less important they are, the more contemptible they are. Besides, you will find the whole patriotic Reich mob in New York; I have no doubt that you will be able to establish yourself there. Outside of New York the only endurable place is St. Louis; Philadelphia and Boston are terrible provincial holes. It would be splendid if you could manage to establish a newspaper of your own; otherwise try to get a job with the *New-Yorker Staatszeitung,* which is very well disposed toward us — its European correspondence has always been under our control.

It is best to send correspondence from over there through me; I then let the firm pay for the postage. . . .

In any event, write me once again before your departure. Let me know the name of the ship on which you are sailing, for then I shall be able to see by the local paper when it arrives in New York. From New York send me your address at once. Marx's address is 28, Dean Street, Soho Square, London.

Best regards,

Yours,

F. E.

MARX TO WEYDEMEYER

[London] September 11 [1851]

Dear Weydemeyer:

. . . Signor Mazzini has also had to learn that this is the time of the dissolution of "democratic" provisional governments. The minority has resigned from the Italian committee after violent battles. They are supposed to be the more advanced ones.

I consider Mazzini's policy fundamentally wrong. By inciting Italy to a breach now he is working entirely in the interest of Austria. On the other hand, he fails to appeal to that part of Italy that has been oppressed for centuries, the peasants, and thus prepares new resources for the counter-revolution. M. Mazzini knows only the cities with their liberal aristocracy and their *citoyens éclairés* [enlightened citizens]. The material needs of the Italian rural population—as impoverished and systematically enfeebled and besotted as the Irish—are, of course, too low for the heaven-in-words of his cosmopolitan-neo-Catholic-ideological manifestos. But it would have required courage, to be sure, to tell the bourgeoisie and the aristocracy that the first step toward the independence of Italy is the complete emancipation of the peasants and the transformation of their sharecropping system into free bourgeois property. Mazzini seems to think that a loan of ten million francs is more revolutionary than winning over ten million human beings. I am very much afraid that if worse comes to the worst the Austrian government will change the system of land ownership *itself* and reform it in the "Galician" manner. . . .[1]

Yours,

K. Marx

MARX TO WEYDEMEYER

London, October 16, 1851

Dear Weydemeyer:

I wrote to A. Charles Dana [Charles Anderson Dana], one of the editors of the *New York Tribune,* and also enclosed a letter from Freiligrath, in which he recommends you. Hence, all you have to do is to go to him and mention our names.

---

[1] After the annexation of Galicia, the Austrian government abrogated many of the feudal privileges of the Galician aristocracy in order to play off the peasants against the rebellious aristocrats in a demagogic fashion, thus creating a social basis for the exploitation of this province, which was still dominated by the big landowners. Austria had introduced a system of the bitterest national oppression in Northern Italy.

You ask me about a statistical handbook. I recommend *The Commercial Dictionary* by MacCulloch, 1845, since it provides economic information as well. There are also more recent works, such as the books by MacGregor, whose statistical handbooks are, I dare say, the best in all of Europe. But they are very expensive. You will doubtless find them in one of the New York libraries. MacCulloch, on the other hand, is the kind of manual that anyone writing for the newspapers must own. For England, in particular, I can also recommend: Porter, *The Progress of the Nation*, new edition, 1851.

For the history of trade in general: Tooke, *History of Prices*, 3 vols., covering up to 1848. For North America I especially recommend MacGregor, who has written a special statistical work on the United States. For Germany: Freiherr von Reden, *Vergleichende Kulturstatistiken*. For France: Moreau.

I have one more commission for you. At the request of an ex-German Catholic priest, Koch (whom you can locate at the *Staatszeitung*, for which he writes from time to time), I sent him 20 copies of the *Manifesto* [*Communist Manifesto*] (in German) and one copy of the English translation, authorizing him to publish it as a pamphlet with a preface by Harney, attached to the English translation. After this I didn't hear a thing from Koch. First, ask him to explain this extremely suspicious silence after sending me so detailed a letter; second, take from him the English translation and see whether it cannot be issued as a pamphlet—in other words, printed, distributed, and sold. It stands to reason that the profits, if any, belong to you; all I want is 20-50 copies for my own use. . . .

Write soon. Regards from my wife, from me, and from all your friends to you and your wife.

I trust you have taken the ocean voyage well and that your affairs in the United States will prosper.

Yours,
K. M.

MARX TO WEYDEMEYER

London, October 31, 1851

Dear Weydemeyer:

I am sending you my second letter to America. After mature deliberation of this matter with Lupus, I decided that we might arrange one transaction together.

First: The old *Neue Rheinische Zeitung* was not widely circulated in America. If you could get hold of some bourgeois or manage to obtain the necessary credit from the owner of a printshop and a paper dealer, it would be profitable to publish a sort of pocket library of articles from the *Neue Rheinische Zeitung* — little booklets, like those that Becker published in Cologne. For instance, W. Wolff's "The Silesian Billion"; Engels' "Hungary"; my "Prussian Bourgeoisie"; some of Weerth's feuilletons, etc. If you can't find them over there, I shall send you the articles, choosing those that are most suitable; you will have to write a brief general foreword to this *Pocket Library of the "Neue Rheinische Zeitung,"* as well as footnotes or postscripts to the individual booklets, wherever you feel they are necessary.

Second: You could publish Engels' and my articles against K. Heinzen that appeared in the *Deutsche Brüsseler Zeitung* in the same format and with explanatory notes. I think they would sell very well.

We would share the profits remaining after the costs of production have been covered.

Third: I have received a number of inquiries and orders from America concerning the six published numbers of my *Revue*,[1] but I have not entered into any arrangements, as I do not trust the rogues over there. You might publish an announcement that they can be obtained from you, but you must have a fair number of orders before they are shipped out from here.

Fourth: The little library I spoke of above might include timely pamphlets written by you as well as by us when the occasion calls. From the commercial standpoint it is safer and more convenient, of course, to begin with material that is ready and at hand. You could wage the necessary polemics, against the Right or the Left, in your little prefaces and postscripts.

And so I suggest that you become a book publisher. Less money is needed for this than for a newspaper, while you would be accomplishing the same ends. You will be spared the long, time-killing preparatory work involved in getting out a newspaper. I think that if you outline this plan in the proper way to Reich, who has money, he will agree to go into this business with you.

My family, as well as Freiligrath, Lupus, and the rest, send your family our best regards.

Yours,

K. Marx

---

[1] *Neue Rheinische Zeitung—Politisch-ökonomische Revue.*

MARX TO WEYDEMEYER

[London] December 19, 1851

Dear Weydemeyer:

I, that is Engels, received your letter the day before yesterday. First of all, my best New Year's wishes for you and your wife. My wife also sends you hers.

I am now at my desk, working on an article for you. Your request came too late, and that is why I was unable to comply with it that very day. On Tuesday (*December 23*) you will be sent: (1) "The Eighteenth Brumaire of Louis Bonaparte," by K. Marx; (2) "The Coup d'Etat in France," by F. Wolff; and (3) "Nemesis," by Wilhelm Wolff. *Engels* will send you his article — about Prussia, I think — by today's mail, perhaps. *Freiligrath* has nothing ready yet, but he authorizes you to use his name as one of your contributors.

Negotiations are going on with *Weerth*, as well as with *Eccarius*. You are now established in the United States for a year at least. "It" [the revolution] won't start on May 2, 1852.

I think you should wait with your first number[1] until the articles listed above arrive. The difference is only five days anyhow. For the forthcoming numbers you can announce the serial publication in article form of a work of mine: "*Neueste Offenbarungen des Sozialismus, oder Idée générale de la Révolution au XIX siècle par P. J. Proudhon. [Latest Revelations of Socialism, or the General Notion of Revolution in the Nineteenth Century, by P. J. Proudhon.]* Critique by K. M." . . .

Tout à toi [At your service]

K. Marx

If you are not already bound by contract, don't buy the *Arbeiter-republik* [*Workers' Republic*] from the wretched Weitling. You will gain about 200 *Straubinger* [apprentices], but you will lose the great reading public. Always appear under the old name. *Règle générale* [general rule].

MARX TO WEYDEMEYER

[London] January 1, 1852

Dear Weywey:

Happy New Year! Best wishes to your wife from my wife and me. It is only today that I am able to send you the article, as I was

[1] Of *Die Revolution,* a weekly published briefly by Weydemeyer in New York in 1852.

interrupted not only by the tempestuous events of the time, but even more so by private affairs. From now on—regularity.

Lupus[1] is seriously ill and therefore hasn't been able to send you a thing as yet. I considered the article by Red Wolff to be unsuitable and therefore did not send it off.

In case—*let's hope it won't be the case*—you have to put off your venture for a time owing to financial circumstances, give the article to Dana, so that he can have it translated into English for his paper. I hope, however, that this won't be necessary.

Give Dana my regards. Tell him that I received his paper and his letter and shall send him a new article next week. As for the numbers of the *Revue,* please write me how big a market, roughly, you, think I can count on in America. I do not have them here; I should have to get them from Hamburg, and this involves well-known difficulties of a financial nature.

I shall send you *Notes to the People* by our friend Ernest Jones, the most influential leader of the British party. They will be a veritable treasure for you, since they can be used as fillers for your paper. Send me at once and keep on sending me in the future a few copies of your weekly.

Salut et fraternité   Yours,

K. Marx

Yesterday I hammered away at Freiligrath, and he promised me that he would cook up a poem for you on the latest events.

MRS. MARX TO WEYDEMEYER

[London, *ca.* January 10, 1852]

Dear Mr. Wedemeyer:

My husband has been very sick all week, in bed most of the time. . . .

Karl is too weak now to write you, which is why he asks me to tell you that you ought to write in your newspaper about our poor friends in Cologne, especially since Kinkel's party, together with the court-writers and mongrels of the *Lithographische Korrespondenz,* is deliberately keeping completely silent about all their suffering and their very existence. This is all the more despicable inasmuch as Kinkel owes his popularity mainly to Becker and Bürgers, and the paper they published at the time.[2] And here these men are languishing in jail, being treated abominably, and now they'll have

---

[1] Nickname for Wilhelm Wolff, to whom Vol. I of *Capital* is dedicated.
[2] The *Westdeutsche Zeitung.*

to serve an extra three months, while the "great men of the future" are coining thousands in the name of the new revolution, and are already dividing up their future governmental posts.

How does your dear wife feel after her terrible journey? How are your children getting on? Have you all gotten acclimatized, if only a bit?

Best regards,

Cordially yours,
Jenny Marx

Lupus is feeling better again. He too is sending something along soon, as is Engels. An urgent request has also been sent to Weerth. Red Wolff has married, and since he is now on his honeymoon, he can't send you anything for the time being.

MARX TO WEYDEMEYER

London, January 16, 1852

Dear Weydemeyer:

Today I got out of bed for the first time in two weeks. From this you realize that my indisposition, which isn't entirely over even now, was a serious one. That is why, with the best intentions, I wasn't able to send you the third installment of my article on Bonaparte this week.

On the other hand, I am enclosing a poem and a private letter by Freiligrath. Now I ask you to: (1) Have the poem printed carefully; the stanzas separated at adequate intervals, and the whole thing printed without an eye to saving space. Poetry loses much when the verses are printed all crowded together. (2) Write a friendly letter to Freiligrath. Don't be afraid to compliment him, for all poets, even the best of them, are *plus ou moins des courtisanes, et il faut les cajoler, pour les faire chanter* [courtisans, more or less, and they have to be cajoled to make them sing]. Our F[reiligrath] is the kindest, must unassuming man in private life, who conceals *un esprit tres fin et tres railleur* [a very subtle and mocking spirit] underneath his genuine simplicity, and whose pathos is "genuine" without making him "uncritical" and "superstitious." He is a real revolutionary and an honest man through and through — praise that I would not mete out to many. Nevertheless, a poet — no matter what he may be as a man—requires applause, admiration. I think it lies in the very nature of the species. I am telling you all this merely to call your attention to the fact that in your correspondence with Freiligrath you must not forget the difference between a "poet" and a "critic." Moreover, it is very nice of him to address his poetic letter directly to you. I think this will give you something by way of contrast in New York.

I don't know whether I can send you another article today. Pieper promised me an article for you. He hasn't appeared up to the present time, but if he does, the article will still have to pass muster—does it go into the fire, or is it worthy of making the trip across the ocean?

I am still too weak to write any longer. More in a week. Regards from my family to yours.

Lupus is also not entirely well as yet, and that is why he hasn't sent anything.

Yours,
K. Marx

. . . The case of Daniels, Becker, et al.[1] wasn't heard at the January session of the court either, on the pretext that the investigation is so difficult that it has to be begun all over again, from the beginning. They have been in jail for nine months already.

ENGELS TO WEYDEMEYER

Manchester, January 23, 1852

Dear Weydemeyer:

. . . For the present I am here in Manchester to stay, luckily in a very independent job and with many advantages; Marx and other friends come to visit me now and then from London, and so long as Weerth is in Bradford, we have established a regular switchback service between the two cities, since the rail trip takes only two and a half hours. But he will probably be leaving soon; he can't stand that filthy hole Bradford, and he hasn't the composure to stay in any one place for a whole year. I am thinking of a trip to the United States either next summer or, if no change occurs in the interim, during the following summer: to New York and, especially, to New Orleans. But that depends on my old man, not on me, and also upon the state of the cotton market.[2] . . .

In France affairs are proceeding splendidly. Yesterday evening La Patrie reported that the establishment of a Ministry of Police for Maupas will be announced in today's Moniteur. De Morny, who, together with Fould and others, represents the material interests of the bourgeoisie (but not its participation in political power) in the

---

[1] The Cologne Communist Trial. See pp. 31-32, 36, 49-52.
[2] It was 1888 before Engels visited America. See pp. 200-01.

Cabinet, will be fired, and there will begin the rule of the pure adventurers Maupas, Persigny and Co. This will open the era of imperial, true socialism. The first socialist measure will be the confiscation of the property of Louis Philippe, since the document by which he transferred his property to his children on August 6, 1830, instead of presenting it to the state in accordance with the traditional custom, is juridically invalid. The Duc d'Aumale's share of the Condé fortune will also be seized. If events unfold rapidly enough, next Saturday's steamship will bring the news. They are still hunting down insurgents like wild beasts in the southern departments.

The British press, and now and then the Augsburg *Allgemeine Zeitung,* is the only dependable source for French news. The best information on France is found in the London *Daily News,* which I am therefore specially recommending to you. The *Tribune* subscribes to it, and you can also get it elsewhere; it is too expensive to subscribe to it yourself. You can certainly get it easily in the cafés of the business sections of the city.

Dronke will probably call on you soon; I have heard that all those who have to quit Switzerland are being shipped across France to America, and not to England. Dronke is supposed to leave now; he is probably in hiding, since nothing has been heard of him. . . .

Here are some additional points by way of comment on the possibility of invading Britain, to clear up the matter for you:

1. Any landing west of Portsmouth runs the risk of being driven into the angle of Cornwall — hence impracticable.

2. Any landing further to the north of, or too close to, Dover runs the risk of suffering the same fate between the Thames and the sea.

3. The initial objectives of the operation would be London and Woolwich. Detachments would have to be assigned to take Portsmouth and Sheerness (Chatham). A strong garrison would have to be kept in London, with strong detachments between London and the coast. With a landing force of 150,000 men, this would require at least 60,000 (and even that would be insufficient). Hence, *90,000 men* would be available for the advance.

4. The second objective of the operation would be Birmingham (the arms factories are located there). The area south of Bristol Channel and the Wash would have to be secured, *i.e.,* the line from Gloucester to King's Lynn, together with a powerful attack on Birmingham. No matter how weak and overwhelmed the enemy's army might be, I think that to deal with it with a force of 90,000 men would be impossible. But even if this should succeed, it would

not gain a tenable defensive position, especially if British sea power came into play. The line is too long and too weak. That is why the advance would have to be maintained.

5. The third objective of the operation would be Manchester. The whole area south of the Mersey (or the Ribble) and the Aire (the Humber) must be secured, and this line held. It is shorter and easier to defend; but here too the invading forces would be greatly weakened by the detaching of troops. Since the defense would still have enough territory and adequate facilities to reorganize its forces, the invaders would have to either advance or soon retreat.

6. The first line that could be held in the extremely narrow north of England is either the Tees or, even better, the Tyne, from Carlisle to Newcastle (the line of the Roman Wall, erected against the Picts). But then the defenders would still have the agricultural, industrial, and commercial resources of the Scottish Lowlands.

7. The conquest of *England proper* may be considered complete, *even though only temporarily,* only when Glasgow and Edinburgh are taken, the defenders are forced back into the Highlands, and the invaders occupy the excellent, short, strong line between the Clyde and the Firth of Forth, which is adequately provided with rail lines to the rear.

But the real difficulties — the difficulties of maintaining the position — begin after the conquest, since communications with France will certainly be cut off.

How many men would be required, under these conditions, to conquer the whole country from Dover to the Clyde and to set up a decent front on the Clyde?

I think 400,000 would not be too high a figure.

These considerations are too detailed for the newspaper, and I am setting them down for you solely as a professional man. Take a look at the map of England and tell me what you think of this. This is one side of the question that the British lose sight of completely.[1]

The mails are closing. I have to conclude. Regards to your wife.

Yours,

F. E.

---

[1] A panicky fear of war and invasion swept England after the rise of Louis Bonaparte to power in France.

ENGELS TO WEYDEMEYER

[Manchester] January 30, 1852

Dear Weydemeyer:

. . . My expectations concerning the confiscation of Louis-Philippe's property and the formation of the Persigny cabinet were borne out sooner than could have been expected. If the information channels are in good working order, this news should have arrived in New York by Liverpool steamer together with my letter.[1] The letter had hardly been sent off when the telegraphic reports of the event reached us here. So much the better—affairs are going splendidly, and they will go even better.

The situation of the Cologne prisoners is very distressing. Since there is absolutely no evidence against them, the criminal court has neither set them free nor turned them over for jury trial, but returned the case to the initial examining magistrate for a new inquiry! In other words, they will remain in jail for the present — without books, without letters, without communication with one another or with the outside world—until a new supreme court has been created. We are trying to expose this infamy in the British bourgeois press.

Best regards,

Yours,

F. E.

MARX TO WEYDEMEYER

[London] February 13, 1852

Dear Weydemeyer:

Enclosed the continuation of my article. The thing is expanding as I work on it, and you will get two more articles on this subject. ["The Eighteenth Brumaire of Louis Bonaparte."] Besides this, I am sending you something on Signor Mazzini in the next mail. Copies of your paper should have arrived long ago. In order to write for a paper, one must get to see it, as you know; and if my collaborators see their things in print, it will increase their zeal.

I enclose a note on the situation of our friends in jail in Cologne. Make an article out of this note.

They have been imprisoned for ten months by now.

In November the case came before the court of inquiry, which decided to hold them for jury trial. After this the case was transferred to the criminal court. The latter handed down its decision

[1] See pp. 33-34.

just before Christmas; it reads: "In view of the absence of facts constituting a crime, there is no basis for sustaining the indictment" (but in view of the importance that the government attaches to this case, we are afraid we might lose our jobs if the judicial prosecution of the defendants were dismissed), "we therefore return the case to the examining magistrate for the elucidation of various matters." The principal reason for the delay is the government's conviction that it would be disgracefully defeated in a jury trial. In the interim it hopes to set up a supreme court to try cases of treason or, at the very least, to abolish trial by jury for all political offenses — a bill to that effect has already been introduced into the Prussian Upper House. Our friends are held in solitary confinement, isolated from one another and from the world outside; they are not allowed mail or visitors, and they don't even get books, which have never been denied to common criminals in Prussia.

The brazen verdict of the criminal court would have been impossible if the press had been in the least interested in the case. But the liberal papers, like the *Kölnische Zeitung,* kept silent out of cowardice, while the "democratic" ones (including the lithographed *Korrespondenz,* which Kinkel is printing with American funds) were silent out of hatred of the Communists, fear of losing their own authority, and envy of the "new" martyrs. That is the gratitude of these brutes toward the *Neue Rheinische Zeitung,* which always supported these democratic scoundrels in their conflicts with the government (Temme, for instance, and others). That is Kinkel's gratitude to the *Westdeutsche Zeitung,* where Becker made a man of him and Bürgers sheltered him.[1] Canaille! These men must be fought to a finish.

Best regards from my family to yours.

Yours,

K. Marx

MARX TO WEYDEMEYER

[London] February 20, 1852

Dear Weydemeyer:

This week I can't send you anything for the simple reason that for more than a week I have been so plagued by money worries that I haven't even been able to continue my studies at the library, much less write articles.

But I hope that I can send you the fifth and sixth articles, which

[1] A play on words: "Becker ihn gebacken und Bürgers ihn geborgen hat."

comprise the concluding portion of the work,[1] on Tuesday (the 24th) and Friday (the 27th), respectively.

I received your letter with the postscript by Cluss. You faced two particular obstacles: 1. unemployment in New York; 2. the stormy west winds that carried the ships sailing from London to New York off their course. For except during the first few days, articles were sent you from England (by me, by Engels, by Freiligrath, by Eccarius, and others) as *regularly* as any paper could have wished. On the other hand, the people over here cooled off somewhat, because many ships arrived from America without word from you. I did not think it necessary to inform anyone, with the exception of Engels and Lupus, about the temporary suspension of your paper. That would have cooled off the contributors even more.

If you want to get regular support from here, you must fulfill the following conditions:

1. Write *every* week, indicating the dates of all the letters of ours that you have received.

2. Keep us currently informed of local conditions, regularly sending over pertinent documents, clippings, etc.

You know, my friend, how hard it is to write for a paper appearing on the other side of the ocean, without knowing its reading public, etc. But if you comply with the foregoing conditions, I guarantee you the necessary articles. I am standing behind all of them with a whip, and I'll know how to make them work. In Germany they have also promised me to send you articles and to write for your paper. If I only knew that the paper would continue, I'd have *an unpaid correspondent available in Paris,* who would write for you *weekly.* I am writing this man—he is one of my best and most intelligent friends. The only trouble is that no one wants to do work in vain, while timely reports lose all value if they are not printed immediately upon receipt. And, moreover, since you can't pay, it is all the more necessary to convince people that they are doing *effective* party work and that their letters are not lying around in some desk drawer.

I think you are making a mistake in waiting for your mail to be delivered to your home; instead of that you ought to notify the post-office that when ships arrive you will regularly pick up your letters yourself, as all newspapers do. That will make it easier to avoid misunderstandings and delays. . . .

As for Dana, I think it was foolish of him to print Simon's article. If it were financially possible for me to do so, I would have immediately declared that I refused to write for him any longer. He

---

[1] *The Eighteenth Brumaire of Louis Bonaparte.*

may allow attacks to be made on Engels and me, but not by that sort of grimy schoolboy. It is ridiculous for him to permit "Agitation" and "Emigration"—those two fictions existing solely in newspaper columns—to be presented to the American public as historical realities, and, what is more, that it be done by an empty-headed individual who granted Germany a Prussian Kaiser, the March societies and the Imperial Regent Vogt and now would like to hand the people over to *himself,* together with his accomplices, Parliament, and a somewhat altered imperial constitution. There is nothing more ridiculous than this rascal making a statesman's pronouncement from his Alpine heights. I thought Dana had more tact. Ludwig Simon *von Trier!* When will that fellow give up this parliamentary title of nobility?

You realize, of course, that in London these rascals have fallen out completely. The only thing that holds them together to some extent is the hope of the *saviour's* funds of the Christ Gottfried Kinkel. On the other side there are the idiot Ruge together with Ronge and two or three other jackasses, concealing their idle vegetating under the word "Agitation." It's as if a stagnant swamp were to call itself "the open sea."

At present, Europe is not concerned with these inanities, but with other matters. After the 2d of December[1] and after the arrival here of new revolutionary elements from France, even Ledru-Rollin has shrunk like an empty balloon. Mazzini is making ultrareactionary speeches; I shall send you an analysis of one of them in the near future.

As for Ernest Jones's *Notes to the People,* where you will find the everyday history of the contemporary British proletariat, I shall send it to you as soon as the state of my finances permits. I have to pay eight shillings to send a package to America.

Give Cluss my best wishes. We are waiting for a letter from him with great impatience. Why didn't you send us his statement? My wife and I, Freiligrath and his wife, and Lupus all send our best wishes to your wife; she has our warmest sympathy. We hope that the new citizen of the world will come into the world safely in the New World.

Adieu,

Your

K. Marx

If nothing comes of the newspaper, couldn't you publish my brochure in separate issues, each one printer's sheet long, or in the parts I sent you? Considerable time will be lost otherwise.

[1] On December 2, 1852, Louis Bonaparte was proclaimed hereditary "Emperor of the French," with the title of Napoleon III.

ENGELS TO WEYDEMEYER
                                    Manchester, February 27, 1852
Dear Weydemeyer:

   ... As for the question of a war against England, it interests me
for the present chiefly as a military problem that one tries to explain
and solve, like a problem in geometry. But I do not consider a
coalition war of this sort impossible, although now it will doubtless
be postponed as long as Derby is at the helm of the government. The
gentlemen of the Holy Alliance now evaluate their own strength
just as falsely as they did in the period of the various coalitions from
1792 to 1807. As for Russia's dependence upon Britain: (1) It must
not be expected that the Tsar feels this dependence; and (2) though
the cessation of trade would cause a serious depression, poverty, and
the spoilage of foodstuffs, this could be stood for two or three years
just like a business crisis, which lasts about the same length of
time. Remember that in Russia money hardly circulates at all in
the rural localities, among the peasants, who comprise the overwhelming majority of the population, and that all the necessities
of life of these barbarians can be made in every village. The cities
and the aristocracy would suffer, of course, but the foundation of
the Russian Empire is the peasantry and the minor nobility, who
live like peasants. It would be very hard for Britain to get the
Continent to revolt; in Spain this was facilitated by the terrain,
the wide expanse, and the sparse population of the country, the
shortage of foodstuffs, and the sea, which surrounds the country
on almost all sides. But Hungary and Poland are inland countries,
while Italy, except for the islands, could hardly defend itself against
the superior forces of the coalition, even with the aid of the British
and the insurgents. Besides, Britain is unable today, and will be
unable even one year after the declaration of war, to raise the kind
of army that was sent to Spain for Wellington. And ships without
landing parties cannot gain a firm foothold anywhere.

   It is really fortunate that the Tories have come to power. The
manufacturers have grown quite soft as a result of their constant
success in the field of trade policy and the continuing of prosperity.
Not a single one was interested in Parliamentary reform, even a
much wider reform than the pitiable Russell bill. Now they are
on the horns of the devil's own dilemma, and already devilishly
apprehensive, particularly as *each* of the new ministers is crassly
advocating one sort of protective tariff or another. The Anti-
Corn-Law League is being re-established here. Parliamentary reform, extension of the suffrage, equalizing the electoral constitu-

encies, and secret voting have now become *questions of life or death for the industrial bourgeoisie,* whereas formerly they directly interested only the lower middle class. Derby is compelled to dissolve Parliament, and he will probably do so as soon as the military budget and the taxes for the coming year have been voted. We shall most likely have new elections in May. The protectionists will gain some votes and will throw some Peelites out of Parliament. But they will remain in the minority, and if Derby dares to introduce a straightforward bill for the establishment of protective tariffs, he will fall beyond the shadow of a doubt. But he may be clever enough to put off this question.

In any event, the British movement has come to life again. Palmerston's dismissal was followed by the whole sequence of events that had to occur after the unceasing Cabinet defeats during the past session. Derby is Act II, the dissolution of Parliament will be Act III. As for British foreign policy under Derby, it will, of course, be reactionary too, but very little of a decisive character will occur. It is possible that they will initiate some sort of refugee trials, but in these trials the government will lose. Endeavors will be made to introduce bills for the control of aliens, which will likewise fall through. Possibly, assistance will be given to the effort to form a coalition against Louis Napoleon, but this too will come to nought. The hands of the British Tories are bound, and unless they try to re-establish the Sidmouth-Castlereagh despotism of 1815-1821 — in so doing they may burn their fingers devilishly, since the British bourgeoisie is rabid about legality and free trade — Messrs. Conservatives will make laughingstocks of themselves. But Derby (while his father was alive, he bore the title of Lord Stanley) is a hothead and may easily resort to extreme and even unlawful measures.

Now all that is lacking is a business crisis, and ever since Derby came to power I have had a presentiment that it will soon break out. The free-trade measures of the British, following one another in rapid succession, with the subsequent opening up of the Dutch colonies, the lowering of tariffs in Spain, Sardinia, etc., and the drop in the price of cotton (since September, 1850, cotton prices have fallen to half the previous level) are supporting prosperity longer than could have been previously expected. But the condition of the Indian and, in part, the American markets (much less manufactured goods were exported to the United States last month than during the corresponding period of the previous year) does not give one any reason to believe that it will last much longer. If the crisis were to break out as early as May — which is hardly likely, however — the dance would begin. But it will hardly break out before September or October.

Give my regards to your wife.

Yours,

F. E.

In the near future I shall send you an article on the position of the British industrial bourgeoisie and on the history of trade—I shall be very busy for about another two weeks.

MRS. MARX TO WEYDEMEYER

[London, February 27, 1852]

Dear Mr. Weydemeyer:

For a week now my husband's eyes have been hurting him so much because of his intensive work at night—he has to spend the day running around on domestic errands—that he is unable to write you, and I have to perform all the functions of a secretary. He asks me to tell you that he could not look through Eccarius' article closely enough, and that you will have to correct the spelling errors in it: that remarkable man writes excellently, but it is only over here that he learned to handle words, and he doesn't recognize periods and commas. In addition, my husband is sending you an article by a Hungarian, who is closely acquainted with the innermost secrets of the Hungarian emigrés. Decide for yourself whether this article can be used and printed at the present time. In any event, the man must be encouraged, since he has promised to send special correspondence by Perczel, Szemere, and others, who are close friends of his, later on. My husband thinks that you will have to correct the bad grammatical errors in the article, but that the peculiarities of style, which give it the stamp of a genuine Hungarian composition, should not be tampered with at all. Furthermore, he asks you to send back his articles on Napoleon[1] at once if you are unable to print them. We may perhaps be able to place them somewhere, translated into French, though it would be a pity, of course, to give up the German. It would be best of all if you could manage to print them in America, and if it were possible to distribute them in Germany as well. The brochure ought to go well, no doubt, as it gives a historical appraisal of the most important event of the present time. I hope, dear Mr. Weydemeyer, to get good news from you, news that your dear wife has undergone the great event, and that

---

[1] *The Eighteenth Brumaire of Louis Bonaparte.*

there are two newborn children in your house—your son and your paper. I send your dear wife my most heartfelt greetings, and I remain,

Yours sincerely,

Jenny Marx

In order not to delay matters too long, you might print each article separately, for the problem is extremely timely. Later on they might all be collected together. No. 5 is going off today. He is sending off No. 6, the concluding article, next Friday. And so, I repeat: *try to make a brochure of it.*

If this can't be done, send the work back—it has to be printed in one way or another.

Give our regards to Cluss, and write us soon how you are getting along.

Lupus has just brought us another little article on the latest events in London.

MARX TO WEYDEMEYER

London, March 5, 1852

Dear Weywey:

. . . Your article against Heinzen, which Engels unfortunately sent me too late, is very good, both brutal and *subtle*—a combination that belongs in any polemic worthy of the name. I gave this article to Ernest Jones, and enclosed you will find a communication for you from him intended for publication.[1] As Jones writes very illegibly, with abbreviations, and as I assume that you are not an out-and-out Englishman as yet, I am sending you together with the original a copy made by my wife, and at the same time the German translation, as you must have them both printed side by side, original and translation. After the letter from Jones you can add the following: With regard to George Julian Harney, who is also one of Herr Heinzen's authorities, Harney published our *Communist Manifesto* in English in his *Red Republican* with a marginal note that it was "the most revolutionary document ever given to the world," and in his *Democratic Review* he translated the wisdom "discarded" by Heinzen, to wit, the articles I wrote in the *Revue of the Neue Rheinische Zeitung* on the French revolution. In

---

[1] Weydemeyer had written an article against Heinzen in an American periodical, *The Democrat.* In the letter to Weydemeyer enclosed by Marx, Jones wrote that it was impossible for anyone with the faintest knowledge of English conditions to ignore the class war.

an article on Louis Blanc he refers his readers to these articles as the "true criticism" of the French affair. For the rest, in England there is no need to cite only the "extremists." If a member of Parliament in England becomes a Minister, he has to be re-elected. So *Disraeli*, the new Chancellor of the Exchequer, writes to his constituents on March 1:

"We shall endeavor to put an end to a class struggle which in recent years has had such a harmful effect on the well-being of this kingdom."

On which *The Times* comments on March 2: "If anything would ever divide classes in this country beyond reconciliation and leave no chance of a just and honorable peace, it would be a tax on foreign corn."

And to keep an ignorant "man of character" like Heinzen from imagining that the aristocracy are *for* and the bourgeoisie *against* corn laws, because the former want *"monopoly"* and the latter *"freedom"* — a philistine sees contradictions only in this abstract form — it is to be noted that in the eighteenth century the English aristocracy were for "freedom" (of trade) and the bourgeoisie for "monopoly" — the same relative position that we find at this very moment between these two classes in Prussia with regard to "corn laws." The *Neue Preussische Zeitung* is the most rabid free-trader.

Finally, in your place I should in general tell the democratic gentlemen that they would do better first to acquaint themselves with the bourgeois literature before they presume to yap out their contradictions of it. For instance, these gentlemen should study the historical works of Thierry, Guizot, John Wade, etc., in order to enlighten themselves as to the past history of classes. Before they try to criticize the critique of political economy they should acquaint themselves with the first elements of political economy. One has only to open Ricardo's great work, for example, to find these words on the first page: "The produce of the earth — all that is derived from its surface by the united application of labor, machinery and capital — is divided among *three classes* of the community, namely, the proprietor of the land, the owner of the stock or capital necessary for its cultivation, and the laborers by whose industry it is culti-vated." [1]

That bourgeois society in the United States has not yet developed far enough to make the class struggle obvious and comprehensible is most strikingly proved by *H. C. Carey* (of Philadelphia), the only American economist of importance. He attacks *Ricardo*, the most

[1] David Ricardo, *On the Principles of Political Economy and Taxation*, 1817, author's preface.

classical representative (interpreter) of the bourgeoisie and the most stoical adversary of the proletariat, as a man whose works are an arsenal for anarchists, socialists, and all the enemies of bourgeois society. He accuses not only him, but Malthus, Mill, Say, Torrens, Wakefield, McCulloch, Senior, Wakley, R. Jones, etc., in short, the economic masterminds of Europe, of tearing society apart and paving the way for civil war by their proof that the economic bases of the different classes must give rise to a necessary and ever-growing antagonism between them. He tries to refute them, not like the fatuous Heinzen, to be sure, by linking the existence of classes to the existence of *political* privileges and *monopolies,* but by attempting to demonstrate that *economic* conditions—rent (landed property), *profit* (capital), and wages (wage labor)—are conditions of co-operation and harmony rather than conditions of struggle and antagonism. All he proves, of course, is that he takes the "undeveloped" social conditions of the United States to be "normal" social conditions.

As for me, no credit is due me for discovering either the existence of classes in modern society or the struggle between them. Bourgeois historians had described the historical development of this struggle of the classes long before me, and bourgeois economists had portrayed their economic anatomy. What I did that was new was to prove: (1) that the *existence of classes* is bound up only with *specific historical phases in the development of production;* (2) that the class struggle necessarily leads to the *dictatorship of the proletariat;* (3) that this dictatorship itself only constitutes the transition to the *abolition of all classes* and to a *classless society.* Ignorant louts like Heinzen, who deny not only the struggle, but even the existence, of classes, merely prove that, despite all their bloodcurdling yelps and humanitarian airs, they regard the social conditions under which the bourgeoisie rules as the final product, the *non plus ultra* [acme] of history, and that they are merely the servitors of the bourgeoisie. And the less these louts themselves comprehend the greatness and the temporary necessity of the bourgeois regime, the more repulsive is their servitude.

From the foregoing notes take whatever you consider suitable. Moreover, Heinzen has adopted from us "centralization" instead of his "federative republic," etc. When the views that we are now spreading about classes have become trite and part of the equipment of "common sense," the boor will proclaim them, with a lot of noise, as the latest product of his "own sagacity" and start barking against our further development. That is how, with his "own sagacity," he yelped against the Hegelian philosophy so long as it was progressive. Now he feeds on its stale crumbs as spewed out, undigested, by Ruge.

Together with this letter you will receive the conclusion of the Hungarian article. If your paper exists, try to use some of it, especially as *Szemere,* the ex-Premier of Hungary, has promised me to write a regular article for you from Paris *over his own signature.*

If your paper has started publication, send *more* copies so that it can be given a wider circulation.

Yours,

K. Marx

MARX TO WEYDEMEYER

London, March 25, 1852

Dear Weydemeyer:

Best wishes to the new citizen of the world! One can't be born at a better time than today. By the time the trip from London to Calcutta will take seven days, the two of us will either be beheaded or have heads that totter with age. And Australia and California and the Pacific Ocean! The new citizens of the world won't be able to comprehend how small our world was. . . .

Very good that you've taken a job as a surveyor. Now you'll be able to operate with greater quiet and security.

Now I am going after Mazzini. Herr Kinkel, who according to his own admissions, draws his surpassing wisdom from "old wives' tales" and pursues the unity of the "great men" wherever he goes, finds upon his return that the struggle is at its height. The fact is that Ledru [Ledru-Rollin] and Mazzini bought the Brussels newspaper *La Nation* for 10,000 francs, out of the proceeds of the Italian loan. And then Signor Mazzini let fly with his first articles, full of the most odious and stupid attacks on France and on socialism, and apropos of the fact that France has lost the initiative. His attacks were so violent that Ledru himself now has to take a stand against them; they say he has already decided to do so. On the other hand, the socialists Louis Blanc, Pierre Leroux, Cabet, Malarmet, and others have gotten together and issued a venomous reply, written by the toad Louis Blanc. Moreover, most of the French emigrés are unbelievably infuriated with Ledru, whom they rightfully hold responsible for Mazzini's blunders. Fire has broken out within the very center of their camp.

If you get hold of the book by that vile priest Dulon, *Der Tag ist Angebrochen* ["Day is Breaking"], give the cur (who would like to play the role of Lamennais) a sound thrashing.

Dronke has been arrested in Paris. He tarried there too long on his way back from Switzerland, instead of passing through France quickly.

I am greatly pleased with your selections. Pieper's article would have been all right for the newspaper, but it is written too hurriedly and superficially for a pamphlet.

Couldn't you get some news of Edgar[1] from Braunfels? That do-nothing never writes a word, and his mother is greatly worried. A madcap!

Cluss's protest met with general approval here at the league meeting, while your *Revolution* was well-liked both in Stechan's society and in ours.

Best regards to your family from all of us,   Yours,

K. Marx

ENGELS TO WEYDEMEYER

Manchester, April 16, 1852

Dear Weydemeyer:

Yesterday I received your letter of March 30 (?) , together with the letter about the "revolutionary meeting." I see that you have begun to paste stamps on your letters; that is senseless, for the "concern" here, *i.e.*, Ermen and Engels, can pay the postal fees here. What I received I sent on to Marx.

The day before yesterday I returned from London, where I spent Easter. Marx's youngest child was very ill and, as Marx now writes me, died; this is the second death in London. You can understand, of course, that his wife is taking it very hard. There also was sickness in the Freiligrath family, but there the patients are on the mend.

You probably know that during his trip across France Dronke was arrested in Paris, partly through his own fault: the youngster stayed there for three weeks, in spite of his previous deportation. Now he writes that he has been transferred from Mazas Prison back to the prefecture of police and that on Good Friday he was to be sent to Boulogne and from there to England. But we haven't heard a word from him since. The youngster has a remarkable talent for getting into a scrape, but he most likely will show up within a day or two. The whole *Neue Rheinische Zeitung* is assembling in England. To be sure, Weerth is in Hamburg at the present time, but nevertheless he is in touch with Bradford and, despite all his reluctance, he regularly returns there.

[1] Edgar von Westphalen, Marx's brother-in-law.

In May our Cologne friends will most likely face a jury, since the criminal court is supposed to consider their case on April 5th and will not set them free, of course. But I dare say, this is all for the best, since the state prosecutor would immediately appeal a verdict of not guilty. . . . If a certain workman by the name of Hansen should arrive in New York from Cologne, treat him as he deserves. This fellow, a member of the League since 1848, administered the funds collected for the benefit of the prisoners, that is, he spent the money on drink and then skipped off to America. . . .

It would be very useful if Dana sent copies of the printed articles by Marx over here. We received only the first six articles and would have liked to get the subsequent ones. If Dana should evade the issue, on the pretext that this would involve a lot of work, procure these copies yourself and send them over here. Marx wanted to write you about this long ago, but most likely he is hardly in a frame of mind to think about it now. See what can be done in this respect. We ought to have a full set of the articles here—it is important to preserve them as documents.

My article on strategy is of no value any more and is quite unsuitable for the symposium, especially since the major points are deduced not in the article, but in my letters to you. File it quietly away. As soon as I have some free time and there is any chance of having it printed, I shall send you an article on the development of trade and on the position of the British industrial bourgeoisie. For the next two or three weeks I shall be devoting all my time to Russian and Sanskrit, which I am now studying, and later, when I get the material from Germany, I shall get down to military problems. But there's no hurry, and that is easier work.

It's time for me to mail this letter. Best regards to your wife and Cluss.

Yours,

F.E.

MARX TO WEYDEMEYER

London, April 30, 1852

Dear Weydemeyer:

It gave me much pleasure to hear about the publication.[1] Lupus' letter needn't be taken so seriously.[2] You know that in our quite

---

[1] Weydemeyer had finally managed to publish Marx's *The Eighteenth Brumaire of Louis Bonaparte* in an edition of one thousand copies.

[2] Wilhelm Wolff (Lupus) had written Weydemeyer a vehement letter on April 16, the day that Marx's infant daughter Franziska had been buried. bitterly reproaching Weydemeyer for his alleged inactivity.

distressing circumstances there always is a certain excessive irritability, which has to be "discounted" to get a true balance.

Neither Engels nor I have as yet received your article in the *Turnzeitung* attacking Kinkel. I am looking forward to it eagerly, as your polemic against Heinzen was excellent. . . .

The status of big commerce and industry in England, and hence on the Continent, is better than ever. As a result of special circumstances (California, Australia, the trade penetration of the British into the Punjab, Sind, and other recently conquered parts of the Indies) the crisis may be postponed until 1853. But when it does break out, it will be frightful. And until then revolutionary upheavals are out of the question. The Cologne trial has again been put off to the July session of court. By that time jury trials will probably have been abolished altogether in Prussia. . . .

Yours,

K. M.

MRS. MARX TO CLUSS

[London, October 28, 1852]

Dear Mr. Cluss:

You will, no doubt, have been following the monster trial of the communists in the *Kölnische Zeitung*. The session of October 23 gave the whole trial an imposing and interesting turn, so favorable for the defendants that we are all beginning to feel a little better. You may imagine that the "Marx Party" is active day and night and has to work with head, hands, and feet. . . . All the assertions of the police are lies. They steal, forge, break open desks, swear false oaths, perjure themselves, claiming they have the right to do so against the communists who stand *hors la société* [outside society]! It is truly hair-raising to see all this, and how the police, in their most villainous form, are taking over all the functions of the Ministry of Justice, pushing Saedt into the background, introducing unauthenticated slips of paper, mere rumors, reports, and hearsay as actually judicially proven facts, as evidence. All the proofs of forgery had to be submitted from here; thus, my husband has to work all day at it, far into the night. Affidavits by the landlords had to be submitted, and the handwriting of Liebknecht and Rings, the men who are alleged to have written the minutes, had to be officially certified to prove the forgery by the police. Then all the papers, in six to eight copies, must be sent to Germany by the most devious channels, via Frankfurt, Paris, etc., as all letters addressed to my husband, as well as all letters sent from here to Cologne, are opened and confiscated. The whole thing is now a struggle between the police and my husband, who is being blamed for everything: the whole revolution, even the conduct of the trial. . . .

Freiligrath, Marx, Engels, and Wolff issued the enclosed statement. We are sending it to the *Tribune* today. You can publish it, too. . . .

Jenny Marx

Stieber has now denounced my husband as an Austrian spy. By way of reply, my husband dug up a wonderful letter that Stieber wrote to him during the period of the *Neue Rheinische Zeitung,* which really compromises Stieber. . . . In brief, things will come to pass that would be unbelievable if one didn't actually witness them. All these police tales divert the public and thus the jurors from the indictment itself, and the bourgeoisie's hatred of these dreadful incendiaries is paralyzed by their horror of the police villainy, so that by now we may even count on our friends' acquittal. The battle against this official power, buttressed with gold and all the weapons, is very interesting, of course, and all the more glorious if we should end up victorious, since on one side there are money and power and everything else, whereas we often didn't know where to get the paper we needed to write letters, etc., etc. . . .

ENCLOSURE

PUBLIC STATEMENT OF FREILIGRATH, MARX, ENGELS, AND WOLFF[1]

To the Editor of . . . . . .

Sir:

The undersigned call your attention to the attitude of the Prussian press, even including the most reactionary papers, such as the *Neue Preussische Zeitung,* during the pending trial of the Communists at Cologne and to the honorable discretion they observed at a moment when scarcely a third part of the witnesses have been examined, where none of the produced documents has been verified, and not a word has fallen yet from the defense. While those papers, at the worst, represent the Cologne prisoners and the undersigned, their London friends, as dangerous conspirators, who alone are responsible for the whole European history of the last four years and for all the revolutionary commotions of 1848 and 1849, there are two public organs, the *Times* and the *Daily News,*

---

[1] This statement was written in English.

which have not hesitated to represent the Cologne prisoners and the undersigned as a gang of swindlers, "sturdy beggars," etc.

The undersigned address to the English public the same demand which the defenders of the accused have addressed to the public in Germany — to suspend their judgment and to wait for the end of the trial. Were they to give further explanations at the present time, the Prussian government might obtain the means of baffling a revelation of police-tricks, perjury, forgery of documents, falsifications of dates, thefts, etc., unprecedented even in the records of Prussian political justice. When those revelations shall have been made in the course of the present proceedings, public opinion in England will know how to qualify the anonymous scribes of the *Times* and the *Daily News,* who make themselves the advocates and mouthpieces of the most infamous and subaltern government spies.

Fr. Engels, F. Freiligrath, K. Marx, W. Wolff

MARX TO CLUSS[1]

London, December 7, 1852

Enclosed: (1) my manuscript of *Enthüllungen über den Kommunistenprozess zu Köln* [*Revelations of the Communist Trial in* Cologne]. This manuscript was sent to Switzerland yesterday; it is being printed there and will be distributed in Germany as a New Year's gift for Messrs. Prussians. Print it in America, *if* you think you can recover at least its *production costs* in the American market. If you can make more, so much the better. In that event, an advance announcement should be made in the press to arouse the public's curiosity. If the brochure can appear in America, it must be printed *anonymously,* as is being done in Switzerland. You will appreciate the humor of the brochure better when you realize that its author is as good as interned because he lacks pants and shoes and that, moreover, *his family* risked and still risks being plunged into *really distressing poverty.* The trial dragged me even deeper into penury, for I had to spend five weeks working for the party against the government's machinations, instead of earning some money. In addition, it has totally estranged the German booksellers with whom I had hoped to sign a contract for my "Political Economy." Lastly, the arrest of Bermbach deprived me of the opportunity of realizing the proceeds of the copies of the *Eighteenth Brumaire* sent by you, for 300 copies were ordered through him as long ago as May. In short — I'm on the rocks. . . .

[1] Text as transcribed by F. A. Sorge.

(2) I am sending you an appeal for donations on behalf of the Cologne prisoners and their families. Place it in various newspapers. It would be good if committees were formed in America, perhaps. . . .

A more extensive statement on the shameful behavior of the government in the Cologne trial (signed by me, Lupus, Freiligrath, and Engels) appeared in various London newspapers. The Prussian Legation is particularly offended by the fact that this unvarnished denunciation of the Prussian government was printed in the *most refined* and *respectable* London weeklies — the *Spectator* and the *Examiner*. . . .

As for Proudhon, you are both right. Massol's illusions arise from the fact that Proudhon, with his customary professional charlatanry, has borrowed some ideas from me, as *his own* "latest discoveries." For example, that there is *no absolute science,* that everything must be explained as founded on material conditions, etc., etc. In his book on Louis Bonaparte, he frankly admits what I first had to deduce from his *Philosophie de la Misère* [*Philosophy of Poverty*], namely, that his ideal is the petty bourgeoisie. France, he says, consists of three classes: (1) the bourgeoisie; (2) the middle class (the petty bourgeoisie); and (3) the proletariat. The purpose of history, and of the revolution in particular, is to dissolve the extremes — the first and third classes — into the second class, the golden mean; this can be done by means of the Proudhonist credit operations, the end result of which must be abolition of interest in all its various forms. . . .

In the proceedings before the Cologne court, Becker has compromised himself and the party. It had been arranged with him beforehand that he was to appear as a non-member of the League and not to lose his following among the democratic petty bourgeoisie. But he suddenly became involved in the deception himself (he is very weak as far as theoretical education is concerned, but strong enough where petty ambition is involved) and decided to play the leader of the democrats at the expense of the communists. Not only does he want to be acquitted, but to exploit the laurels of the trial for his own personal ends. He is not only brazen; he is turning into a blackguard.

In conclusion, a few words about France: Bonaparte, who has always lived by borrowing, assumes that the golden age will be most easily established in France if he establishes credit institutions everywhere and makes them as accessible as possible to all classes of society. His operations have two good sides to them: they are paving the way for a terrible financial crisis; and they demonstrate what the Proudhonist tricks lead to once they are roused from their theoretical sleep and put into practice, *viz.*, to fraudulent stock-jobbing without precedent since John Law.

The Orleanists — I know one of their agents very well — are displaying unusual activity. Thiers is here now. They have many allies in the army and in Bonaparte's immediate entourage. They would like to kill him in his bed (in January). We shall see. In any event, I shall be informed of this two weeks *before* their attempt and shall warn the revolutionary-proletarian party in Paris through the secret society of *"frères et amis"* ["brothers and friends"] to which I belong. Even if the Orleanists pull the chestnuts out of the fire, they won't be able to eat them in any event. . . .

K. M.

MARX TO CLUSS[1]

[London, April 1853]

. . . Today I received the first five issues [of *Die Reform*] from New York—I don't know whether from Weydemeyer or Kellner. I was already acquainted with most of them through you. This is at least an honest paper, something rare in America, and a workingman's paper. I can't say that the editor-in-chief's affected disdain of *questions personelles* [personal questions], which are also party questions, his make-believe naïve simplicity, or his Biblical solemnity are much to my taste. But one has to take the paper as it is. What I liked best of all was Weydemeyer's introduction to the "Economic Sketches." That is good. I have appealed to the people here. . . . On the whole, it's hard to get collaborators. I myself am overworked. The others are still a little frightened by previous experiences. Our party is unfortunately very *pauvre* [poor]. . . .

ENGELS TO WEYDEMEYER

Manchester, April 12, 1853

Dear Weydemeyer:

. . . I have perfected my knowledge of Slavic languages and military science this winter, and by the end of the year I shall understand Russian and South Slavic fairly well. I purchased the library of a retired Prussian artillery officer in Cologne cheaply, and for a time I again felt like a bombardier, among the Plümicke, the brigade

---

[1] This letter is translated from the fragment published by Franz Mehring in *Die Neue Zeit*, Vol. 25 (1907), Pt. 2.

school handbook, and the other old volumes you recollect. There is no doubt that Prussian military literature is the very worst of the lot; the only tolerable stuff is what was written in the immediate, fresh recollection of the campaigns of '13-'15. But after 1822 there sets in an abominable pretentious, military pedantry that isn't worth a damn. A few tolerable things have recently been published in Prussia again, but not many. Since I am not familiar with the specialized literature, the French works are completely inaccessible to me, unfortunately.

I have just about boned my way through the old campaigns (those since 1792); the Napoleonic campaigns are so easy that it is hard to go astray in them. *Au bout du compte* [all things considered], Jomini is the best historian of these campaigns; the natural genius Clausewitz doesn't quite appeal to me, despite the many fine pieces he has written.

For the immediate future, *i.e.*, for *us*, the most important is the Russian campaign of 1812—it is the only one where there are major strategic problems still unsolved. In Germany and Italy there are no other lines of operations feasible other than those established by Napoleon; in Russia, on the other hand, everything is still obscure and unclear. When we seek an answer to the problem of what a revolutionary army should do in the event of a successful offensive against Russia, the question whether Napoleon's plan of operations in 1812 envisaged from the very start a direct advance on Moscow or an advance only to the Dnieper and the Dvina in the first campaign again rises to face us. This question can now be solved, it seems to me, solely by sea: in the Skaggerak and the Dardanelles, and at St. Petersburg, Riga, and Odessa — that is, of course, if we leave chance out of our reckoning and start only with an approximate balance of forces as a basis. Another condition, of course, is that we leave aside any *internal* movement in Russia, whereas a noble-bourgeois revolution in St. Petersburg, with an ensuing civil war inside the country, is quite within the realm of possibility. Mr. Hertzen made the problem much easier for himself (*Du Développement des idées révolutionnaires en Russie* [*The Development of Revolutionary Ideas in Russia*]), by propounding the Hegelian construction of a democratic-social-communist-Proudhonist Russian republic headed by the triumvirate of Bakunin-Hertzen-Golovin, so that it can't miss. By the way, it is very uncertain whether Bakunin is still alive. In any event, it is extremely difficult to conquer vast, widespread, sparsely populated Russia. As for the former Polish provinces this side of the Dvina and the Dnieper, I haven't wanted to hear about them ever since I learned that all the peasants there are Ukrainians while only the nobles and some of the bourgeois are Poles, and that for the peasant there the restoration of Poland would mean merely the restoration of the old rule of the nobility in full force, as was the case in Ukrainian Galicia in 1846. In all these areas, not counting the Kingdom of Poland proper, there are hardly 500,000 Poles!

However, it's good that the revolution this time encounters a sturdy antagonist in the shape of Russia, and not such feeble scarecrows as in 1848.

In the meanwhile all sorts of symptoms are making their appearance. The cotton prosperity over here is actually attaining such heights as to make one dizzy, while individual branches of the cotton industry (coarse material, domestics) are in a state of complete slump. The speculators are counting on saving themselves from the dizzy swindle by swindling wholesale (building railways with British money) only in America and France, while swindling over here at retail, on a small scale, thus gradually infecting *all* commodities with the swindle. The quite abnormal winter and spring weather over here have most likely damaged the grain crop, and if, as is usually the case, this is followed by an abnormal summer, the crop will be a failure. The present prosperity, in my opinion, cannot last beyond autumn. In the meantime, the third British cabinet in the course of a single year is now making a fool of itself — and this is the last possible cabinet without the direct intervention of the radical bourgeoisie. The Whigs, the Tories, the coalitionists are all suffering defeat in turn, not because of a tax deficit, but because of surplus. This characterizes the whole policy as well as the extreme impotence of the old parties. If the present ministers fall, Britain cannot be governed without a considerable extension of the electorate; in all likelihood this will coincide with the onset of the crisis. The prolonged boredom of prosperity makes it almost impossible for the unlucky Bonaparte to preserve his dignity — the world is bored, and Bonaparte bores the world. Unfortunately, he cannot get married again every month. That swindler, drunkard, and cheat will break his neck, because he is compelled to put Engels' *Fürstenspiegel* [*Princely Mirror*] into practice, if only for appearance's sake. The blackguard, playing the role of "Father of his country," is at his wits' end. He can't even start a war; at his slightest move he comes up against serried ranks, a solid wall of bayonets. Besides, peace gives the peasants the highly desired time to reflect on how the man who promised to crush Paris for the sake of the peasants is now beautifying Paris at the expense of the peasants, while mortgages and assessments are growing rather than diminishing, in spite of everything. In a word, this time events are developing methodically, and that is very promising.

In Prussia the government, with its income tax, has nicely gotten itself into trouble with the bourgeoisie. The tax assessments are being raised by the bureaucrats with the greatest arrogance, and you can imagine the delight with which these noble inkslingers are now snooping around in the trade secrets and ledgers of all businessmen. Even my father, the inveterate Prussian, is boiling with rage. These people must now taste the blessings of the *à bon marché* [bargain] constitutional-paternal-Prussian government down to the very dregs. The Prussian government debt, which was about 67 million talers before 1848, must have quadrupled since then, and they now want to borrow again! It should be said that the stout king had agreed to sweat a little again, as in the days of March [1848], if he were only assured these credits until his blissful death. But Louis Napoleon again helped him to re-establish the Zollverein, Austria yielded a bit out of fear of war, "and now, Lord, allow your servant to go to his grave in peace!"

The Austrians are doing their best to get Italy into motion again; up to the Milan putsch the country was entirely engrossed in trade and prosperity, to the extent that the latter was compatible with taxes. If all this continues for a couple of months more, Europe is splendidly prepared and needs only the impetus of the crisis. In addition, the unprecedentedly long and universal prosperity — ever since the beginning of 1849 — has restored the strength of the exhausted parties (in so far as they are not completely worn out, like the monarchists in France) much more quickly than was the case after 1830, for example, when business conditions were, on the whole, mixed and colorless for a long time. In 1848, moreover, only the Paris proletariat and, later, Hungary and Italy, were exhausted by serious struggles; the insurrections in France after June 1848 were almost not worth mentioning, ultimately *ruining* only the old monarchist parties. Then there is the comical result of the movement in *all* countries, nothing being serious or important but the colossal historical irony and the concentration of Russian war resources. In view of all this, it seems quite impossible to me, even from the most dispassionate point of view, for the present situation to outlast the spring of 1854.

It is very good that this time *our party* comes forward under altogether different auspices. All the socialist stupidities, that had to be championed in 1848 as against the pure democrats and South German republicans, L. Blanc's nonsense, etc., even things that *we* were compelled to put forward in order to obtain support for our views in the confused German situation—all that is now championed by our opponents—Ruge, Heinzen, Kinkel, *et al.* The preliminaries of the proletarian revolution, the measures that prepare the battle-ground and clear the way for us, such as a single and indivisible republic, etc., things that *we* had to champion *against* the people whose natural, normal job it should have been to achieve or, at least, to demand them — all that is now *convenu* [taken for granted]. The gentlemen have learned. This time we start right off with the *Manifesto* [*Manifesto of the Communist Party*] thanks to the Cologne trial in particular, in which German communism passed its baccalaureate examination (especially in the person of Röser).

All this, of course, concerns only the theory; in practice we shall always be reduced to pressing for resolute measures and absolute ruthlessness above all. And that's the trouble. I have a presentiment that, thanks to the perplexity and flabbiness of all the others, our party will be forced into the government one fine morning to carry out ultimately the measures that are of no direct interest to us, but are in the general interests of the revolution and the specific interests of the petty-bourgeoisie; on which occasion, driven by the proletarian populace, bound by our own printed declarations and plans — more or less falsely interpreted, more or less passionately put forward in the partisan struggle — we shall be constrained to undertake communist experiments and extravagant measures, the untimeliness of which we know better than anyone else. In so doing we lose our heads—only *physiquement parlant* [physically speaking], let us hope —a reaction sets in, and until the world is able to form a *historical* judgment of such events, we are considered not only beasts, which wouldn't matter, but also *bête* [stupid], which is much worse.

I don't see how it can turn out otherwise. In a backward country like Germany, which possesses an advanced party and is involved in an advanced revolution with an advanced country like France, the advanced party must take over at the first serious conflict and as soon as *actual danger* is present, and that is, in any event, *ahead of* its normal time. All that is unimportant, however, and the best thing we can do is for our party to have established its historical rehabilitation in its *literature* ahead of time, should events take such a turn.

Moreover, we shall appear on the historical stage much more respectably than last time. First, we are rid of all the old good-for-nothings *in personalibus* [in point of personnel]—the Schappers, Willichs, and their ilk; second, we have grown somewhat stronger; third, we can count on a rising young generation in Germany (if nothing else, the Cologne trial alone suffices to assure us that); and finally, we have all profited considerably from our exile. To be sure, we also have people among us who live by the principle: "What do we have to study for, that's what *père* [Father] Marx is for, whose job it is to know everything." But, on the whole, the Marx party studies pretty hard, and when one looks at the other jackasses among the emigrés, who have picked up new phrases here and there and thus made themselves more confused than ever, it is obvious that the superiority of our party has increased absolutely and relatively. But that is needed, too, for *la besogne sera rude* [the job will be hard].

Before the coming revolution I wish I had time to study at least the Italian and Hungarian campaigns of 1848-49. On the whole, this story is clear enough to me, despite unsatisfactory maps, etc., but lots of work and money are required to establish the details with the accuracy required for a description. In both instances the Italians behaved like jackasses. In general, Willisen's description and critique are correct in most cases, but sometimes they are stupid. The complete superiority of Austrian strategy, which Willisen stresses as early as 1848, is revealed only in the Novara campaign, which is actually the most brilliant campaign fought in Europe since Napoleon. (*Outside* Europe, old General Charles Napier accomplished feats in India in 1842 that really remind one of Alexander the Great. By and large, I consider him the best of the generals alive today.) The traditional faith in positions established in the campaigns of the 1790's that was prevalent in Italy, as in Baden, in 1849 is comical. Herr Sigel would never fight from any other position than that rendered classical by Moreau, while Charles Albert believed in the miraculous power of the Rivoli plateau no less firmly than in the virginity of Mary. In Italy this tradition was so unshakable that each major maneuver of the Austrians began with a feigned attack on Rivoli, and *each time* the Piedmontese fell into the trap. The gist of the matter, of course, was that the corresponding positions and lines of communications of the Austrians were quite different. In Hungary, Monsieur Görgei stands out above all the others, no matter who, and they all envied and hated him for it; if Görgei, with his great military talent, had not possessed a slight amount of vainglory, it is quite likely that these largely stupid attacks would have ended up by making a traitor of him. After the Világos affair, fully justified from the *military* (though *not* from the revolutionary) *standpoint,* these gentlemen made such stupid and senseless charges against Görgei, as to compel one to take an interest in this man willy-nilly. The real "treason" occurred after the withdrawal of the troops from Komárom even before the Russians got there, but Kossuth is as much to blame for this as Görgei. The role of Bayer, Görgei's chief of staff, who is now in London, has not been cleared up at all as yet. To judge from Görgei's memoirs and other documents, *he* was the soul of Görgei's *strategic* plans. B[ayer], as Pleyel told me, was the principal author of the official *Austrian* book on this campaign. (Bayer was a prisoner in Pest, but escaped.) They say that this book is very good, but I haven't been able to get it yet. Görgei speaks of Klapka with great respect, but everybody admits his extreme weakness of character. Perczel is generally recognized to be a fool, a "democratic" Hungarian general. Old man Bem considered himself to be merely a good guerrilla fighter and a good commander of a single detachment with specific assignments. As far as I can judge, he fulfilled only this function, but did so excellently. He committed two blunders: once when, after the Banat, he undertook his fruitless expedition into the unknown, and, later, when he repeated the skillful maneuver toward Hermanstadt, with which he had once been successful, during the great Russian invasion and was defeated. Papa Dembinski was simply a dreamer and a braggart, a guerrilla fighter who imagined that he was fit to be a leader in a major war and committed all sorts of extravaganzas. Amusing stories are told about him in Smit's book on the Polish campaign of 1831. . . .

Yours,

F. Engels

MARX TO CLUSS[1]

[London, June 1853]

. . . You have no other paper in New York. Wouldn't it therefore be impolitic to abandon Kellner and the paper? In the final analysis, you will be doing the fellow a service. Pretend to be naïve, and continue writing. That's the worst thing you could do to him. Don't free him from influences that, from all appearances, have become damned intolerable to him. Act like the citizens of Prussia. The government and its Manteuffel are doing their very best to get rid of the citizens' friendship. The latter act as if they believed in the constitutionality of their government, *et le gouvernement est constitutionel malgré lui-même* [and the government is constitutional in spite of itself]. That is wordly wisdom. . . .

---

[1] This letter is translated from the fragment published by Franz Mehring in *Die Neue Zeit*, Vol. 25 (1907), Pt. 2, p. 165.

MARX TO WEYDEMEYER

London, February 1, 1859

Dear Weiwi:

Your letter, dated February 28, 1858, got here (or at any rate reached me) at the end of May, and here I am replying in February 1859. The reason is very simple. I had liver trouble all spring and summer and it was only with difficulty that I managed to find time for the work I had to do. It was out of the question for me to write unless it was absolutely necessary. And later on I was swamped with work.

First of all, the most cordial regards to you and yours from all the members of my family, as well as from Engels, Lupus, and Freiligrath. And my especial compliments to your wife. Engels is, as always, in Manchester; Lupus lives there too, giving lessons, and is fairly well off. Freiligrath, in London, is the manager of a branch of the Swiss *Crédit Mobilier:* Dronke is a commission agent in Glasgow; Imandt (I don't know whether you know him) is a professor in Dundee; our good friend Weerth died in Haiti, unfortunately—an irreplaceable loss.

Things have been going badly rather than well with me for the past two years. On the one hand, the good old *Tribune* cut my income in half because of the crisis, though it never gave me an extra penny in times of prosperity; on the other hand, the time I needed for my study of political economy (more of that below) forced me to turn down (though with a heavy heart) very remunerative offers made to me in London and Vienna. But I must pursue my goal through thick and thin, and I must not allow bourgeois society to turn me into a money-making machine.

Last May Herr Cluss was here. It happened that I was with Engels in Manchester at the time. He visited my wife and accepted the invitation to return next day, but he didn't show up [. . . .][1] from London and wasn't seen again. Instead of a visit, he sent my wife a letter, written "because of embarrassment" in a rather "uncivil" manner. Nor did he show up in Manchester. We later found out that he had formed an alliance with Herr Willich. This explains the mysterious suspension of his correspondence. If we were conceited, we would have felt pretty well chastised at learning that a fool like Willich had won a victory over us even in the eyes of a man as bright as Cluss, but this whole episode had so much that was comical about it that it stifled any chagrin.

I have broken with Ernest Jones. Despite my repeated warnings

[1] Manuscript torn at this point.

and despite the fact that I accurately predicted what would happen, namely, that he would ruin himself and disorganize the Chartist party, he nevertheless took the course of trying to reach an agreement with the radical bourgeoisie. Now he is a ruined man, and the harm he has caused the British proletariat is enormous. The mistake will be corrected, of course, but an extremely favorable moment for action has been allowed to slip by. Imagine an army whose general crosses over to the camp of the enemy on the eve of a battle. . . .

The revolutionary wind blowing over the Continent of Europe has, of course, awakened all the great men from their winter sleep. I am sending off another letter together with this one—my first letter to Komp. I have given up my organizational contacts. I found them compromising for my German friends. *Over here,* after the dirty tricks played on me by the boors who let themselves be used as the tools of Kinkel and other humbugs against me, I retired completely to my study ever since the Cologne trial. My time was too valuable for me to waste in futile exertions and petty squabbles.

And now to essentials!

My *Critique of Political Economy* will be published in parts (the first part in eight or ten days from now) by Franz Duncker (Besser's publishing house) in Berlin. It is only thanks to Lassalle's extraordinary zeal and powers of persuasion that Duncker was gotten to take this step. For all that, he left a back door open for himself. *The definitive contract depends on the sale of the initial parts.*

I divide all political economy into six books:

Capital; Landed Property; Wage Labor; State; Foreign Trade; World Market.

Book I on capital consists of four sections.

Section I—Capital in general—consists of three chapters: (1) *The Commodity;* (2) *Money or Simple Circulation;* (3) *Capital.*[1] (1) and (2), about ten printer's sheets, represent the contents of the first parts to be published. You understand the *political* reasons that moved me to hold back the third chapter, on "Capital," until I have got a firm footing again.

The contents of the parts now being published are as follows:

Chapter I: The Commodity.

A. *Historical notes on the analysis of commodities.* [William Petty (an Englishman of the time of Charles II); Boisguillebert

---

[1] This plan was altered somewhat by Marx by the time Vol. I of *Capital* was published, in 1867. *Cf.* Karl Marx, *Capital,* Vol. I, International Publishers, New York, 1939.

(period of Louis XIV); B. Franklin (his first published work, 1719); the physiocrats, Sir James Steuart, Adam Smith, Ricardo, and Sismondi.]

Chapter II: Money or Simple Circulation.
   1. The measure of values.

B. *Theories of the unit of measurement of money.* [End of the seventeenth century. Locke and Lowndes; Bishop Berkeley (1750); Sir James Steuart; Lord Castlereagh; Thomas Attwood; John Gray; the Proudhonists.]

   2. *The medium of circulation.*
      a. *The metamorphosis of commodities.*
      b. *The circulation of money.*
      c. *The coin. The token of value.*
   3. *Money.*
      a. *Hoarding.*
      b. *Means of payment.*
      c. *World money.*
   4. *The precious metals.*

C. *Theories of the medium of circulation and of money.* [Monetary system; *The Spectator,* Montesquieu, David Hume; Sir James Steuart, A. Smith, J. B. Say, the Bullion Committee, Ricardo; James Mill; Lord Overstone and his school; Thomas Tooke, James Wilson, John Fullartone.]

In these two chapters, the Proudhonist socialism now fashionable in France, which proposes to let private production continue to exist, *but* proposes to *organize* the exchange of private products, which wants *commodities* but not *money,* is likewise destroyed root and branch. Communism must first of all rid itself of this "false brother." But aside from any polemical aim, you know that the analysis of the simple money-forms is the most difficult, because it is the most abstract, part of political economy. I hope to gain a scientific victory for our party. But the party itself must now show whether its membership is big enough to buy enough copies to ease the bookseller's "scruples of conscience." The continuation of the project depends upon the sale of the first few parts. Once I have a definitive contract, everything will be all right.

   Best regards.

Yours,
K. Marx

ENGELS TO WEYDEMEYER

Manchester, November 24, 1864

Dear Weydemeyer:

. . . These are boring times here in Europe. The crushing of the Polish insurrection was the last significant event; for his assistance in this affair Bismarck received permission from the Tsar to seize Schleswig-Holstein from the Danes. It will be a long time before Poland can rise again—even with outside help—and Poland is absolutely indispensable to us. The cowardice of the German liberal philistines is to blame for the whole thing. If these dogs had displayed more understanding and courage in the Prussian Diet, everything might have turned out all right. Austria was ready to come to Poland's defense at any time. The only factors that prevented it were Prussia's position and the treason of Bonaparte, who, in these circumstances, would, of course have kept his promises to the Poles only if he could have played it *safely, i.e.,* if he had been backed up by Prussia and Austria.

Your war over there is one of the most imposing experiences one can ever live through. Despite the numerous blunders committed by the Northern armies (and the South has committed its share), the conquering wave is slowly but surely rolling on, and the time must come in 1865 when the *organized* resistance of the South will suddenly fold up like a pocket knife, and the war will degenerate into banditry, as was the case in the Carlist War in Spain and, more recently, in Naples. A people's war of this sort, on both sides, is unprecedented ever since the establishment of powerful states; its outcome will doubtless determine the future of America for hundreds of years to come. As soon as slavery — that greatest of obstacles to the political and social development of the United States — has been smashed, the country will experience a boom that will very soon assure it an altogether different place in the history of the world, and the army and navy created during the war will then soon find employment.

Moreover, it is easy to see why the North found it hard to create an army and generals. From the start the Southern oligarchy placed the country's small armed forces under its own control—it supplied the officers and also robbed the arsenals. The North was left without any military cadres, except for the militia, while the South had been preparing over the course of several years. From the outset the South had available a population accustomed to the saddle for use as light cavalry, while the North lagged behind in this respect. The North adopted the method, introduced by the South, of alloting posts to adherents of a certain party; the South, engulfed in a revolution and under the rule of a military dictatorship, was able to disregard this. Hence all the blunders. I do not deny that Lee is better than all the generals of the North and that his latest campaigns around the fortified Richmond encampment are masterpieces, from which the glorious Prince Friedrich Karl of Prussia could learn a great deal. But the resolute attacks of Grant and Sherman finally rendered all this strategy useless.

It is obvious that Grant is sacrificing an enormous number of men—but could he have acted otherwise? I haven't the slightest idea of the state of discipline of your army, its steadfastness under fire, its capacity and readiness to endure hardships, and, in particular, its *morale, i.e.,* what can be demanded of it without risking its demoralization. One must know all that before venturing a judgment, especially if one is on the other side of the ocean, without adequate information, and without any decent maps. But it seems to me certain that the army now commanded by Sherman is the best of your armies, as superior to Hood's army as Lee's army is to Grant's.

Your tables of organization and your elementary tactics are borrowed entirely from the French, as I have heard—thus the basic formation is the column, with spaces between the platoons. What is your field artillery like now? If you could give me some information on this point, I should be very grateful. What happened to the great man Anneke? I lost sight of him after he almost lost the battle of Pittsburg Landing because he hadn't been issued everything he was supposed to have according to the Prussian table of organization. Of the Germans participating in all the campaigns, Willich has apparently made the best showing; Sigel, on the other hand, demonstrated his mediocrity. And Schurz, the valiant Schurz, who p . . . . . under a hail of bullets, what enemies is he annihilating now?

By the way, the Prussian guns that leveled Düppel and Sonderburg[1] at a range of 6500 paces were old, long, bronze 24-pounders rifled and adapted for breech loading, the shell weighing 54 pounds, and the charge — 4 pounds! I have seen them myself.

Best regards to your wife.

Yours,
F. Engels

---

[1] Two Danish fortresses captured in the Prusso-Danish War of 1864.

MARX TO WEYDEMEYER

London, November 29, 1864

Dear Weywey:

I am sending you simultaneously by mail four copies of a printed address drafted by me.[1] The newly established International Workingmen's Committee, in whose name it is issued, is not without importance. Its English members consist mostly of the chiefs of the local trade unions, that is, the actual labor kings of London, the same fellows who prepared the gigantic reception for Garibaldi and prevented Palmerston from declaring *war* upon the *United States,* as he was on the point of doing, through the monster meeting in St. James's Hall (under Bright's chairmanship). The members from the French are insignificant, but they are the direct organs of the leading "workmen" in Paris.

There is likewise a connection with the Italian societies, which recently held their congress in Naples. Although for years I systematically declined all participation in all "organizations," I accepted *this time,* because it involved a matter where it is possible to do some important work. . . .

Yours,

K. Marx

ADDRESS OF THE INTERNATIONAL WORKINGMEN'S ASSOCIATION TO ABRAHAM LINCOLN [2]

To Abraham Lincoln,
President of the United States of America.

Sir: — We congratulate the American people upon your re-election by a large majority. If resistance to the Slave Power was the reserved watchword of your first election, the triumphant war-cry of your re-election is, Death to Slavery.

From the commencement of the titanic American strife the workingmen of Europe felt instinctively that the star-spangled banner carried the destiny of their class. The contest for the territories which

[1] Marx's *Inaugural Address* of the First International. See *Founding of the First International,* International Publishers, New York, 1937.

[2] This address was signed by all the members of the General Council of the International Workingmen's Association (the First International) and was forwarded to President Lincoln through Charles Francis Adams, the Minister of the United States in London. It was published in *The Bee-Hive,* London, January 7, 1865.

opened the dire epopee, was it not to decide whether the virgin soil
of immense tracts should be wedded to the labor of the emigrant
or prostituted by the tramp of the slave driver?

When an oligarchy of 300,000 slaveholders dared to inscribe, for
the first time in the annals of the world, "slavery" on the banner of
armed revolt; when on the very spots where hardly a century ago the
idea of one great democratic republic had first sprung up, whence
the first declaration of the Rights of Man was issued, and the first
impulse given to the European revolution of the eighteenth century;
when on those very spots counter-revolution, with systematic thor-
oughness, gloried in rescinding "the ideas entertained at the time of
the formation of the old Constitution," and maintained "slavery to
be a beneficent institution, indeed the only solution of the great
problem of the relation of labor to capital," and cynically proclaimed
property in man "the cornerstone of the new edifice"; then the
working classes of Europe understood at once, even before the
fanatic partisanship of the upper classes for the Confederate gentry
had given its dismal warning, that the slaveholders' rebellion was
to sound the tocsin for a general holy crusade of property against
labor, and that for the men of labor, with their hopes for the future,
even their past conquests were at stake in that tremendous conflict
on the other side of the Atlantic. Everywhere they bore therefore
patiently the hardships imposed upon them by the cotton crisis,
opposed enthusiastically the pro-slavery intervention, importunities
of their "betters," and from most parts of Europe contributed their
quota of blood to the good cause.

While the workingmen, the true political power of the North,
allowed slavery to defile their own republic; while before the Negro,
mastered and sold without his concurrence, they boasted it the
highest prerogative of the white-skinned laborer to sell himself and
choose his own master; they were unable to attain the true freedom
of labor or to support their European brethren in their struggle for
emancipation, but this barrier to progress has been swept off by
the red sea of civil war.

The workingmen of Europe feel sure that as the American War
of Independence initiated a new era of ascendancy for the middle
class, so the American anti-slavery War will do for the working
classes. They consider it an earnest of the epoch to come, that it fell
to the lot of Abraham Lincoln, the single-minded son of the working
class, to lead his country through the matchless struggle for the rescue
of an enchained race and the reconstruction of a social world.

ENGELS TO WEYDEMEYER

Manchester, March 10, 1865

Dear Weydemeyer:

At last I have gotten down to answering your letter of January 20. I sent it to Marx, who kept it for a very long time—partly because he was ill—and returned it to me only last week. I was unable to write you by the previous steamer, as I was too busy with the firm's affairs on that day.

Many thanks for the detailed answer to my questions. I had lost the thread of the "combined" operations because of the careless war reporting in the local press. The Red River expedition remained entirely incomprehensible to me, and even Sherman's movement eastward from Vicksburg was very obscure, as no one over here had written about the southern corps advancing from New Orleans. These combined operations, with a junction point not only in the enemy's territory, but even behind his lines, indicate how primitive are the strategic notions of a people wholly inexperienced in military affairs. Nevertheless, if the honorable Wrangel and Prince Friedrich Karl had not commanded forces twice as large as the enemy's in the war with Denmark, they would have done exactly the same. The battle of Missund and the two incomprehensible "demonstrations" (I use that word as some sort of name for a thing not having a name) against Düppel before the offensive were even more childish.

As for Grant's conduct before Richmond, I endeavor to explain it otherwise. I fully share your opinion that it would have been *strategically* correct to attack Richmond from the *west*. But it seems to me—in so far as one can judge, at such a distance and without accurate information—that Grant chose the eastern approach for two reasons:

1. Because it was easier for him to secure supplies there. In the west the only railroads he could use were the ones to Fredericksburg and Tennessee (both of these roads passed through regions exhausted by the war), while in the east he had the Fredericksburg railroad, as well as the York and the James Rivers. Bearing in mind the difficulty of supplying large armies, which played so important a part throughout the war, I cannot condemn Grant unqualifiedly until I am clear on this point. You upbraid him for having turned his back to the *sea*, but when you command the sea and possess secured embarkation points for troops (Monroe and Norfolk), that is an *advantage*. Compare Wellington's campaigns in Spain and the Crimean campaign, during which the Allies, after their victory at the Alma, actually *fled*, in order to

have the sea protect their rear south of Sebastopol. It is quite obvious that possession of the Shenandoah Valley was the best guarantee of the security of Washington.

2. But the question arises: did Grant (or, for that matter, Lincoln) *want* to have Washington secured against all danger? On the contrary, it seems to me that with the looseness of the Federal Constitution and the rather indifferent attitude toward the war of some regions in the North, Lincoln really never seriously wanted to drive the Confederates out of Richmond, but rather wanted to keep them in positions from which they threatened Washington, Pennsylvania, and even New York to some extent. I believe that otherwise he never would have gotten the recruits or the money to finish the war. I readily believe that Grant has very much wanted to capture Richmond for the past 3-4 months, but he hasn't been strong enough. I estimate his forces are 70-90,000 men, while Lee has 50-70,000. If this ratio is approximately correct, then he achieved the maximum possible in his offensive, which was known to be strategically incorrect beforehand, by wresting from Lee any possibility of waging an offensive defense and by surrounding Richmond on at least three sides. I do not think that Lee, after having distinguished himself among all the other Northern and Southern generals by his brilliant counter-offensives during the past two years, would now give up this method of waging war unless he were *compelled* to do so. On the other hand, the North has gained an extraordinary advantage in having been able to pin the South's best army down to Richmond, to one corner of the South's terrain because of a childish point of honor, until all the adjoining territory had been cut off and disorganized militarily for the Southerners as a result of the conquest of the Mississippi Valley and of Sherman's campaign, and until it was possible for all the Union's available troops to advance on Richmond to finish the business with one decisive blow. This, apparently, is now taking place.

The latest news received from New York is dated February 25. They report the capture of Charleston and Wilmington and Sherman's march from Columbia to Winnsboro. Obviously, Sherman is the only man in the North who is able to hammer victories out of his soldiers' feet. The men under his command must be splendid fellows. I await the development of events with impatience. If Lee evaluates his desperate situation correctly, there is nothing left for him but to break camp and move south. But whither? The only road *open* to him is the road to Lynchburg and Tennessee; but it is too risky to enter a narrow mountain valley with a single rail line, fronting on the fortifications of Knoxville and Chattanooga. Moreover, this would most likely mean simply sacrificing the troops of Beauregard and Hardee, as well as the other Confederate forces in North Carolina, and exposing his flank to Sherman. Or debouching on Petersburg, turning Grant's left flank, and moving directly south against Sherman? This is risky, but it is the most advantageous move, the only way of gathering around him the remnants of the fleeing armies, holding up Grant by destroying the rail lines and bridges, and falling upon Sherman with superior forces. If Sherman accepts battle, with the whole Southern army against him, he will doubtless be defeated, while if he falls back to the coast, he opens Lee's road to Augusta, where the latter can give his army its first breathing spell. But in that event Sherman and Grant would certainly join forces, and Lee would again be faced with superior forces, and this time he would have to fight in the open field, as I do not believe the Confederates can again assemble enough fortress guns at any point within the country to organize a new Richmond. But even if they did so, they would have escaped one trap only to fall into another. The last alternative is an invasion of the North. Jefferson Davis is fully capable of it, but if they did this, everything would be over in two weeks.

Lee might also send only part of his forces southward to stop Sherman, together with Beauregard and the others. This seems to to me to be the most likely way out. In that event, Sherman will probably "give them a thrashing," as they say in Southern Germany, and then there will be nothing more that Lee can do. But even if Sherman should be defeated, Lee would have gained only one month's respite, and the troops advancing up from the coast on all sides — not to mention Grant's victories over the weakened Richmond army in the meanwhile—would soon make his position as bad as it had been before. Come what may, the war is coming to an end, and I wait for every steamer with the greatest impatience, for exciting news reports are now raining down. The strategic speculations of the numerous southern sympathizers over here are extremely funny: they all boil down to the maxim of the Polish-Palatine General Sznayde, who, every time he ran away, said: "We are acting exactly like Kossuth."

I am very grateful for your information on the American armed forces—without it I could not have gotten a clear picture of a number of problems of the war being fought over there. I have known the "Napoleon" guns for a long time; the British *had already abandoned them* (they are light, smooth-bore 12-pounder cannon, with a charge weighing one-quarter that of the shell) when Louis Bonaparte invented them anew. You can purchase as many Prussian howitzers as you want, as they have all been withdrawn from service and replaced by the rifled 4-pounders and 6-pounders (which fire 13-pound and 9-pound shells). I am not at all surprised that the angle of elevation of your howitzers is only 5°; for the angle of elevation was no higher in the old French long howitzers (before 1856), while, if I am not mistaken, the British are not much better. For a long time the Germans have been the only ones to use high-angle fire with howitzers, but the latter's inaccuracy, especially in range, brought them into disrepute.

I come now to other matters.

A Frankfurt lawyer by the name of von Schweitzer established himself in Berlin with a little newspaper, *Der Social-Demokrat,* and asked us to write for it. As Liebknecht, who is in Berlin, was to join the editorial board, we accepted. But then an insufferable Lassalle cult began to develop in the paper, while we learned positively (old lady Hatzfeldt told it to Liebknecht and asked him to work along those lines) that Lassalle was involved with Bismarck *much more deeply* than we had ever known. An actual alliance existed between them, which had gone so far that Lassalle was to go to Schleswig-Holstein and there advocate the annexation of the duchies to Prussia, whereas Bismarck had made less definite promises concerning the introduction of a sort of universal suffrage, and more specific promises regarding the right of coalition and social concessions, government support for workers' associations, and the like. The stupid Lassalle *had absolutely no guarantees* from Bismarck; *au contraire* [on the contrary], he would have been thrown into jail *sans façon* [unceremoniously] as soon as he became troublesome. The gentlemen of the *Social-Demokrat knew this* and nevertheless continued with the Lassalle cult more and more intensively. And then these fellows let themselves be intimidated by the *threats* made by Wagener (of the *Kreuzzeitung),* and began to pay court to Bismarck, flirt with him, etc., etc. This began to be too much. We printed the enclosed declaration and withdrew, Liebknecht also resigning. The *Social-Demokrat* then declared that we did not belong to the Social-Democratic Party; this excommunication set us at ease, of course. The whole Lassallean Allgemeiner Deutscher Arbeiterverein [General Association of German Workers] is on such a false track that nothing can be done; moreover, it won't last long.

I was asked to write on military problems, which I did, but in the meanwhile the tensions increased, and the article turned into a pamphlet, which I have had printed separately; I am sending you a copy by this steamer.[1] According to the papers I receive, the thing seems to be causing a considerable scandal, particularly along the Rhine; in any event it will do a lot to keep the workers from joining up with reaction right away.

The International Association in London is progressing splendidly. Especially in Paris, but no less so in London. It is doing well in Switzerland and Italy, too. Only the German Lassalleans refuse to bite, especially not under the present circumstances. We are getting letters and offers, however, from all over Germany; things have taken a definite turn, and the rest will follow. . . .

Yours,

F. Engels

ADDRESS OF THE INTERNATIONAL WORKINGMEN'S ASSOCIATION TO PRESIDENT JOHNSON [2]

To Andrew Johnson,
President of the United States.
Sir:

The demon of the "peculiar institution," for the supremacy of which the South rose in arms, would not allow his worshippers to honorably succumb on the open field. What he had begun in treason, he must needs end in infamy. As Philip II.'s war for the Inquisition bred a Gérard, thus Jefferson Davis' pro-slavery war a Booth.[3]

It is not our part to call words of sorrow and horror, while the heart of two worlds heaves with emotion. Even the sycophants who, year after year, and day by day, stuck to their Sisyphus work of morally assassinating Abraham Lincoln and the great republic he headed stand now aghast at this universal outburst of popular feeling, and rival with each other to strew rhetorical flowers on his open grave. They have now at last found out that he was a man neither to be browbeaten by adversity nor intoxicated by success, inflexibly pressing on to his great goal, never compromising it by blind haste, slowly maturing his steps, never retracing them, carried away by no

[1] *Die preussische Militärfrage und die deutsche Arbeiterpartei* [*The Military Question in Prussia and the German Workers Party*], Hamburg, 1865.

[2] Written in English by Marx and adopted by the General Council of the International Workingmen's Association on May 13, 1865. Published in *The Bee-Hive*, London, May 20, 1865.

[3] Balthazar Gérard, the agent of Philip II of Spain, on July 10, 1584, assassinated William of Orange, leader of the Netherlands Seven United Provinces which were engaged in a mortal struggle for independence from Spain. John Wilkes Booth was the assassin of Abraham Lincoln.

surge of popular favor, disheartened by no slackening of the popular pulse, tempering stern acts by the gleams of a kind heart, illuminating scenes dark with passion by the smile of humor, doing his titanic work as humbly and homely as heaven-born rulers do little things with the grandiloquence of pomp and state; in one word, one of the rare men who succeed in becoming great without ceasing to be good. Such, indeed, was the modesty of this great and good man that the world only discovered him a hero after he had fallen a martyr.

To be singled out by the side of such a chief, the second victim to the infernal gods of slavery, was an honor due to Mr. Seward. Had he not, at a time of general hesitation, the sagacity to foresee and the manliness to foretell "the irrepressible conflict"? Did he not, in the darkest hours of that conflict, prove true to the Roman duty to never despair of the republic and its stars? We earnestly hope that he and his son will be restored to health, public activity, and well-deserved honors within much less than "90 days."

After a tremendous war, but which, if we consider its vast dimensions, and its broad scope, and compare it to the Old World's Hundred Years' Wars, and Thirty Years' Wars, and Twenty-Three Years' Wars,[1] can hardly be said to have lasted 90 days, yours, Sir, has become the task to uproot by the law what has been felled by the sword, to preside over the arduous work of political reconstruction and social regeneration. A profound sense of your great mission will save you from any compromise with stern duties. You will never forget that to initiate the new era of the emancipation of labor, the American people devolved the responsibilities of leadership upon two men of labor—the one Abraham Lincoln, the other Andrew Johnson.

---

[1] The Hundred Years' War is the name given the series of contests waged by the English kings between 1337 and 1453 for possession of the French crown and French territory. The great religious struggles between 1618 and 1648 are called the Thirty Years' War. These struggles marked the climax of the Reformation and closed the period of distinctively religious wars in Europe. The Twenty-Three Years' War refers to the period of almost uninterrupted European warfare from 1740 to 1763. It includes the First Silesian War (1740-42), the War of the Austrian Succession (1741-48), the Second Silesian War (1744-45), the raid of the Young Pretender into England (1745-46), and the Seven Years' War (1756-63), which began in 1751 in India and in 1754 in North America, where it is known as the French and Indian War.

MARX TO MEYER

Hannover, April 30, 1867

Dear Friend:

You must have a very bad opinion of me, the more so when I tell you that your letters not only gave me *great pleasure,* but were a *real solace* for me during the harrowing period when I received them. Knowing that an able man, *à la hauteur des principes* [of high principle], is secured for the party compensates me for the worst. Moreover, your letters were filled with the kindest friendship for me personally, and you will understand that I, who am engaged in the bitterest conflict with the whole (official) world, can least underestimate this.

Well, why didn't I answer you? Because I was constantly hovering at the edge of the grave. Hence I had to make use of EVERY moment when I was able to work to complete my book, to which I have sacrificed health, happiness, and family. I trust that this explanation needs no further postscript. I laugh at the so-called "practical" men and their wisdom. If one chose to be an ox, one could of course turn one's back on the sufferings of mankind and look after one's own skin. But I should have really regarded myself as *impractical* if I had pegged out without completely finishing my book, at least in manuscript.

The first volume of the work will be published in a few weeks by *Otto Meissner* in Hamburg. The title is: *Capital, a Critique of Political Economy.* I have come to Germany in order to bring the manuscript across and am staying for a few weeks with a friend [Dr. Ludwig Kugelmann] in Hannover on my way back to London.

Volume I comprises the *"Process of Capitalist Production."* Besides the general theoretical exposition, I describe in great detail, from hitherto unused *official* sources, the condition of the English agricultural and industrial proletariat *during the last 20 years,* ditto *Irish* conditions. You will, of course, understand that all this only serves me as an *"argumentum ad hominem."*[1] I hope that the whole work will have been published in a year from now. *Volume II* gives the continuation and conclusion of the theories, *Volume III the history of political economy from the middle of the seventeenth century.*[2]

As for the International Workingmen's Association, it has become

[1] Turning the weapons of the adversary (*i.e.,* the English bourgeoisie) against itself.

[2] Marx intended to publish the continuation of the first volume of *Capital* in *one* volume; this volume grew into two. Consequently the volume that had been planned as Volume III (Theories of Surplus Value), was later numbered IV. (See Engels' Preface to Vol. II of *Capital.*)

a power in England, France, Switzerland, and Belgium. Establish as many branches as possible in America. Dues per member one penny (about one silbergroschen) per annum, but every group contributes what it can. Congress this year in Lausanne, September 3rd. Write me about these things, about how you yourself are getting on in America, and about general conditions. If you keep silent, I shall consider it proof that you still haven't forgiven me.

Cordially yours,
Karl Marx

MARX TO MEYER

London, July 4, 1868

Dear Friend:

. . . I enclose credentials for Sorge. We are in direct communication with Whaley, Sylvis, and Jessup.

The Commonwealth ceased publication a long time ago. Weekly reports on the meetings of the General Council [of the First International] are printed in the *Bee-Hive*. But this paper is a narrow-minded trade-union organ, which is far from representing our views.

Up to now German press reviews of my book [*Capital*]—most of them quite favorable—have appeared in the following newspapers: *Die Zukunft,* the Stuttgart *Beobachter,* the Württemberg *Staatsanzeiger,* the *Frankfurter Börsenzeitung,* the *Hamburger Börsenzeitung,* the Hamburg *Anzeiger,* etc., and in Hannover papers and papers in the Rhine Province and Westphalia. Especially comprehensive reviews in the form of a series of articles were published in Schweitzer's *Social-Demokrat* (Berlin) and in the *Elberfelder Zeitung.* Both of these papers (though the latter is a liberal bourgeois newspaper) openly took my side.

The big bourgeois and reactionary papers, such as the *Kölnische* [*Zeitung*], the *Augsburger* [*Zeitung*], the *Neue Preussische* [*Zeitung*], the *Vossische* [*Zeitung*], etc., are careful to keep their mouths shut.

The only thing that has appeared in the camp of official political economy is the report by Dr. Dühring (privatdozent at the University of Berlin, an adherent of Carey's) , printed at the beginning of the year in the *Hildburghauser Ergänzungsblätter.* (The report is fainthearted, but on the whole sympathetic.) An article was also published in the July issue of the economic journal edited by Faucher and Michaelis. But Faucher's comments are, of course, what one would expect from the buffoon and hired jester of Bastiat's German disciples.

I should be very glad to have you send me newspapers from time to time, but it would be particularly useful to me if you could collect some anti-bourgeois material on land-ownership and agricultural conditions in the United States. As I am dealing with *land rent* in Volume II [*Capital*], material attacking H. Carey's harmonies would be particularly welcome.

Best regards.

Salut,

Yours,

K. Marx

ENCLOSURE London, July 4, 1868

We recommend Mr. Sorge to all the friends of the International Workingmen's Association, and we likewise empower him to act in the name of and on the behalf of this Association.

For the General Council of the International Workingmen's Association,

Karl Marx

Secretary for Germany

ADDRESS OF THE INTERNATIONAL WORKINGMEN'S ASSOCIATION TO THE NATIONAL LABOR UNION [1]

Fellow Workmen:

In the inaugural address of our association we said: "It was not the wisdom of the ruling classes, but the heroic resistance to their criminal folly by the working classes of England that saved the West of Europe from plunging headlong into an infamous crusade for the perpetuation and propagation of slavery on the other side of the Atlantic." It is now your turn to prevent a war whose direct result would be to throw back, for an indefinite period, the rising labor movement on both sides of the Atlantic.

We need hardly tell you that there are European powers anxiously engaged in fomenting a war between the United States and England. A glance at the statistics of commerce shows that the Russian export of raw products — and Russia has nothing else to export — was giving way to American competition when the Civil War tipped the scales. To turn the American ploughshare into a sword would at this time save from impending bankruptcy a power whom your republican statesmen in their wisdom had chosen for their confidential adviser. But disregarding the particular interests of this or that government,

[1] Written in English by Marx and adopted by the General Council of the International Workingmen's Association on May 11, 1869.

is it not in the general interest of our oppressors to disturb by a war the movement of rapidly extending international cooperation?

In our congratulatory address to Mr. Lincoln on the occasion of his re-election to the Presidency[1] we expressed it as our conviction that the Civil War would prove to be as important to the progress of the working class as the War of Independence has been to the elevation of the middle class. And the successful close of the war against slavery has indeed inaugurated a new era in the annals of the working class. In the United States itself an independent labor movement has since arisen which the old parties and the professional politicians view with distrust. But to bear fruit it needs years of peace. To suppress it, a war between the United States and England would be the sure means.

The immediate tangible result of the Civil War was of course a deterioration of the condition of the American workingmen. Both in the United States and in Europe the colossal burden of a public debt was shifted from hand to hand in order to settle it upon the shoulders of the working class. The prices of necessaries, remarks one of your statesmen, have risen 78 per cent since 1860, while the wages of simple manual labor have risen 50 and those of skilled labor 60 per cent. "Pauperism," he complains, "is increasing in America more rapidly than population." Moreover the sufferings of the working class are in glaring contrast to the newfangled luxury of financial aristocrats, shoddy aristocrats, and other vermin bred by war. Still the Civil War offered a compensation in the liberation of the slaves and the impulse which it thereby gave to your own class movement. Another war, not sanctified by a sublime aim or a social necessity but like the wars of the Old World, would forge chains for the free workingmen instead of sundering those of the slave. The accumulated misery which it would leave in its wake would furnish your capitalists at once with the motive and the means of separating the working class from their courageous and just aspirations by the soulless sword of a standing army. Yours, then, is the glorious task of seeing to it that at last the working class shall enter upon the scene of history, no longer as a servile following, but as an independent power, as a power imbued with a sense of its responsibility and capable of commanding peace where their would-be masters cry war.

[1] See pp. 65-66.

MARX TO MEYER AND VOGT

London, April 9, 1870

Dear Meyer and Dear Vogt:

... After occupying myself with the Irish question for many years I have come to the conclusion that the decisive blow against the English ruling classes (and it will be decisive for the workers' movement all over the world) can *not* be delivered *in England* but *only in Ireland.* On December 1, 1869, the General Council issued a confidential circular drawn up by me in French (for the reaction upon England only the French, not the German, papers are important), on the relation of the Irish national struggle to the emancipation of the working class, and therefore on the attitude which the International Workingmen's Association should take toward the Irish question.

I will here only give you in brief the decisive points.

Ireland is the bulwark of the *English landed aristocracy.* The exploitation of this country is not only one of the main sources of their material wealth, it is their greatest *moral* strength. They, in fact, represent the *domination of England over Ireland.* Ireland is therefore the *grand moyen* [great means] by which the English aristocracy maintains *its domination in England* itself.

On the other hand, should the English army and police move out of Ireland tomorrow, you would at once have an agrarian revolution in Ireland. But the overthrow of the English aristocracy in Ireland involves and has as a necessary consequence its overthrow in England. And this would fulfill the prerequisite for the proletarian revolution in England. The destruction of the English landed aristocracy in Ireland is an infinitely easier operation than in England itself, because the *land question* has hitherto been the *exclusive form* of the social question in Ireland, because it is a question of existence, of *life and death,* for the immense majority of the Irish people, and because it is at the same time inseparable from the *national* question. Quite apart from the passionate character of the Irish and the fact that they are more revolutionary than the English.

As for the English *bourgeoisie,* they have *d'abord* [in the first place] a common interest with the aristocracy in transforming Ireland into a mere pasture land, which provides the English market with meat and wool at the cheapest possible prices. It has the same interest in reducing the Irish population to such a small number, by eviction and forcible emigration, that *English capital* (leasehold capital) can function with "security" in that country. They have the same interest in clearing the estate of Ireland as they had in the clearing of the agricultural districts of England and Scotland. The £6000—£8000 absentee and other Irish revenues which at present flow annually to London have likewise to be taken into account.[1]

But the English bourgeoisie has also much more important interests in the present Irish regime. Owing to the constantly increasing concentration of leaseholds, Ireland constantly supplies its own surplus to the English labor market and thus forces down wages and the moral and material position of the English working class.

And most important of all! Every industrial and commercial center in England now possesses a working-class population *divided* into two *hostile* camps, English proletarians and Irish proletarians. The ordinary English worker hates the Irish worker as a competitor who lowers his standard of life. In relation to the Irish worker he feels himself a member of the *ruling* nation and so turns himself into a tool of the aristocrats and capitalists *against Ireland,* thus strengthening their domination *over himself.* He cherishes religious, social, and national prejudices against the Irish worker. His attitude towards him is much the same as that of the "poor whites" to the Negroes in the former slave states of the U. S. A. The Irishman pays him back with interest in his own money. He regards the English worker as both the accomplice and the stupid tool of *English rule in Ireland.*

This antagonism is artificially kept alive and intensified by the press, the pulpit, the comic papers, in short by all the means at the disposal of the ruling classes. *This antagonism* is the *secret of the impotence of the English working class,* despite their organization. It is the secret by which the capitalist class maintains its power. The latter is well aware of this.

But the evil does not stop here. It continues across the ocean. The antagonism between English and Irish is the hidden basis of the conflict between the United States and England. It makes any honest and serious co-operation between the working classes of the two countries impossible. It enables the governments of both countries to break the edge of the social conflict, whenever they think fit, by their mutual bullying and, in case of need, by war between the two countries.

England, as the metropolis of capital, as the power that has hitherto ruled the world market, is for the time being the most important country for the workers' revolution, and moreover the

---

[1] "£6000—£8000" refers to the average income of an absentee landlord.

only country in which the material conditions for this revolution have developed to a certain degree of maturity. Therefore to hasten the social revolution in England is the most important object of the International Workingmen's Association. The sole means of hastening it is to make Ireland independent.

Hence the task of the International is everywhere to put the conflict between England and Ireland in the foreground, and everywhere to side openly with Ireland. The special task of the Central Council in London is to awaken the English workers to a realization of the fact that *for them* the *national emancipation of Ireland* is no question of abstract justice or humanitarian sentiment but *the first condition of their own emancipation.*

These are, roughly, the principal points made in the circular letter, which thereby likewise set forth the *raisons d'être* [motives] for the General Council's resolutions on the Irish Amnesty. Shortly thereafter I sent a sharp anonymous article on how the British were treating the Fenians, etc., attacking Gladstone, etc.—to the *Internationale* (the organ of our Belgian Central Committee in Brussels). In the same article, I accused the French republicans (the *Marseillaise* had printed a stupid article on Ireland written over here by the miserable Talandier) of centering all their *colères* [indignation], in their national egotism, on the French Empire.

This worked. My daughter Jenny, over the signature of "J. Williams" (in a private letter to the editors she had used the name of Jenny Williams), wrote a series of articles for the *Marseillaise* and also published a letter from O'Donovan Rossa. Hence immense noise.

After years of cynical refusal, *Gladstone* was *thereby* finally compelled to agree to a *Parliamentary inquiry* into the treatment of the Fenian prisoners. Jenny is now the regular correspondent on Irish affairs for the *Marseillaise. (This is between us, of course.)* The British government and the British press are murderously furious that the Irish problem is now on the *ordre du jour* [order of the day] in France and that this *canaille* is now being watched and exposed throughout the Continent, via Paris.

This stone also brought down another bird. We thus forced the Irish leaders, journalists, and the like in Dublin to enter into relations with us, something that the *General Council* had been unable to achieve previously!

In America you have a broader field for work along the same lines. *A coalition of the German workers with the Irish* (as well as with those English and American workers who are ready to do so) is the most important job you could start on at the present time.

This must be done in the name of the International. The social significance of the Irish problem must be made clear. . . .

Salut et fraternité!

Karl Marx

MARX TO SORGE

[London] September 1, 1870

Dear Mr. Sorge:

My continued silence in the face of your several letters was due to two circumstances: at first "overwork," later very serious illness. At the beginning of August the doctors sent me to the seashore. But there a violent sciatica bent me double for weeks. I have been back in London only since yesterday, by no means fully recovered.

First of all, my best thanks for what you have sent me, especially the Labor Statistics, which are of great value to me.

Now I shall briefly answer the questions in your various letters.

Hume [1] was empowered to carry on propaganda among the Yankees, but has exceeded his powers. I shall submit the matter to the General Council next Tuesday, with an exhibition of his "cards."

As for the "secretaryship" for the U. S., the matter stands as follows: I am secretary for the *German* branches over there, Dupont for the *French,* and lastly Eccarius for the *Yankees* and the English-speaking section. In our public declarations, therefore, Eccarius figures as "Secretary for the U. S." Otherwise we should have to employ useless circumlocutions. I, for instance, would also have to sign as "Secretary for the *Russian* Branch" in Geneva, and so on. Moreover, Eccarius himself plainly set forth the state of affairs in a New York paper — in connection with Cluseret. [2]

Next week I shall send you a pack of membership cards.

The miserable behavior of Paris during the war [Franco-Prussian War of 1870-71]—still allowing itself to be ruled by the mamelukes of Louis Bonaparte and of the *Spanish* adventuress Eugenie after these appalling defeats—shows how much the French need a tragic lesson in order to regain their manhood.

What the Prussian jackasses do not see is that the present war is

---

[1] Hume was an American reformer and had had membership cards of the International Workingmen's Association printed for himself with all sorts of phraseology of the French Revolution.

[2] Gustave Cluseret, Minister of War in the Paris Commune from April 3 to April 30, 1871, claimed to represent the International Workingmen's Association in the United States.

leading just as inevitably to a war between Germany and Russia as the War of 1866 led to the war between Prussia and France. This is the *best result* that I expect from Germany. "Prussianism" as such never has existed, and can never exist, except in alliance with and in subjection to Russia. And such a war No. 2 will act as the midwife of the inevitable social revolution in Russia.

I regret that some misunderstanding on the part of my friend Vogt which is incomprehensible to me has led to a wrong opinion regarding Schily. Schily is not only one of my oldest and most intimate personal friends; he is one of the ablest, most courageous, and most reliable members of the party.

I am very glad that Meyer is going to Cincinnati as a delegate.[1]

Most faithfully yours,

Karl Marx

I should like to have a look at the Kellogg money nonsense [2] (merely a variety of Bray, Gray, Bronterre O'Brien, etc., in England and of Proudhon in France) in the original. The stuff cannot be gotten here.

K. M.

MARX TO MEYER

[London] January 21, 1871

Dear Meyer:

... We have worked up a powerful movement among the working class over here against Gladstone (in support of the French Republic), which will probably bring about his downfall. At the present time Prussia is wholly under the sway of the Russian Cabinet. If it gains a conclusive victory, the heroic German philistine will get what he deserves. Unfortunately, the present French government thinks it can wage a revolutionary war without a revolution. . . .

The semiofficial *Archives of Forensic Medicine* is published in St. Petersburg (in Russian). One of the physicians writing for this journal published an article, "On the Hygienic Conditions of the Western European Proletariat," in the last quarto issue, chiefly quoting my book [*Capital*], and mentioning the source. This re-

[1] To the August 1870 convention of the National Labor Union.
[2] Edward Kellogg, a small merchant in New York, having lost his property in the crisis of 1837, developed a plan for financial reform which he first published in 1848 under the title, *Labor and Other Capital*. Kellogg's ideas began to win influence in the labor movement during the Civil War. During the period from 1867 to 1872, when Greenbackism or monetary reform dominated the ideology of the labor movement, Kellogg's influence was at its height.

sulted in the following calamity: the censor was severely rebuked by the Minister of the Interior, the editor-in-chief was fired, and that issue of the journal—all the copies they could still get hold of —was consigned to the flames!

I don't know whether I told you that at the beginning of 1870 I began to study Russian, which I now read fairly fluently. This came about after I had received Flerovsky's very important work on *The Condition of the Working Class* (*Especially the Peasants*) *in Russia* from St. Petersburg; I also wanted to familiarize myself with the (excellent) economic works of Chernyshevsky (who was rewarded by being sentenced to the Siberian mines for the past seven years). The result was worth the effort that a man of my age must make to master a language, differing so greatly from the classical, Germanic, and Romance languages. The intellectual movement now taking place in Russia testifies to the fact that fermentation is occurring deep below the surface. Minds are always connected by invisible threads with the body of the people. . . .

Regards to you and Vogt,

Yours,
Karl Marx

I wrote to my old friend G. J. Harney, who is now Assistant Secretary of State of Massachusetts, concerning the public lands.

MARX TO BOLTE

Brighton, August 25, 1871

Dear Mr. Bolte:

I have been here for about two weeks, sent by the doctor because my health was very much impaired as a result of overwork. I shall probably return to London next week, however.

Next week you will receive an appeal from the General Council for the refugee Communards. Most of them are *in London* (over 80 to 90 by now). The General Council has kept them above water up to now, but in the past two weeks our funds have melted away so fast, while the number of arrivals increases daily, that they are in a very deplorable condition. I hope that everything possible will be done in New York. In Germany all the resources of the party are still absorbed by the victims of the police persecution there, as is the case in Austria, as well as in Spain and Italy. In Switzerland they not only have a part of the refugees themselves to support, though only a small part, but they also have to aid the Internationals as a result of the St. Gall lockout.[1] Lastly, in Belgium there also are some of the refugees, though only a few of them, and, what is more, the Belgians have to aid them, particularly in getting them through to London.

Owing to these circumstances, up to the present all the funds for the bulk of the refugees in London have been raised exclusively in England.

The *General Council* now includes the following members of the Commune: Serraillier, Vaillant, Theisz, Longuet, and Fränkel, and the *following agents of the Commune:* Delahaye, Rochat, Bastelica and Chalain.

I have sent the *New York Herald* a statement in which I disclaim all responsibility for its correspondent's absurd and wholly falsified report of his conversation with me. I do not know whether it has printed the statement.[2]

Give Sorge my regards. I shall answer his letter next week.

Faithfully yours,

Karl Marx

MARX TO CONWAY[3]

[London, August 29, 1871]

Dear Sir:

Upon my return from Brighton I found your note, dated August 24.[4] The next session of the General Council will take place today, but as it will continue debate on the courts-martial in France, no outside visitors will be allowed to be present, in accordance with a resolution adopted last Tuesday. This strict regulation was made necessary by the penetration of detectives and spies of the French police into our sessions.

I have the honor to enclose a list of the French refugees. Their number (about 80-90 at the present time) is constantly increasing, day by day, while our funds are completely exhausted. The situation

[1] A strike of textile finishers in St. Gall, Switzerland, that began on June 13, 1871, was countered by a city-wide employers' lockout of all workers who refused to sign affidavits that they were not members of the International Workingmen's Association.

[2] The statement was not carried in the *New York Herald.*

[3] This letter was written in English.

[4] Moncure D. Conway had inquired about the date of the next session of the General Council.

is truly deplorable. It would be best to form a special committee, if possible, to take over the job of finding work for the refugees, most of whom are skilled workers and professional men.

Sincerely yours,
Karl Marx

MARX TO SORGE

[London] September 12, 1871

Dear Mr. Sorge:

Kindly transmit the enclosed letter from our Irish secretary, McDonnell, to J. Devoy.

I had no time to reply to you in greater detail. We are so extremely busy here at the present time that I have been compelled for the past three months (and still am) to interrupt some very urgent theoretical work.

I shall merely say in regard to the Statutes that the *English edition* is the sole authentic one.[1] The conference[2] will issue authentic versions in English, French, and German, which is also necessary because several congress decisions relating to the Statutes must be incorporated in them.

The Central Committee in New York must not forget:

1. That the General Council had contacts in America long before the Committee was established;[3]

2. That, as far as the Address is concerned,[4] it was on sale in London, and hence anybody had the right to send it to his friend in America at his own expense. The first shipment to New York was so small because the first edition was sold out in two days, which is why I did not get the number of copies allotted for my shipments.

3. In Par. 6 of the Statutes it is expressly stated that: "no independent local society shall be precluded from directly corresponding

[1] The French version of the Statutes did not fully correspond with the English version.

[2] The Franco-Prussian War and the suppression of the Commune had prevented the convening of the regular congress of the International Workingmen's Association on the scheduled date. The General Council had therefore decided to hold a conference in London. It was held September 17-23, 1871.

[3] The North American Central Committee had complained of the damage to its work caused by the private correspondence of various members of the General Council, particularly Eccarius, with persons in the United States.

[4] The Address of the International Workingmen's Association on the Civil War in France, which Marx wrote in defense of the Paris Commune.

with the General Council," and in Washington, for example, the branch declared that it did not want to enter into contact with New York.

Salut fraternel,
Karl Marx

MARX TO SORGE

[London] November 6, 1871

Dear Friend:

Today 100 copies (50 French and 50 English) of the conference resolutions are being sent off to New York. The decisions not intended for publication will be communicated to you later.

A new, *revised* edition of the Statutes and Regulations is being published in English tomorrow, and you will receive 1,000 copies for sale in America (1 d. each). The text must not be translated into French and German in New York, as we are issuing *official* editions in both languages. Write us how many copies in each language will be wanted.

I have turned over the correspondence with the German Section and the New York Committee to *Eccarius* (he has been appointed to handle that at my suggestion), since my time does not allow me to perform this function properly.

Section 12 (New York)[1] has submitted proposals to the General Council that it be constituted the leader in America. Eccarius will have sent the decisions against these pretensions and for the present Committee to Section 12.

As for the Washington branch[2] (which has sent the General Council a list of its members), the New York Committee went too far.

---

[1] Section 12, dominated by the Woodhull-Claflin sisters and their supporters, had issued a bombastic appeal to the citizens of the Union. Section 1 protested against this appeal and fought against the efforts of Section 12 to pervert the proletarian character of the International. The Woodhull-Claflin section called for women's suffrage, the right of women to hold public office, free love, a world language, and pantarchy (the rule of all). It bitterly attacked all those who resisted its attempt to capture the leadership of the International in the United States. But the proletarian sections combated the maneuvers of these petty-bourgeois reformers, and when on November 19, 1871, the Central Committee of the International in New York was dissolved, the representatives of the proletarian sections immediately formed a Provisional Federal Council and appealed to the General Council in London.

[2] This was Section No. 23, consisting of journalists and government employees in Washington, native-born Americans, who took a vigorous stand against the Woodhull-Claflin clique.

It had no right to demand anything but the number of members and the name, etc., of the corresponding secretary.

More in the next letter (this week).

Yours,

K.M.

MARX TO SORGE

[London] November 9, 1871

Dear Friend:

I sent you 100 Conference Resolutions day before yesterday, 50 English and 50 French.

This week 1,000 copies of the English Revised and Official Statutes and Regulations will be sent to you. Try to sell them. The General Council has large expenditures to make as a result of the various tasks set it by the conference.

We shall have an official French edition of the Revised Statutes, etc., printed in Geneva, and the official German edition printed in Leipzig. Write us approximately how many copies of each will be required in the United States.

A section of the International, *Section francaise de 1871* (about 24 strong), has been formed here among the French refugees, which immediately clashed with the General Council because we demanded changes in its statutes. It will probably result in a split. These people are working together with some of the French refugees in Switzerland, who in turn are intriguing with the men of the *Alliance de la Démocratie Socialiste,*[1] which we dissolved. The object of their attack is not the governments and ruling classes of Europe, allied against us, but the General Council of London, and particularly my humble self. This is their gratitude for my having lost nearly five months in work for the refugees and having acted as their vindicator through the *Address on the Civil War.*

I defended them even at the conference, where the delegates from Spain, Belgium, Switzerland, and Holland expressed their misgivings lest the General Council endanger its international character through too large an admixture of French refugees. But in the eyes of these "Internationalists" it is in itself a sin for "German" influence (because of German science) to predominate in the General Council.

---

[1] The Alliance of Socialist Democracy, which attempted to take over the International Workingmen's Association and transform it into an anarchist center, was organized by Michael Bakunin in 1868.

As for the New York Central Committee, the following:

1. According to the conference decisions, see II:1, in the future, it must call itself *Federal Council* or *Federal Committee* of the United States.

2. As soon as a much LARGER number of branches has been established in the different states, the most practical thing to do is to call a congress of the different sections — following the example of Belgium, Switzerland, and Spain — to elect a Federal Council or Committee in New York.

3. Federal committees can in turn be established in the many states — as soon as they have a sufficient number of branches — for which the New York Committee functions as the central point.

4. The definitive special statutes, both of the New York Federal Committee and of the committees yet to be established, must be submitted to the General Council for sanction before their publication.

We are making rapid progress in Italy. A great triumph over the Mazzini party. The progress in Spain is also considerable. A new section has been established in Copenhagen, which already has 1,500 members and publishes its own paper, *Sozialisten*.

The Braunschweig court's indictment of the local Executive Committee, Bracke *et al.*, has been transmitted to me — an infamous document.

All of us regret that you intend to resign from the Committee. I trust, however, that your decision is not final. I myself often think of doing the same, as international affairs take too much of my time and interrupt my theoretical work.

Apropos. I should like to have 12 copies of Woodhull's, etc. *Weekly* of October 31, containing my daughter's story.[1] Only by accident did we see a copy of this number.

Salut fraternel,
Karl Marx

ENGELS TO CUNO

London, November 13, 1871

Esteemed Friend:

In reply to your kind letter of the 1st instant, I must, unfortunately, tell you that we have no contacts in Milan at the present time,

---

[1] Marx's daughter reported how the French police of the Versailles Government shadowed and molested her at every step during a visit to France.

with the exception of *Gazz[ettino] Rosa,* to which we send documents for publication, but which has made no suggestions to us for the establishment of sections, etc. The movement in an internationalist spirit began in Italy so quickly and so unexpectedly that everything is still in a quite unorganized state over there, and moreover, as you know, the Mardocheans [the police] are doing all they can to hamper the organization. That there are suitable elements in Milan is evident from the very fact that the *Gazz[ettino] R[osa]* has readers; for the present the only thing you can do is to seek them out. I promise to send you the address of the first one to write me. This will most likely happen soon, since my name, as secretary for Italy, will probably be well known everywhere soon enough, thanks to the numerous forthcoming publications of the General Council. Milan, as the principal center of Mazzinism up to now and as a large industrial city, is also of especial importance to us because with Milan we gain the industrial silk-manufacturing district of Lombardy. Therefore, whatever you and your friends may be able to do for the common cause in Milan will be *particularly worthwhile.*

We have a strong section in Turin (its address: *Proletario Italiano*); letters from Lodi (from the *Plebe*) that quite likely also reported the formation of sections have been lost.

This morning I saw Ricciotti Garibaldi at Marx's; he is a very intelligent young man, very even-tempered, but a soldier rather than a thinker. He may turn out to be very useful, however. Even the old man [Giuseppe Garibaldi] displayed more good-will than clarity in his theoretical views, but none the less his last letter to Petroni is of tremendous value to us. If his son manifests as true an instinct as the old man in all great crises, he will be able to accomplish a great deal. Can you get us a reliable address in Genoa? We need a reliable way of getting our publications to the old man in Caprera, and R[icciotti Garibaldi] says that a lot is being confiscated. . . .

Salut et fraternité,

F. Engels

MARX TO BOLTE

[London] November 23, 1871

Friend Bolte:

I received your letter yesterday together with Sorge's report.

1. First of all, as to the attitude of the General Council towards

the New York Federal Council, I trust that my letter already sent to Sorge (and a letter to Speyer, which I authorized him to communicate to Sorge *confidentially*) will have disposed of the extremely wrong viewpoint of the German Section which you represent.

In the United States, as in every other country where the *International* first has to be established, the General Council originally had to authorize separate individuals and appoint them as its official correspondents. But from the moment the New York Committee had gained some consistency, these correspondents were dropped one after the other, although they could not be eliminated all at once.

For some time past the *official* correspondence with formerly appointed authorized representatives has been confined to Eccarius' correspondence with Jessup, and I see by your own letter that you have no complaint at all to make regarding the latter.

Except for Eccarius, however, no one was to carry on official correspondence with the United States but myself and Dupont as correspondent (at the time) for the *French sections,* and whatever correspondence he conducted was confined *to the latter*.

With the exception of yourself and Sorge, I have not carried on any official correspondence at all. My correspondence with S. Meyer is private correspondence, of which *he has never published the slightest detail,* and which by its very nature could *in no way* be troublesome or harmful to the New York Committee.

There is no doubt, on the other hand, that G. Harris and perhaps Boon — two English members of the General Council — are carrying on private correspondence with Internationals in New York, etc. Both of them belong to the sect of the late Bronterre O'Brien, and are full of follies and crotchets, such as currency quackery, false emancipation of women, and the like. They are thus by nature allies of Section 12 in New York and its kindred souls.

The General Council has no right to forbid its members to conduct private correspondence. But if it could be *proved* to us:

Either that this private correspondence pretends to be *official,*

Or that it conteracts the activity of the General Council — whether for publication or for quarrels with the New York Committee — the necessary measures would be taken to prevent such mischief.

These O'Brienites, in spite of their follies, constitute an often necessary counterweight to trade unionists in the Council. They are more revolutionary, firmer on the land question, less nationalistic, and not susceptible to bourgeois bribery in one form or another. Otherwise they would have been kicked out long ago.

2. I was greatly astonished to see that German Section No. 1 suspects the General Council of any preference for bourgeois philan-

thropists, sectarians, or amateur groups. The mattter is quite the contrary.

The *International* was founded in order to replace the socialist or semi-socialist sects by a real organization of the working class for struggle. The original Statutes and the Inaugural Address show this at a glance. On the other hand, the International could not have maintained itself if the course of history had not already smashed sectarianism. The development of socialist sectarianism and that of the real labor movement always stand in inverse ratio to each other. So long as the sects are justified (historically), the working class is not yet ripe for an independent historical movement. As soon as it has attained this maturity all sects are essentially reactionary. For all that, what history exhibits everywhere was repeated in the history of the International. What is antiquated tries to reconstitute and assert itself within the newly acquired form.

And the history of the International was a *continual struggle of the General Council* against the sects and against amateur experiments, which sought to assert themselves within the International against the real movement of the working class. This struggle was conducted at the congresses, but far more in the private dealings of the General Council with the individual sections.

In Paris, as the Proudhonists (Mutualists) were cofounders of the Association, they naturally held the reins there for the first few years. Later, of course, collectivist, positivist, etc., groups were formed in opposition to them.

In Germany — the Lassalle clique. I myself corresponded with the notorious Schweitzer for two years and irrefutably proved to him that Lassalle's organization[1] is a mere sectarian organization and, as such, hostile to the organization of the *real* workers' movement aimed at by the International. He had his "reasons" for not understanding.

At the end of 1868 the Russian, Bakunin, joined the *International* with the aim of forming inside it *a second International* under the name of *Alliance de la Démocratie Socialiste, with himself as leader.* He — a man devoid of theoretical knowledge — claimed that this separate body was to represent the *scientific* propaganda of the International, and that this propaganda was to become the special function of this *second International within the International.*

His program was a hash superficially scraped together from the

[1] After Lassalle's death in 1864, the leadership of his organization, the *Allgemeiner Deutscher Arbeiterverein* (General Association of German Workers) was taken over by J. B. von Schweitzer, a Frankfurt lawyer, who had become a follower of Lassalle in the early sixties. See p. 70.

Right and the Left — EQUALITY OF CLASSES (!), *abolition of the right of inheritance* as the *starting point* of the social movement (St. Simonist nonsense), *atheism* as a *dogma* dictated to the members, etc., and as the main dogma *(Proudhonist), abstention from the political movement.*

This children's primer found favor (and still has a certain hold) in Italy and Spain, where the real conditions for the workers' movement are as yet little developed, and among a few vain, ambitious, and empty doctrinaires in French Switzerland and Belgium.

For Mr. Bakunin the doctrine (the rubbish he has scraped together from Proudhon, St. Simon, etc.) was and is a secondary matter — merely a means to his personal self-assertion. Though a nonentity theoretically, he is in his element as an intriguer.

For years the General Council had had to fight against this conspiracy (which was supported up to a certain point by the French Proudhonists, especially in *southern France*). At last, by means of conference resolutions I:2-3, IX, XVI, and XVII, it delivered its long-prepared blow.[1]

Obviously the General Council does not support in America what it combats in Europe. Resolutions I:2-3 and IX now give the New York Committee the legal weapons with which to put an end to all sectarianism and amateur groups, and, if necessary, to expel them.

3. The New York Committee will do well to express its full agreement with the conference decisions in an *official letter to the General Council.*

Bakunin, personally threatened moreover by Resolution XIV (publication of the Nechayev trial in *Égalité*) which will bring to light his infamous doings in Russia, is making every possible effort to get protests started against the conference among the remnants of his following.

For this purpose he has got into contact with the demoralized portion of the French refugees in Geneva and London (a numerically weak component, anyway). The slogan issued is that the General Council is dominated by *Pan-Germanism* (or Bismarckism). This

---

[1] Resolutions I:2 and 3 of the London Conference forbade all sectarian names for sections, branches, etc., and prescribed that they should be exclusively designated as branches or sections of the International Workingmen's Association with the addition of the name of their locality. Resolution IX stressed the necessity of the political activity of the working class and declared that its economic movement and its political activity are inseparably connected. Resolution XVI declared the question of the *Alliance de la Démocratie Socialiste* disposed of since its secretary, N. Joukovsky, had declared the Alliance dissolved. Resolution XVII permitted the Jura sections in Switzerland to adopt the name of *Fédération Jurassienne* and censured its organs, *Progrès* and *Solidarité*.

refers to the *unpardonable* fact that *I* am by birth a German and actually do exercise a decisive intellectual influence upon the General Council. (*N. B.* The *German* element in the Council is two-thirds weaker *numerically* than either the *English* or the *French.* The crime therefore consists in the fact that the English and French elements are dominated by the German element *theoretically* (!) and find this domination, *i.e.*, German science, very useful and even indispensable.)

In Geneva, under the patronage of the bourgeoise, Madame Andrée Leo (who at the Lausanne Congress was so shameless as to denounce Ferré to his Versailles executioners), they have published a paper, *La Révolution Sociale,* which polemizes against us in almost literally the same words as the *Journal de Genève,* the most reactionary paper in Europe.

In London they tried to establish a French Section, of whose activities you will find an example in No. 42 of *Qui Vive?,* which I enclose. (Likewise the issue containing the letter from our French Secretary, Serraillier.) This Section, consisting of twenty people (including many *mouchards* [police spies]), has not been recognized by the General Council, but another, a much larger section, has.

In fact, despite the intrigues of this bunch of scoundrels, we are carrying on great propaganda in France — and in Russia, where they know what value to place on Bakunin, and where my book on capital is just being published in Russian.

The secretary of the first-mentioned French Section (the one not recognized by us and now in process of complete dissolution) was the same *Durand* whom we expelled from the Association as a *mouchard.*

The Bakuninist abstentionists from politics, Blanc and Albert Richard of Lyons, are now *paid Bonapartist agents.* The evidence is in our hands. Bousquet (of the same clique in Geneva), the correspondent in *Béziers* (Southern France), has been denounced to us by the section there as a police agent.

4. With regard to the *resolutions* of the Conference, let me say that the whole edition was in my hands, and that I sent them *first* to New York (Sorge) as the most distant point.

If reports of the Conference — half true and half false — appeared in the press before this, the blame for this rests on a delegate to the Conference, against whom the General Council has instituted an inquiry.[1]

5. As for the Washington Section, it applied first to the General

---

[1] This refers to reports by Eccarius in the New York *World.*

Council in order to maintain contact with it as an independent section. If the affair is settled, it is useless to return to it.

With regard to sections the following general remarks apply:

(a) According to Art. 7 of the Statutes, sections that wish to be "independent" can apply directly to the General Council for admission ("no independent local society shall be precluded from directly corresponding with the General Council"). *II: Arts. 4 and 5 of the Regulations:* "Every new branch or society (this refers to 'independent local societies') intending to join the International is bound immediately to announce its adhesion to the General Council!" (II: Art. 4) and "The General Council has the right to admit or to refuse the affiliation of any new branch, etc." (II: Art. 5.)

(b) According to Art. 5 of the Regulations, however, the General Council has to consult the Federal Councils or Committees beforehand regarding admission, etc., and

(c) According to the decision of the Conference (see V: Art. 3 of the Regulations), as a matter of course no section will be admitted any more that takes a sectarian name, etc., or (V: Art. 2) does not constitute itself simply as "Section of the International Workingmen's Association."

Kindly communicate this letter to the German Section you represent, and make use of its contents for action but not for publication.

Salut et fraternité,

Karl Marx

Capital has not been published in English or French as yet. A French edition was being worked on but was discontinued as a result of recent events.

Eccarius has been appointed, at my request, secretary for *all* sections in the United States (with the exception of the French, for which Le Moussu is secretary). Nevertheless I shall be glad to answer any private questions that you or Sorge may address to me. Engels has sent the article on the International from the *Irish Republic* to Italy for publication there.

In the future the *Eastern Post,* which contains the reports of the General Council's sessions, will be sent to New York regularly, addressed to Sorge.

N.B. as to political movement: The political movement of the working class has, of course, as its final object the conquest of political power for this class, and this requires, of course, a previous organization of the working class developed up to a certain point, which itself arises from its economic struggles.

But on the other hand, every movement in which the working class comes out as a *class* against the ruling classes and tries to coerce them by pressure from without is a political movement. For instance, the attempt in a particular factory, or even in a particular trade, to force a shorter working day out of the individual capitalists by strikes, etc., is a purely economic movement. The movement to force through an eight-hour *law,* etc., however, is a *political* movement. And in this way, out of the separate economic movements of the workers there grows up everywhere a *political* movement, that is to say a movement of the *class,* with the object of achieving its interests in a general form, in a form possessing general, socially coercive force. Though these movements presuppose a certain degree of previous organization, they are in turn equally a means of developing this organization.

Where the working class is not yet far enough advanced in its organization to undertake a decisive campaign against the collective power, *i.e.,* the political power, of the ruling classes, it must at any rate be trained for this by continual agitation against, and a hostile attitude toward, the policies of the ruling classes. Otherwise it remains a plaything in their hands, as the September revolution in French [1] showed, and as is also proved up to a certain degree by the game that Messrs. Gladstone and Co. still succeed in playing in England up to the present time.

MARX TO SORGE [2]

London, November 29, 1871

My dear Sorge:

I hope you have at last received at New York the resolutions of the Conference and the different letters I sent you. Together with this letter I am sending the three last *Eastern Post* reports on the sittings of the General Council. They contain, of course, only what is meant for public use.

In regard to financial matters I have only to remark:

1. The New York Committee need pay only 2d. per piece for the pamphlets on the *Civil War* [3] it has received. It will pay 1d. per piece for the *Statutes and Regulations à fur et mesure* [in proportion] that they are sold. But you ought to write us how many French and German editions of the *Statutes, etc.,* you need. Besides what you

---

[1] This refers to the Revolution in Paris on September 4, 1870, following the collapse of the Second Empire.

[2] This letter was written in English.

[3] *The Civil War in France,* the famous address of the General Council of the International on the Paris Commune.

want immediately, perhaps you will find it useful to have some stock in reserve.

2. With regard to the money sent us for the refugees, the General Council wants an express written declaration that the General Council alone is responsible for its distribution among the French refugees and that the so-called "*Society* of French Refugees at London" has no right of control over the Council.

This is necessary because, although the mass of the above-named society are honest people, the committee at their head are *ruffians,* so that a great part — and the most meritorious part of the refugees — does not want to have anything to do with the "Society," but to be relieved directly by the Council. We, therefore, give a weekly sum for distribution to the Society and distribute another sum directly.

It is the above-said ruffians who have spread the most atrocious calumnies against the General Council without whose aid (and many of its members have not only given their time, but paid out of their own purse) the French refugees would have *crevé de faim* [perished of hunger].

I come now to the question of McDonnell.[1]

Before admitting him, the Council instituted a most searching inquiry as to his integrity, he, like *all* other Irish politicians, being much calumniated by his own countrymen.

The Council — after most incontrovertible evidence on his private character — chose him because the *mass of the Irish workmen in England* have more confidence in him than in *any other person*. He is a man quite above religious prejudices, and as to his general views, it is absurd to say that he has any "bourgeois" predilections. He is a proletarian, by the circumstances of his life and by his ideas.

If any accusation is to be brought forward against him, let it be done in exact terms, and not by vague insinuation. My opinion is that the Irishmen, removed for long periods by imprisonment, are not competent judges. The best proof: their relations with the *Irishman,* whose editor, Pigott, is a mere speculator, and whose manager, Murphy, is a ruffian. That paper—despite the exertions of the General Council for the Irish cause—has always intrigued against us. McDonnell was constantly attacked in that paper by an Irishman (O'Donnell) connected with Campbell (an officer of the London *police*) and a habitual drunkard, who for a glass of gin will tell the first constable all the secrets he may have to dispose of.

After the nomination of McDonnell, Murphy attacked and ca-

---

[1] The Irishmen in the Central Committee and in the Provisional Federal Council had objected to the appointment of McDonnell as secretary for Ireland.

lumniated the *International* (not only McDonnell) in the *Irishman,* and, *at the same time,* secretly, asked us to nominate him secretary for Ireland.

As to O'Donovan Rossa, I wonder that you quote him still as an authority after what you have written me about him. If any man was obliged, personally, to the *International* and the French Communards, it was he,[1] and you have seen what thanks we have received at his hands.

Let the Irish members of the New York Committee not forget that, to be useful to them, we want above all *influence* on the *Irish in England,* and that for that purpose there exists, as far as we have been able to ascertain, no better man than McDonnell.

Yours fraternally,

Karl Marx

Train [2] has never received credentials on the part of the General Council.

ENGELS TO CUNO

[London] January 24, 1872

Dear Cuno:

. . . Bakunin, who up to 1868 had intrigued against the International, joined it after he had suffered a fiasco at the Berne Peace Congress [3] and at once began to conspire *within it* against the General Council. B[akunin] has a singular theory, a potpourri of Proudhonism and communism, the chief point of which is, first of all, that he does not regard capital, and hence the class antagonism between capitalists and wage earners which has arisen through social development, as the main evil to be abolished, but instead the *state.* While the great mass of the Social-Democratic workers hold our view that state power is nothing more than the organization with

---

[1] The imprisoned Fenians, and O'Donovan Rossa, in particular, had been atrociously mistreated in the English prisons, and the General Council (that is, Marx) had publicized this in English and French newspapers, whereupon the British Government pardoned the Fenians on condition that they emigrate.

[2] George Francis Train had pretended to be an Internationalist in Chicago.

[3] In 1867, at the congress of the League of Peace and Freedom, a bourgeois organization, Bakunin was elected a member of its executive committee. At the second congress of the League, which took place in Berne in 1868, Bakunin and his colleagues advanced certain anarchist proposals, which were rejected by the congress. As a result, Bakunin and his supporters seceded from the League and established the Alliance of Socialist Democracy.

which the ruling classes — landowners and capitalists — have provided themselves in order to protect their social privileges, Bakunin maintains that the *state* has created capital, that the capitalist has his capital *only by the grace of the state.* And since the state is the chief evil, the state above all must be abolished; then capital will go to hell of itself. We, on the contrary, say: Abolish capital, the appropriation of all the means of production in the hands of the few, and the state will fall of itself.

The difference is an essential one: the abolition of the state is nonsense without a previous social revolution; the abolition of capital *is* the social revolution and involves a change in the whole mode of production. However, since for Bakunin the state is the main evil, nothing must be done that can keep alive the state, *i.e.,* any state, republic, monarchy, or whatever it may be. Hence, *complete abstention from all politics.* To commit a political action, especially to take part in an election, would be a betrayal of principle. The thing to do is to conduct propaganda, revile the state, organize, and when *all* the workers are won over, that is, the majority, depose the authorities, abolish the state, and replace it by the organization of the International. This great act, with which the millenium begins, is called *social liquidation.*

All this sounds extremely radical and is so simple that it can be learned by heart in five minutes, and that is why this Bakuninist theory has also rapidly found favor in Italy and Spain, among young lawyers, doctors, and other doctrinaires. But the mass of the workers will never allow themselves to be persuaded that the public affairs of their country are not also their own affairs; they are by nature *political* and whoever tries to convince them that they should leave politics alone will in the end be left in the lurch. To preach that the workers should abstain from politics under all circumstances means to drive them into the arms of the priests or the bourgeois republicans.

Now as, according to B[akunin], the International is not supposed to be formed for political struggle but in order that it may at once replace the old social organization when social liquidation occurs, it follows that it must come as near as possible to the Bakuninist ideal of future society. In this society there will above all be no *authority,* for authority = state = absolutely evil. (How these people propose to operate a factory, run a railroad, or steer a ship without one will that decides in the last resort, without unified direction, they do not indeed tell us.) The authority of the majority over the minority also ceases. Every individual, every community, is autonomous, but how a society of even two people is possible unless each gives up some of his autonomy, Bakunin again keeps to himself.

Well, the International must be organized according to this pattern as well. Every section is autonomous, and in every section every individual. To hell with the *Basel resolutions,* which conferred upon the General Council a pernicious authority demoralizing even to itself! Even if this authority is *voluntarily* conferred, it must cease just *because* it is authority.

Here you have in brief the main points of the swindle. But who were the authors of the Basel resolutions? The same *Mr. Bakunin and Co.!*

When these gentlemen saw that at the Basel Congress they would be unable to realize their plan for transferring the General Council to Geneva, *i.e.,* getting it in their hands, they adopted another course. They founded the Alliance of Socialist Democracy, an international society *within* the large International under the pretext that you now encounter in the Bakuninist Italian press, in the *Proletario* and the *Gazzettino Rosa,* for example: the ardent Latin races require a more striking program than the chilly, deliberate Northerners. This little plan failed owing to the resistance of the General Council, which naturally could not tolerate the existence of any separate *international* organization *within the* International. Since then, the same plan has appeared in various forms in connection with the efforts of Bakunin and his adherents to substitute Bakunin's program for the program of the International. On the other hand, reaction—beginning with Jules Favre and Bismarck and ending with Mazzini—has always come down hard upon the empty and vainglorious Bakuninist phrasemongering when it wanted to attack the International. Hence the necessity of the declaration of December 5 against Mazzini and Bakunin, which was likewise printed in the *Gazz[ettino] Rosa.*

The core of the Bakunin conspiracy consists of a few score Jurassians, who have scarcely two hundred workers behind them; its vanguard in Italy consists of young lawyers, doctors, and journalists, who now come forward everywhere as the representatives of the Italian workers, with a few of the same breed in Barcelona and Madrid, and a few individuals elsewhere—in Lyon and Brussels. There are almost no workers among them; they have only one worker here, Robin. The conference (convened out of necessity, because of their inability to convoke a congress) served as a pretext; and since most of the French refugees in Switzerland went over to their side—they (the Proudhonists) had much in common with them, while personal motives also played a part—they were the ones to start the campaign. To be sure, a dissatisfied minority and unrecognized geniuses are to be found everywhere within the International—and they counted on them, not without reason.

At the present time their fighting forces are:

1. Bakunin himself—the Napoleon of this campaign.

2. Two hundred Jurassians and 40-50 members of the French sections (refugees in Geneva).

3. In Brussels, Hins, editor of the *Liberté,* who does *not* support them *openly,* however.

4. Here, the remnants of the French Section of 1871, never recognized by us, which has already split into three mutually hostile parts; then about twenty Lassalleans of the type of Herr von Schweitzer, expelled from the German Section (for proposing *resignation en masse* from the International), who, as defenders of extreme centralization and a strong organization, surprisingly enough enter into an alliance with the anarchists and autonomists.

5. In Spain, a few individual friends and adherents of Bakunin, who exert a strong influence, at least theoretically, upon the workers, particularly in Barcelona. But, on the other hand, the Spaniards attach great importance to organization, and its absence among the others is obvious to them. How much success Bakunin may expect here will be revealed only at the Spanish Congress in April, but as the workers will predominate at this congress, I have no fears about it.

6. Lastly, in Italy, as far as I know, the Turin, Bologna, and Girgenti sections have voted for convening a *special* congress.

The Bakuninist press asserts that twenty Italian sections have affiliated with them; I have no knowledge of them. In any event, the leadership is in the hands of Bakunin's friends and adherents almost everywhere, and they are raising a terrific hubbub. But it will most likely be found that they haven't much of a following, since a more exhaustive investigation of the matter will prove that in the last analysis the overwhelming mass of Italian workers are still Mazzinists and will remain so as long as the International is identified there with abstention from politics.

At any rate, the situation in Italy is such that the Bakuninists are for the present the masters of the situation within the International. Nor does the General Council think of complaining about this; the Italians have the right to make as many mistakes as they please, and the General Council will oppose this only in peaceable debates. They likewise have the right to express themselves in favor of a congress in the Jurassian spirit, although it is extremely peculiar, to be sure, that sections that have just joined [the International] and can have no knowledge of anything should immediately take a definite stand on a question of this sort without even hearing *both*

sides! I have already given the Turinese my opinion of this quite
frankly, and I shall do the same with other sections taking a similar
stand. For every such statement of affiliation represents an indirect
approval of the false slanders and charges against the General
Council contained in the circular[1]; the General Council, however,
will soon issue its own circular on this question. If you can prevent
a similar declaration by the Milanese *until this latter appears,* you
will be acting in accordance with our desires. . . .

And the General Council, of course, will not call an extraordinary
congress for the benefit of a few intriguing and vainglorious individuals. As long as these individuals stay within legal bounds, the
General Council will gladly allow them freedom of action, and this
coalition of quite heterogeneous elements will soon fall apart itself.
But as soon as they undertake anything contrary to the statutes or
the resolutions of the congress, the General Council will do its duty.

If one bears in mind at what a time these people began their
conspiracy—precisely when the International is everywhere subjected
to the fiercest persecution—it is impossible not to think that the
gentlemen of the international police are involved in this affair.
And this is actually the case. In Béziers the Geneva Bakuninists
have as their correspondent the Chief Commissioner of Police!
Two prominent Bakuninists, Albert Richard of London and
Leblanc, were here and told a worker, Scholl of Lyon, with whom
they had gotten in touch, that the only way to overthrow Thiers
was to put Bonaparte back on the throne, and that was why they
were traveling about at *Bonaparte's expense* to carry on *propaganda*
among the emigrés on behalf of a *Bonapartist restoration!* That is
what these gentlemen call absention from politics! In Berlin the
Neuer Sozial-Demokrat, subsidized by Bismarck, is singing the same
tune. I shall leave as a moot point the extent to which the Russian
police is involved in this affair, though Bakunin was deeply em-
broiled in the Nechayev affair (he denies this, to be sure, but we
have authentic Russian reports here, and since Marx and I understand Russian, he cannot bluff us). Nechayev was either a Russian
agent-provocateur or, at any rate, acted like one; moreover, there
are all sorts of suspicious characters among Bakunin's Russian
friends. . . .

I again ask you to be discreet with *all* persons closely connected
with Bakunin. All sects are characterized by the fact that they
stick together closely and carry on intrigues. *All of your confidences*
—you may rest assured of this—will be conveyed to Bakunin at once.
One of his principles is the affirmation that keeping a promise and

[1] Issued by the Jura Federation, controlled by Bakunin.

other similar things are nothing but bourgeois prejudices, which a true revolutionary should always disregard in the interests of the cause. In Russia he speaks of this openly, but in Western Europe it is a secret doctrine. . . .

Yours,
F. Engels

ENGELS TO CUNO

London, April 22[-23], 1872

Dear Cuno:

This morning I received your letter, which I had awaited with anxiety. Gandolfi wrote me some time ago that they suspected that the Italian government turned you over to the Prussians. I learned of your arrest, etc., from the newspapers, which also indicated that you were being deported for "lack of visible means of support." A police statement to that effect appeared in a Milan newspaper. This affair is not without significance. It is the first exploit of the international police conspiracy organized by Prussia, Austria, and Italy, and if you haven't been transported by the police via the Bavarian frontier to Duesseldorf as yet, you owe this solely to the *stupidity of the Bavarians.* Tomorrow morning I shall report the matter to the General Council, after which the whole story will be included in the official report, which will be printed in the *Eastern Post* and sent out to every country in the world. In the meantime, write an article about this under your own name and send it to the *Volksstaat,* the Geneva *Égalité,* and the *Gazz[ettino] Rosa.* We shall take care of England, America, and Spain, as well as of France, over here. The rascals will finally have to realize that they cannot do this with impunity and that the International's arms are longer than those of the King of Italy. As soon as the story is printed I shall send you a copy, together with all the newspapers I can collect for you—they won't be too numerous.

The advice Liebknecht gave you—to write to Bismarck—is very good, but for altogether different reasons. First, instead of assisting you to obtain redress, Bismarck will be very *glad* it happened and will merely be irritated that the Bavarians released you, instead of realizing that this gave them a splendid opportunity for the police to transport a member of the International all over Germany. But you should write B[ismarck] simply in order to be able to send his reply—which will be nothing but a lame excuse, of course—to Bebel, who will use it to raise *a row in the Reichstag.* But it is out of the question, of course, that Bismarck will even lift a finger to rebuke Italy for having fulfilled his orders so well.

You must not be surprised that you have gotten so little support from the party comrades. From one of your previous letters I had already realized that you were under youthful illusions concerning the aid you would receive when in need. Unfortunately, my answer to this letter was confiscated by the Mardocheans [the police] and never reached you. I should add that, although our German workers have outstripped all the others as far as theory goes, in practice they are far from having shaken off their *"Knoten"* [handicraft] past, and thanks to the predominantly petty-bourgeois character of life in Germany, they are tremendously narrow-minded, especially in money matters.

That is why I wasn't at all surprised at what you experienced in this respect. If I had money, I should send you some, but we here are quite pinched for funds. We have more than a hundred helpless emigrés of the Paris Commune, *literally helpless,* for no people ever feel as helpless abroad as do the French; and what they didn't eat up, we sent to a fine chap in Cork, Ireland, who founded the International there and was rewarded by being excommunicated by the priests and the bourgeoisie and ultimately ruined. We haven't a cent left. If we get some money from somewhere or other, I shall see to it that you are not forgotten. . . .

The circular of the General Council on Bakunin and Co. is in the press and will probably be ready by the end of next week.[1] I shall send you a copy. It sets forth everything quite bluntly, and it will produce a terrific row. I intend to send you newspapers tomorrow—*Gazzett*[*ino*] *Rosa* and some other Italian items, in general, anything I can lay my hands upon.

A congress of the Spanish members of the International was held in Saragossa on April 8-11, at which our people won a victory over the Bakuninists. It is now discovered that the *Alliance de la Démocrati Socialiste*[2] continued to exist in Spain within the International as a *secret society* under the leadership of Bakunin—a secret society aimed, not at the government, but against the masses of workers! I have every reason to suspect that the same thing is going on in Italy. What information do you have on this subject?

If anything comes of the job in Spain that Becker had in mind for you, let me know at once so that I can give you letters of introduction to our people. That job is probably in Catalonia,

---

[1] *Les Prétendues Scissions dans l'Internationale* [*The Alleged Splits in the International*], Geneva, 1872.
[2] See footnote, p. 86.

the only industrial province of Spain, and you will be able to do very useful work there, since the masses of workers there are good but leave their newspaper (the Barcelona *La Federacion*) and the key jobs in the hands of the Bakuninists.

There is only one newspaper appearing in Turin by now—*L' Anticristo,* something on the order of a weekly *Gazzettino Rosa.* Then there are *La Plebe* in Lodi, *Il Fascio Operaio* in Bologna, and *L'Eguaglianza* in Girgenti—all the other Italian newspapers are dead. Our experiences in other countries made it obvious to me long ago that this would have to happen. It is not enough to have a few persons at the top; the masses in Italy are still too backward to be able to support so many newspapers.

Prolonged and dogged work, with much more theoretical content than the Bakuninists possess, is required to free the masses from the influence of the Mazzinist nonsense. . . .

Write me very soon—especially on what you are able to do in your special profession, so that I can take the necessary steps.

Cordially yours,

F. E.

ENGELS TO CUNO

London, May 7[-8], [18]72

Dear Cuno:

It is very good that you are writing B[ismarck] about your case— this should be done if only to force him to compromise himself and thus afford Bebel an occasion for a Reichstag speech. By now you have most likely received the *Eastern Post* with the report of the meeting of the General Council at which I talked about your case; I sent that issue off on the 2nd of this month. You have probably received the newspapers sent you on April 24 and 27. I also reported on the arson plot,[1] but this is very badly stated in the report, which I am sending you tomorrow, as is usually the case when I don't write these things myself. . . .

The secret society of the Bakuninists in Spain is a fully established fact; you will find the details in the report *(the second one)* on the Saragossa Congress in the Brussels *Liberté,* which you will probably find in the *Volksstaat* one of these days. Luckily enough, the best of the people attending the congress soon realized that the interests of this secret enterprise and the interests of the International were not identical, and as the interests of the International were dearer to

---

[1] The attempt to set fire to the Milan Agricultural Academy, which was imputed to members of the International.

them than everything else, they immediately shifted their stand and remained in the secret society solely in order to check on it and to paralyze its activity. One of them was here as a delegate to the conference and convinced himself that everything they had told him down there about the intrigues, dictatorship, etc., of the General Council was empty twaddle. A short time later one of our best men [Paul Lafargue]—half Frenchman, half Spaniard—left for Madrid, and this settled the matter. The Spaniards have an excellent organization, of which they are rightfully proud, and, as it happens, it has shown itself in the best light during the past six months. . . .

I did not doubt for an instant that the same secret society existed in Italy, though, perhaps, not as rigidly as in formalistic Spain. The best proof of this for me was the almost military precision with which the very same slogan, issued *from above,* was simultaneously proclaimed in every corner of the country (note that these are the very same persons who always preached the principle *"dal basso all'alto"* [from the bottom to the top] to the people, and to the International! It is quite understandable that you were not initiated, for even among the Bakuninists only the *leaders* were admitted to this esoteric society. Meanwhile, some individual symptoms of improvement can be observed in Italy. . . . The damned difficulty in Italy is simply getting into direct contact with the workers. These damned Bak[uninist] doctrinaire lawyers, doctors, and the like penetrate everywhere and behave as if they were the hereditary representatives of the workers. Wherever we have been able to break through this line of skirmishers and get in touch with the masses themselves, everything is all right and soon mended, but it is almost impossible to do this anywhere without addresses. That is why it would have been of great value for you to have remained in M[ilan] and to have been able to visit various cities from time to time—if not now, then at any rate later on. With one or two able comrades at the key points we should have managed to deal with all this rabble in half a year or so.

As for the Spanish police, all I can tell you is that apparently they are frightfully stupid and that there is no unity among them. For instance, one of our best men in Madrid [Paul Lafargue] was ordered to be deported by the Minister of the Interior, but the governor of Madrid would have nothing to do with it, and he remained there undisturbed. . . .

Sincerely yours,

F. E.

May 8, evening. As I had to go into town to get the enclosed fifty-franc banknote (dated October 11, 1871, No. 2,648,626, in the upper left corner—626, in the upper right corner—Z.106), and it was too late to send this letter off by registered mail, which had to be done because of the money, I still have time to tell you the story about Becker, which is another instance of what petty intrigues go to make up world history. For a long time old man Becker has retained his own ideas of organization, dating from the epoch *before* '48: little groups, whose leaders kept in touch in order to give the whole organization a general trend, a little conspiratorial activity on occasion, and the like; another idea, likewise dating from that period, was that the central organ of the German organization had to be located *outside* Germany. When the International was founded, and Becker took over the organization of the Germans in Switzerland and other countries, he established a section in Geneva, which was gradually converted into the "Mother Section of the Groups of German-Language Sections" by organizing new sections in Switzerland, Germany, and elsewhere. It then began to claim the top leadership, not only of the Germans living in Switzerland, America, France, etc., but also of the Germans in Germany and Austria. This was all the old method of revolutionary agitation employed up to '48, and as long as it was based upon the voluntary subordination of the sections, there could be no objection to it. But there was one thing the good soul Becker forgot: that the organization of the International was too big for such methods and goals. Becker and his friends, however, *accomplished* something and always remained direct and avowed sections of the International.

In the meantime the labor movement in Germany was growing, freeing itself from the fetters of Lassalleanism, and, under the leadership of Bebel and Liebknecht, it came out *in principle* for the International. The movement became too powerful and acquired too much independent significance for it to be able to acknowledge the leadership of the Geneva Mother Section; the German workers held their own congresses and elected their own executive organs. The relationship of the German workers' party to the International never was made clear, however. This relationship remained a purely platonic one; there was no actual membership for individuals (with some exceptions), while the formation of sections was forbidden by law. As a result, the following situation developed in Germany: They claimed the *rights* of membership, while they brushed aside its *obligations,* and only after the London Conference did we insist that henceforth they would have to comply with their obligations.

Now you will understand why there not only had to arise a certain rivalry between the leaders in Germany on the one hand,

and the Geneva Mother Section on the other, but that individual conflicts also became unavoidable, especially over the question of the payment of dues. The extent to which the General Council was *dictatorial* in this affair, as in every other, you can see from the fact that it was completely uninterested in the matter and left both sides to shift for themselves. Each was right in some respects and wrong in others. From the very start Becker attached great importance to the International, but wanted to cast it in the long-obsolete mold. Liebknecht and the others were in the right in so far as the German workers wanted to rule themselves, and not be controlled by an obscure council in Geneva; but in the last analysis they wanted to subordinate the International to their own, specifically German, aims and to make it serve them. The General Council could intervene solely at the request of both sides or in the event of a serious conflict.

Liebknecht evidently took you to be a Becker agent, traveling on behalf of the Geneva Mother Section, and *this* explains all the mistrust with which it seems he received you. He is also a man of '48 and attaches more importance to such trifles than they deserve. You may be glad that you did not live through this period—I have in mind not the first revolutionary wave from February to the July battles (that was splendid), but the democratic bourgeois intrigues, beginning with June '48, and the ensuing emigration of '49-51. At the present time the movement is infinitely greater.

This, I trust, will explain the reception you got in Leipzig. No special importance should be attached to such trifles—they are all things that are overcome by themselves in time. When you meet the Belgian members of the International, you will, perhaps, again be disappointed. Above all, don't entertain too great illusions about these people. They are very good elements, but the cause has, by and large, run along in a worn-out rut, and a phrase is more important to them than the thing itself. The big words autonomy and authoritarianism can attract a large audience in Belgium as well. *Eh bien, vous verrez pour vous-même* [well, you will see for yourself].

At your friendly service,

F. E.

ENGELS TO CUNO

London, June 10, 1872

Dear Cuno:

. . . We now possess accurate information on the Spanish secret society, *La Aleanza*—it will be quite a surprise to that gang at the congress. The same society *doubtless* exists in Italy. If only Regis could get down there! But the poor chap is now selling newspapers in Geneva, to earn a living as best he can. Cafiero in Naples and someone else in Turin whom I don't know [Carlo Terzaghi] turned letters of mine over to the Jurassians; that doesn't matter to me, but the very fact of their perfidy is unpleasant. The Italians will still have to pass through a school of experience for them to realize that a peasant people as backward as they are merely makes itself ridiculous when it tries to prescribe to the workers of big industrial countries the road they should take for their emancipation. . . .

We know that affairs are in pretty bad shape in Belgium. The apathy of this neutral nation (*sit venia verbo* [if that word can be used]) is the underlying reason for the fact that the plotters and jackasses can call the tune there. The International is declining in Belgium with every day, thanks to the inertia of the intelligent and reliable men among their leaders. Moreover, the clique's leaders have done us a tremendous service with their new draft statutes. The proposal for the abolition of the General Council has put an end to the last vestiges of their influence (which was far from small, since this was one of the oldest federations). The Spaniards call this downright treason. It's a pity that you're not going to Spain; you would like these people—in the last analysis they are the most gifted of all the Latins, and you could have been very useful there. These people require a certain dose of German theory, and they take it very well; besides, they are distinguished by a fanaticism and a class hatred of the bourgeoisie such as we Northerners or the vacillating Italians cannot imagine. . . .

Your recent description of the impression Duesseldorf made upon you made me laugh heartily. Why, for us, the philistine Wuppertalers, Duesseldorf was always a little Paris, where the pious gentlemen of Barmen and Elberfeld kept their mistresses, went to the theatre, and had a royal good time. But the sky always looks gray where one's own reactionary family lives. Moreover, the process of industrial development, which has spread to Duesseldorf as well, is extremely depressing and deadly boring throughout Germany, so that I can well imagine that the Wuppertal's dreariness and wretchedness have now conquered Duesseldorf as well.

But one fine day we shall send them packing, and then we'll sing the old song again that they used to sing thirty years ago in Milan:

> *Nun, nun, semper nun,*
> *E se ciappem la cioppa*
> *La pagaremo nun!*
> *[We, we, always we,*
> *And if we go out on a spree,*
> *Who'll have to pay for it? We!]*

But the bourgeoisie will have to pay for the *cioppa* [spree].

Yours,

F. Engels

MARX TO SORGE

London, June 21, 1872

Dear Friend:

... As for my *Capital,* the first German installment of the second edition of Vol. I will be published next week, as will the first French installment in Paris. You will get copies of both consecutively from me for you and some of your friends. Of the French edition (the title page of which reads, by no means as a mere phrase, *"entièrement révisée par l'auteur"* [completely revised by the author], for I have had the devil of a job with it), 10,000 copies have been printed and 8,000 already sold, before publication of the first installment.

In Russia, books, after printing is completed but before they are released to the public, must be submitted to the censorship, which must file suit in court if it does not want to pass them.

They write me as follows from Russia regarding the Russian translation of my book (which is a masterly job): "In the censorship office two censors went over the work and laid their conclusions before the censorship committee. Even before the examination it was decided in principle not to hold this book up merely because of the author's name, but to make a close investigation of how far it really corresponds to its title. The following is a summary of the conclusion that was unanimously adopted by the censorship committee and submitted to the Central Administration for decision:

" 'Although the author, according to his convictions, is a thoroughgoing socialist and the whole book has a quite definite socialist character, nevertheless, in view of the fact that the presentation can by no means be called accessible to everyone and that, on the other hand, it possesses the form of a rigidly mathematical scientific demonstration, the Committee declares the prosecution of this book in court to be impossible.' Accordingly it was allowed out into the world. Three thousand copies have been printed. It was made available to the Russian public on March 27th, and 1000 copies had already been sold by May 15th."

In his announcement of my book the primeval know-nothing lout Heinzen made merry of the statement on the title-page: "Translation rights reserved." Who would want to translate such nonsense! The book was obviously written merely in order that Karl Heinzen shouldn't understand it.

We have issued a French translation of the *Address on the Civil War [in France]*, price 2½d. per copy. If wanted in the U.S., please write.

Regarding the Nicholson [1] affair, it is best not to say anything about it in the General Council for the present.

Salut,
Your
K.M.

ENGELS TO CUNO

London, July 5, [18]72

Dear Cuno:

. . . Bakunin & Co. will make every effort to beat us at the congress, and as these gentlemen have no scruples about methods, we must take precautionary measures. They are sending delegates from hundreds of various societies, not belonging to the International at all, and are trying to obtain a seat and a vote for these persons as delegates of the International in order to place the General Council in the minority with the aid of a coalition of the most heterogeneous elements. Schweitzer and Hasenclever have already concluded an avowed alliance with the scoundrels over here—Vésinier, Landeck, Smith, Schneider, and others—while the latter, in turn, are corresponding with the Jurassians and the American rogues (see the *Emancipation* that I sent you yesterday). . . .

The congress will be held in any event. On the Continent there is never any guarantee against police interference; but then they will have to get aboard a steamer, go to England, and hold it there. It would be inexpedient to convene it in England from the very start; though only in England would it be safe from police interference. Nevertheless it would be subjected to attacks

---

[1] Nicholson, who was treasurer of the Provisional Federal Council, had put it in an embarrassing position.

by our enemies. The General Council, they would say, is convening the congress in England because only there do they possess an artificial majority.

Bakunin has issued a furious, but very weak, abusive letter[1] in reply to the *Scissions*.[2] That ponderous elephant is beside himself with rage because he has finally been dragged from his Locarno lair out into the light, where neither machinations nor intrigues are of any more use. Now he declares that he is the victim of a conspiracy of all the European—*Jews!*

The continued existence of the Alliance—at least in Spain—as a *secret society* will break the old scoundrel's neck. Not only do we have proofs of this, but it is now quite officially known in Madrid and elsewhere, so that a denial is out of the question. This man of honor, who everywhere acts as the most devoted champion of the International, organized this secret conspiracy to seize over-all control and, with the assistance of his initiated brother Jesuits, to lead the broad masses of workers by the nose like a blind herd! If this were tolerated, I wouldn't remain in the International for a day. To be Bakunin's sheep—things haven't reached that pass yet! The hardest blow of all for him was our having uncovered this whole story and our threatening to expose him at the congress. And now Lafargue (Marx's son-in-law, who has been in Madrid for eight months) is accusing him, B[akunin], of having drawn up and sent to Spain the secret instructions on how the International was to be controlled there. . . .

Yours,

F. E.

ENGELS TO HEPNER

London, August 4, [18]72

Dear Hepner:

I was about to write a brief article for you on the latest Bakuninist stories, when it developed that the General Council would have to make a statement on the matter itself. Thus the article has

---

[1] An open letter by Bakunin and some of his adherents, published in the *Bulletin de la Fédération Jurassienne* of July 15, 1872. The letter was subsequently published as a pamphlet under the title *La Reponse de quelques Internationaux à la circulaire privée de Conseil Général* [*The Reply of Some Members of the International to the Secret Circular of the General Council*].

[2] *Les Prétendues Scissions dans l'Internationale* [*The Alleged Splits in the International*], Geneva 1872, the General Council's circular on the Bakuninist conspiracy.

turned into an address, the German translation of which you will get by Wednesday.

The latest Spanish documents may well serve as a supplement. Bakunin retained the *Alliance de la Démocratie Socialiste*,[1] which you know of from the *Scissions*, as a *secret society* in order to obtain control of the International. But we learned of this, and now we have the proofs. Thus, the charge will now be made publicly, as otherwise the elections to the Congress would take place in Spain under the management of the Alliance and would have resulted in its victory. B[akunin] will break his neck in this affair. . . .

According to our information, the preparations [for war] are being made on such a colossal scale that the Prussians can be defeated only if they are opposed by Austria, in addition to France and Russia. But Austria will be on Prussia's side, unless some sudden change occurs, which cannot be assumed under the existing circumstances. Moreover, we shall soon witness the odd spectacle of Wilhelm [Kaiser Wilhelm I] issuing an appeal to the Poles and re-establishing some sort of Poland. And with this he, and the whole Prussian regime, will break their necks. The Prusso-German Empire is far from having reached its culminating point; this war (if it ends well, which is to be expected) will swiftly raise it to its climax, and then it will come tumbling down from the dizzy heights of Napoleonic glory. It is quite possible that *this time* the movement will start in Berlin; the contradictions are growing more sharply acute there, and all that is required to bring about an explosion is a change in the political situation. A Berlin revolution of that kind will certainly be pretty shabby, but still it is better for it to come from within than after a Sedan, which never turns out well. . . .

Best regards,
Yours,
F. E.

ENGELS TO HEPNER

London, December 30, 1872

Dear Hepner:

. . . Of the two articles on the revival of the reform movement, the first was good, while the second was straightway contrary to the facts. The many miserable little congresses, which are taken seriously in this article only because they are taken seriously by the *Bee-Hive*, which has sold out to the bourgeoisie, have no other purpose than

[2] See footnote, p. 86.

as preparations for the impending parliamentary elections. All the reform leagues listed in the article are of absolutely no importance and consist, for the most part, of *the very same people*. And what people? With a few exceptions, they consist of the labor leaders whom Marx branded as corrupt at The Hague! It is impossible to judge the movement here from over there, taking the *Bee-Hive* and *Reynold's* [*Newspaper*] as your guides. The fact that a few trade unionists attend such congresses does not mean that the trade unions are thinking of becoming political, which they (at least most of them, and the biggest unions among them) *couldn't* do at all without totally revamping their by-laws. . . .

In fact, things are shockingly bad in the movement here—worse than they ever were, as is to be expected with such industrial prosperity.

[F. E.]

MARX TO SORGE

London, August 4, 1874

Dear Sorge:

My long silence cannot be excused at all; *cependant il y a des circonstances atténuantes* [however, there are extenuating circumstances]. That damned liver complaint has made such headway that I was positively unable to continue the revision of the French translation [Vol. I of *Capital*] (which actually amounts almost to complete rewriting), and I am very unwillingly submitting to the physicians' orders sending me off to Karlsbad.

They assure me that after I return I shall be fully able to work again, and being *unable* to work is indeed a death sentence for any man who is not a beast. The journey is expensive and so is the stay there, and what is more, it is uncertain whether the foolish Austrian government won't expel me! The Prussians would scarcely be so stupid, but they like to talk the Austrians into such compromising measures; and I actually believe that the false newspaper reports that Rochefort wants to go to Karlsbad, and so forth, stem from Herr Stieber and are, in the last analysis, meant for me. I have neither time nor money to lose and have therefore decided to apply for British naturalization, but it is very likely that the British Home Minister, who, like a sultan, decides on naturalization, will upset my plans. The matter will probably be decided this week. In any event, I am going to Karlsbad, if only because of my youngest daughter [Eleanor] who was seriously, dangerously ill, is only now able to travel again, and has also been told by her doctor to go to Karlsbad. . . .

In England the International is as good as dead for the present. The Federal Council in London exists as such only in name, although some of its members are active individually. The great event over here is the reawakening of the agricultural laborers. The miscarriage of their initial efforts does no harm, *au contraire* [on the contrary]. As for the urban workers, it is regrettable that the whole gang of leaders did not get into Parliament. That is the surest way of getting rid of the rascals.

In France workers' syndicates are being organized in the various big cities and are in correspondence with one another. They confine themselves to *purely professional* matters, nor can they do anything else. Otherwise they would be suppressed without further ado. Thus they keep some sort of organization, a point of departure for the time when freer movement will again be possible.

By their own practical importance, Spain, Italy, and Belgium demonstrate the intrinsic value of their super-socialism. In Austria our people are working under the most difficult conditions; they are compelled to move with the greatest caution. Nevertheless they have made one great advance: they have prevailed upon the Slavic workers in Prague and elsewhere to act together with the German workers. During the final period of the General Council in London I tried in vain to achieve an understanding of this sort.

In Germany Bismarck is working for us.

General European conditions are such as to drive more and more toward a *European war*. We shall have to pass through it before any decisive activity of the European working class can be thought of.

My wife and children send you their best regards.

Yours,
Karl Marx

In judging conditions in France, especially those in Paris, it should not be forgotten that alongside the official military and political authorities the gang of epauletted Bonapartist blackguards is still secretly active, out of which the great republican Thiers formed the military courts for slaughtering the Communards. They constitute a sort of secret tribunal of terror; their *mouchards* [police spies] are everywhere, making the Parisian workers' districts, in particular, unsafe.

ENGELS TO SORGE

London, September 12 and 17, 1874

Dear Sorge:

... With your resignation the old International is entirely wound up and at an end anyhow. And that is well. It belonged to the period of the Second Empire, when the oppression throughout Europe prescribed unity and abstention from all internal controversy for the labor movement, then just reawakening. It was the moment when the common, cosmopolitan interests of the proletariat could come to the fore; Germany, Spain, Italy, and Denmark had only just come into the movement or were just coming into it. In reality the theoretical character of the movement in 1864 was still very unclear throughout Europe, that is, among the masses. German communism did not yet exist as a workers' party, Proudhonism was too weak to be able to insist on its particular fads, Bakunin's new trash did not yet exist even in his own head, and even the leaders of the English trade unions thought they could enter the movement on the basis of the program laid down in the Preamble to the Statutes. The first great success was bound to explode this naive conjunction of all fractions. This success was the Commune, which was beyond doubt the child of the International intellectually, though the International did not lift a finger to produce it, and for which the International — to that extent with full justification — was held responsible.

When, thanks to the Commune, the International became a moral force in Europe, the row began at once. Each tendency wanted to exploit the success for itself. The inevitable decomposition set in. Jealousy of the growing power of the only people who were really ready to continue working along the lines of the old comprehensive program — the German Communists — drove the Belgian Proudhonists into the arms of the Bakuninist adventurers. The Hague Congress was actually the end — and for both parties. The only country where something could still be accomplished in the name of the International was America, and by a happy instinct the executive was transferred there. Now its prestige is exhausted there too, and any further effort to galvanize it into new life would be folly and a waste of energy. The International dominated ten years of one side of European history — the side on which the future lies — and can look back upon its work with pride. But in its old form it has outlived itself. In order to produce a new International like the old one — an alliance of all the proletarian parties of all countries — a general suppression of the labor movement like that which prevailed from 1849 to 1864 would be necessary. For this the proletarian world has now become too big, too extensive. I think the next International — after Marx's writings have been at work for some years — will be directly Communist and will openly proclaim our principles. . . .

The squabbles in New York, which made it impossible for you to remain in the General Council any longer, are just as much proof as consequence of the fact that the thing has outlived itself. When circumstances no longer allow a society to act effectively, when the first thing to be done is simply to keep the bond of union tied so that it can be used again upon occasion, there are always people to be found who cannot fit themselves into this situation, definitely want to play the busybody, and demand that "something be done," and this something can then only be folly. And if these people succeed in getting the majority, they compel everyone who does not want to bear the responsibility for their absurdities to resign. What good fortune that we did not send the minute books over! . . .

Best regards,

Yours,
F. Engels

MARX TO SORGE

London, September 27, 1877

Dear Friend:

. . . This crisis [the Russo-Turkish War and Near Eastern crisis] is *a new turning point* in European history. Russia — and I have studied conditions there from the original *Russian* sources, unofficial and official (the latter accessible to but few persons, but obtained for me through friends in St. Petersburg) — has long been standing on the threshold of an upheaval; all the elements for it are prepared. The gallant Turks have hastened the explosion by years through the blows they have dealt not merely to the Russian Army (and Russian finances), but to the very persons of the *dynasty commanding* the army (the Tsar, the heir to the throne, and six other Romanovs). The upheaval will begin *secundum artem* [according to the rules of the art], playing at constitutionalism, *et puis il y aura un beau tapage* [and then there will be a fine row]. If Mother Nature is not particularly hard on us, we shall yet live to see the fun!

The stupid nonsense the Russian students are perpetrating is merely a symptom, worthless in itself. But it is a symptom. All sections of Russian society are in full decomposition economically, morally, and intellectually.

This time the revolution begins in the East, hitherto the unbroken bulwark and reserve army of counter-revolution.

Herr Bismarck was pleased to see the thrashing, but it wasn't to go that far. Russia, too much weakened, could not hold Austria in check again as it did in the Franco-Prussian War! And if it were to go as far as revolution there, what would become of the ultimate guarantee of the Hohenzollern dynasty?

For the present the most important thing is for the Poles (in the Kingdom of Poland) to lie low. Only no risings there at this moment! Bismarck would march in at once, and Russian chauvinism would again side with the Tsar. If on the other hand the Poles wait quietly until things are ablaze in Petersburg and Moscow, and Bismarck then intervenes as a savior, Prussia will meet — its Mexico!

I have rammed this home again and again to any Poles I am in contact with who can influence their fellow-countrymen.

Compared with the crisis in the East, the *French crisis* [1] is quite a secondary event. Still it is to be hoped that the bourgeois republic wins out or else the old game will begin all over again, and no nation can repeat the same stupidities too often.

With the most cordial regards from my wife and myself,

Yours,

Karl Marx

MARX TO SORGE

[London] October 19, 1877

Dear Sorge:

... A rotten spirit is making itself felt in our party in Germany, not so much among the masses as among the leaders (upper class and "workers"). The compromise with the Lassalleans has led to compromise with other halfway elements too; in Berlin (via *Most*) with Dühring and his "admirers," but also with a whole gang of half-mature students and super-wise doctors of philosophy who want to give socialism a "higher, ideal" turn, that is to say, to replace its materialist basis (which calls for serious, objective study by anyone wanting to make use of it) by modern mythology with its goddesses of Justice, Liberty, Equality, and Fraternity. Dr. Höchberg, who publishes the *Zukunft,* is a representative of this tendency and has

[1] In France the monarchist President of the Republic, MacMahon, attempted in 1877 to prepare for a restoration of the monarchy and dissolved the Chamber of Deputies. At the elections in October, however, the victory was gained by a republican majority.

"bought his way" into the party — with the "noblest" intentions, I assume, but I do not give a damn for "intentions." Anything more miserable than his program of the *Zukunft* has seldom seen the light of day with more "modest presumption."

The workers themselves, when, like Herr Most and Co., they give up work and become *professional literary men*, always breed "theoretical" mischief and are always ready to join muddleheads from the allegedly "learned" caste. *Utopian* socialism especially, which for tens of years we have been clearing out of the German workers' heads with so much effort and labor — their freedom from it making them theoretically (and therefore also practically) superior to the French and English — utopian socialism, playing with fantastic pictures of the future structure of society, is again spreading in a much more futile form, not to be compared with the great French and English utopians, but with — Weitling. It is natural that utopianism, which *before* the era of materialist-critical socialism concealed the latter within itself *in nuce* [in a nutshell], coming now *post festum* [after the event] can only be silly — silly, stale, and fundamentally reactionary.

Of late the *Vorwärts* seems to be following the principle of accepting manuscript, *"copie"* as the French call it, no matter where it comes from. In one of the latest numbers, for example, first a fellow who doesn't know the economic ABC makes grotesque *disclosures* regarding the "laws" of crises. He discloses nothing but his own inner "crisis." And then there is the impertinent youngster of Berlin, who is allowed to print his unauthoritative thoughts on England and the shallowest Pan-Slavism nonsense in endless tapeworm articles at the expense of the "sovereign people"! *Satis superque* [enough and more than enough]!

Yours,

Karl Marx

Apropos. A few years ago (not many) a sort of Blue Book was published (I don't know whether official or not) on the conditions of the miners in Pennsylvania, who live, as we know, in the most feudal dependence upon their moneylords (I think the thing was published after a bloody conflict[1]). It is of the greatest importance for me to have this publication, and if you can get it for me I shall send you what it costs. If not, perhaps you can get me the title, and I shall then ask Harney (in Boston).

---

[1] The Pennsylvania miners' "long strike of 1875," broken by the use of troops.

MARX TO SORGE

London, September 19, 1879

Dear Friend:

. . . I did not receive the new edition of *Weitling*.[1] Of the American periodicals I receive only the *Paterson Labor Standard,* which has but very little in it. Thanks for your latest shipments of Pennsylvania, Ohio, and Massachusetts Labor Bureau statistics, as well as for Steward's speech.[2] I am much pleased that the chief of the Massachusetts bureau will, as he writes me, from now on send me their publications (including census) as soon as published.

As for Most and Co, we maintain a "passive" attitude towards them, that is to say, we have no relationship with them, although I see Most now and then at my house. Mr. Lübeck lies when he says that Engels and I have issued any *"statement"* against Most or against the *Freiheit*. . . . Bernstein wrote Engels from Zurich that Most wrote to Germany and Switzerland, saying we backed him. Engels replied: If Bernstein submitted *proofs* of this, he would issue a public statement against this untruth. But Bernstein (nephew of the Berlin rabbi Rebenstein, of the Berlin *Volkszeitung*) had, in fact, not a shred of proof to submit. Instead he whispered the false secret to Lübeck, who immediately sold it to the U.S. with the usual discretion of these penny-a-liners.

Our points of dispute with Most are by no means those of the Zurich gentlemen of the trio, "Dr. Höchberg, Bernstein (his secretary), and C. A. Schramm." We do not reproach Most for his *Freiheit* being *too revolutionary;* what we do hold against him is that it has *no revolutionary content,* but merely deals in *revolutionary phrases.* We reproach him not for *criticizing the party leaders in Germany,* but first, for making a public scandal instead of communicating his views to them in writing, *i.e., by letter,* as we do; and, second, because he merely uses this as an excuse for making himself important and putting the *idiotic secret conspiratorial plans* of Messrs. *Weber Jr. and Kaufmann* into circulation. Long before he arrived these fellows felt themselves destined to take the "general labor movement" under their all-highest direction, and they contrived all sorts of endeavors in every quarter to realize this "charming" venture.

The worthy Johann Most, a man of the most childish vanity, actually believes that world affairs have suffered a tremendous

[1] The new edition of Wilhelm Weitling's *Garantien der Freiheit* (*Guarantees of Freedom*), published by S. Landsberg in 1878.

[2] Ira Steward, founder of the Eight-Hour League, had made a speech to workers in Chicago on July 4, 1879.

change because this same Most no longer lives in Germany, but in London. The man is not without talent, but he kills his talent by too much writing. In addition he is without *esprit de suite* [consistency]. Every change of the wind blows him first in one direction and then in another like a weathercock.

On the other hand, matters may indeed reach the point where Engels and I would be compelled to issue a "public statement" against the Leipzigers[1] and their Zurich allies. This is the state of affairs: Bebel wrote us that they wanted to found a party organ in Zurich and he requested our names as collaborators. Hirsch's name was given us as the responsible editor. Thereupon *we accepted,* and I at once wrote Hirsch (then in Paris, from which he has since been banished, for the second time) to accept the editorial post, since he alone affords us the certainty that a crew of doctors, students, and the like, and professorial socialist rogues, such as strut in the *Zukunft,* etc., and has already begun to penetrate the *Vorwärts,* would be kept out, and the party line would be adhered to strictly. But it turned out that Hirsch had uncovered a hornets' nest in Zurich. The five men: *Dr. Höchberg* (who has bought his way into the party with his money, an emotional driveler, the cousin of Sonnemann); . . . *Bernstein,* his secretary; *C. A. Schramm,* a philistine though meaning well; *Viereck,* sent from Leipzig (also a philistine lout, the natural son of the German Kaiser); and the businessman *Singer* of Berlin (a petty-bourgeois paunch, paid me a visit some months ago)—these five men constituted themselves — with the highest permission of Leipzig — the constituent committee, and appointed the trio: ₓ*ₓ (Höchberg-Bernstein-C. A. Schramm) as the *administrative committee, which was to supervise the editorial board* and have immediate jurisdiction. Bebel, Liebknecht, and a few others of the German leaders stood above them as the final court of appeal. Hirsch demanded to know, first, *from whom the money* is to come. Liebknecht had written: from the "party + Dr. Höchberg"; Hirsch stripped off the rhetorical flourish and reduced this quite correctly to "Höchberg." Second, Hirsch did not want to submit to the trifolium Höchberg-Bernstein-C.A. Schramm, in doing which he was all the more justified since Bernstein, answering a letter in which he had asked for information, had bureaucratically ridden roughshod over him, rejected his *Laterne — mirabile dictu* [wonderful to relate] — as ultra-revolutionary, etc. After a prolonged correspondence, in which Liebknecht did not play a shining part, Hirsch withdrew. Engels

[1] The Executive Committee of the German Social-Democratic Party, headed by August Bebel, Wilhelm Liebknecht, and Wilhelm Bracke, had its seat in Leipzig during the life of Bismarck's Anti-Socialist Law.

wrote to Bebel that *we* are also withdrawing, as we had from the very start refused to write for the *Zukunft* (Höchberg) and *Neue Gesellschaft* (Wiede). These fellows — zeros theoretically, incompetent practically — want to take the teeth out of socialism (which they have trimmed up according to university recipes) and out of the Social-Democratic Party in particular, to enlighten the workers or, as they put it, feed them "the elements of education" through their confused half-knowledge, and, above all, to make the party respectable in the eyes of the philistine. They are poor *counter-revolutionary* windbags.

Well, the weekly organ is now appearing (or is to appear) in Zurich, under their supervision and the higher supervision of the Leipzigers. (Vollmar editor.)

In the meantime, Höchberg came here to entice us. He found only Engels, who made clear to him the deep gulf between us and him by means of a critical review of the *Jahrbuch* issued by Höchberg (under the pseudonym Dr. L. *Richter*). (Take a look at the *miserable* product; the article signed with three ****** is [by] the trio Höchberg-Bernstein-C.A. Schramm.) (But honest Johann Most also figures in it with the groveling article on the book scribbler Schäffle.) Nothing more blameworthy for the party has ever been printed. What a good turn Bismarck did, *not himself, but us,* by making it possible for these fellows to make themselves clearly heard as a result of the enforced silence in Germany.

Höchberg was stunned when Engels told him the unvarnished truth; he is a "peaceable" evolutionary and really expects proletarian emancipation to come only from the "educated bourgeois," *i.e.,* people like himself. He declared Liebknecht had told him that we all agreed *au fond* [at bottom]. All those in Germany — *i.e.,* all the leaders — shared his view, etc. Indeed, after making the great mistake in the transactions with the Lassalleans, Liebknecht has opened the doors wide to all these barbarians, and thus paved the way *malgré lui* [in spite of himself] for a demoralization in the party which could be eliminated *only* by the Socialist Law.

Now if the "weekly" — the party organ — should actually *proceed* along the lines initiated by Höchberg's *Jahrbuch,* we should be compelled to take a public stand against such dissipation of the party and its theory! Engels has drawn up a circular (letter) to Bebel, etc.[1] (only for *private circulation* among the German party leaders, of course), in which our standpoint is set forth without reserve. Thus

[1] See Letter 170 in Marx-Engels, *Selected Correspondence,* International Publishers, 1935, pp. 362-80.

the gentlemen have been warned in advance, and they know us well enough to know that this means: yield or succumb! If they want to compromise themselves, *tant pis* [so much the worse]! In no event will they be allowed to compromise *us*. You can see how low parliamentarism has already brought them from the fact that they are charging Hirsch with a great crime — because of what? Because he has handled the scoundrel Kayser somewhat roughly in the *Laterne* for the latter's disgraceful speech on Bismarck's tariff legislation. But, but now they say the party, *i.e.*, the handful of parliamentary representatives of the party, had authorized Kayser to speak like that! All the more shame for this handful! But even that is a miserable excuse. In fact they were foolish enough to let Kayser speak for himself and on behalf of his constituents; but he spoke in the name of the party. However that may be, they are already so far affected by parliamentary idiocy that they think they are *above criticism,* that they denounce criticism as a *crime de lèse majesté.*

As for the *Communist Manifesto,* nothing has been done about it up to now because first Engels, and then I, had no time. But we must get on with it at last. . . .

Your loyally devoted
Karl Marx

MARX TO SWINTON[1]

[London] November 4, 1880

My dear Sir:

I have sent you today a copy of the French edition of the *Capital.* I have at the same time to thank you for your friendly article in the *Sun.*

Apart Mr. Gladstone's sensational failures abroad — political interest centers here at present on the Irish "Land Question." And why? Mainly because it is the harbinger of the English "Land Question."

Not only that the great landlords of England are also the largest landholders of Ireland, but having once broken down in what is ironically called the "sister" island, the English landed system will no longer be tenable at home. There are arraigned against it the British farmers, wincing under high rents, and — thanks to the American competition — low prices; the British agricultural laborers, at last impatient of their traditional position of ill-used beasts of

---

[1] This letter was written in English.

burden, and — that British party which styles itself *"Radical."* The latter consists of two sets of men; first the *ideologues* of the party, eager to overthrow the political power of the aristocracy by mining its material basis, the semifeudal landed property. But behind these principle-spouters, and hunting them on, looks another set of men — sharp, closefisted, calculating *capitalists,* fully aware that the abolition of the old land laws, in the way proposed by the ideologues, cannot but convert land into a commercial article that must ultimately concentrate in the hands of capital.

On the other side, considered as a natural entity, John Bull has ugly misgivings lest the aristocratic English landed garrison in Ireland once gone — England's political sway over Ireland will go too!

Liebknecht has to enter prison for six months. The *Anti-Socialists' Law* having failed to overthrow or even to weaken the German Social-Democratic organization, Bismarck clings the more desperately to his panacea, and fancies that it *must* work, if only applied on a larger scale. Hence he has extended the *state of siege* to Hamburg, Altona, and three other Northern towns. Under these circumstances, the German friends have written me a letter of which one passage reads thus:

"The Socialist Law, though it could not break and never will break our organization, does impose pecuniary sacrifices almost impossible to bear. To support the families ruined by the police, to keep alive the few papers left to us, to keep up the necessary communications by secret messengers, to fight the battle on the whole line — all this requires money. We are nearly exhausted and forced to appeal to our friends and sympathizers in other countries."

So far this extract.

Now we here at London, Paris, etc., will do our best. At the same time, I believe that a man of your influence might organize a subscription in the United States. Even if the monetary result were not important, denunciations of Bismarck's new *coup d'état* in public meetings held by you, reported in the American press, reproduced on the other side of the Atlantic, would sorely hit the Pomeranian *hobereau* [country squire] and be welcomed by all the socialists of Europe. More information you might get from Mr. Sorge (Hoboken). Any money forthcoming to be sent over to Mr. *Otto Freytag,* Landtagsabgeordneter, *Amtmannshof, Leipzig.* His address ought, of course, not be made public; otherwise the German police would simply — *confiscate.*

Apropos. My youngest daughter [Eleanor]—who was not with us at Ramsgate — just tells me that she has cut my portrait from the copy of the *Capital* I sent you, on the pretext that it was a mere caricaure. Well, I shall make up for it by a photogram to be taken on the first fine day.

Mrs. Marx and the whole family send you their best wishes.

Yours most sincerely,

Karl Marx

MARX TO SORGE

[London] November 5, 1880

Dear Sorge:

You must attribute my long silence (1) to a very great pressure of work, and (2) to the grave illness of my wife, which has already lasted over a year.

You have seen the heights to which Johann Most has developed, and on the other hand, how miserably the so-called party organ, the Zurich *Sozialdemokrat* (not to mention the *Jahrbuch* there) has been managed, *duce* [under the leadership of] Dr. Höchberg. Engels and I have been engaged in constant correspondence with the Leipzigers[1] in this connection, with sharp clashes occurring often. But we have avoided intervening *publicly* in any way. It is not fitting for those who sit quietly, *comparativement parlant* [comparatively speaking], abroad to make the position of those working within the country under the hardest conditions and with the greatest personal sacrifices more difficult, to the delight of the bourgeois and the government. Liebknecht was here a few weeks ago, and "improvement" has been promised in every respect. The party organization has been renewed, which could be done only in a secret manner, *i.e.,* so far as "secret" means a secret to the police.

It is only recently that I fully discovered Most's blackguardism—in a *Russian* socialist paper. He never dared to print in *German* what can be read here in the Russian vernacular. This is no longer an attack upon individual persons, but the dragging of the *whole German labor movement through the mud.* At the same time it grotesquely shows *his absolute lack of understanding* of the doctrine he formerly peddled. It is a babbling, so silly, so illogical, so degenerate, that it finally dissolves into *nothing, viz.,* Johann Most's boundless personal vanity. As he was unable to accomplish anything in Germany in spite of all his ranting, except among a certain Berlin mob, he has allied himself with the younger generation of Bakuninists in Paris, the group that publishes the *Révolution*

[1] See footnote, p. 119.

sociale (whose circle of readers = exactly 210, but which possesses *Pyat's Commune* as its ally. The cowardly, melodramatic *farceur* [comedian] *Pyat* — in whose *Commune* I figure as *Bismarck's* right hand — has a grudge against me because I have always treated him with absolute contempt and thwarted all his attempts to use the *International* for his sensational tricks.) In any event Most has performed the good service of having brought all the ranters — Andreas Scheu, Hasselmann, etc., etc. — together as a group.

As a result of *Bismarck's* new state-of-siege decrees and the persecution of our party organs, it is absolutely necessary to raise *money* for the party. I have therefore written to *John Swinton* (for a well-meaning bourgeois is best suited for this purpose), and told him to apply to you for detailed information regarding German conditions.

Aside from the trifles mentioned on the previous page — and how many of these have we seen burst and vanish again without a trace during our long years of exile — things are going along splendidly on the whole (I mean by this the general developments in Europe), as well as within the circles of the really revolutionary party on the Continent.

You have probably noticed that the *Égalité,* in particular (thanks *en première instance* [principally] to *Guesde's coming over* to us and to the work of my son-in-law Lafargue), has for the first time offered us a French *"workers' paper"* in the wider sense. *Malon,* too, in the *Revue Socialiste,* has had to espouse *socialisme moderne scientifique, i.e., German* socialism, even though with the inconsistencies inseparable from his eclectic nature (we were enemies, as he was originally one of the co-founders of the *Alliance*[1]). I wrote the *"Questionneur"* for him, which was first printed in the *Revue Socialiste* and a reprint of which was then distributed throughout France in a very large edition. Shortly afterward Guesde came to London to draw up a workers' election program, together with us (myself, Engels, Lafargue), for the coming general elections. With the exception of some trivialities which Guesde found it necessary to throw to the French workers, despite my protest, such as fixing the minimum wage by law, and the like (I told him: "If the French proletariat is still so childish as to require such bait, it is not worth while drawing up any program whatever"), the economic section of the very brief document consists solely of demands that have spontaneously arisen out of the labor movement itself, except for the introductory passages where the communist goal is defined in a few words. It was a tremendous

---

[1] *Alliance de la Démocratie Socialiste,* the international secret society established within the First International by Bakunin to seize control of the International for the anarchists. See pp. 86, 97, 102, 111.

step forward to pull the French workers down to earth from their fog of phraseology, and hence it was a violent shock to all the French giddyheads, who live by "fog-making." After the most violent opposition by the anarchists, the program was first adopted in the *Région centrale* — *i.e.,* Paris and its environs — and later in many other workers' centers. The simultaneous formation of opposed groups of workers, which accepted, however, most of the "practical" demands of the program, *sauf les anarchistes* [except the anarchists], who do not consist of actual workers, but of *déclassés* with a few duped workers as their rank-and-file soldiers, and the fact that very divergent standpoints were expressed solely regarding other questions, prove to me that this is *the first real labor movement* in France. Up to the present time only sects existed there, which naturally received their *mot d'ordre* [slogan] from the founder of the sect, whereas the mass of the proletariat followed the radical or pseudo-radical bourgeois and fought for them on the day of decision, only to be slaughtered, deported, etc., the very next day by the fellows they had put into power.

The *Emancipation* that was put out in Lyons a few days ago will be the organ of the *Parti ouvrier* [Workers Party] that has sprung up on the basis of German socialism.

Meanwhile we also have had and have our champions in the camp of the enemy itself — *i.e.,* in the radical camp. *Theisz* has taken up the labor problem in the *Intransigeant,* Rochefort's organ; after the defeat of the Commune he came to London a Proudhonist, like all "thinking" French socialists, and there he changed completely — through personal contact with me and concientious study of *Capital.* On the other hand, my son-in-law [Charles Longuet] gave up his professorship in Kings College, returned to Paris (his family is still here fortunately), and became one of the most influential editors of *Justice,* which belongs to Clemenceau, the leader of the extreme Left. He has done such good work that Clemenceau, who came out publicly as late as last April against socialism and as the advocate of American-democratic-republican views, has swung over to us in his latest speech in Marseilles, against Gambetta. This is true of both its general tendency and its principal points, as contained in the *minimum program.* Whether he will keep what he promises is wholly immaterial. In any event he has introduced our element into the Radical Party, whose organs, comically enough, consider wonderful, now that it comes from the mouth of Clemenceau, what they had ignored or ridiculed as long as it was merely issued as the slogan of the *Parti ouvrier.*

I need hardly tell you — for you know *French chauvinism* — that the secret threads by which the leaders, from Guesde-Malon to Clemenceau, have been set in motion are *entre nous* [between us]. *Il n'en faut pas parler. Quand on veut agir pour Messieurs les Francais, il faut le faire anonymement, pour ne pas choquer le sentiment "national."* [One must not talk about this. When one wishes to influence Messrs. the French, one must do so anonymously in order not to shock "national" feeling.] As it is, the anarchists denounce our co-operators already as *Prussian* agents, under the dictatorship of the "notorious" Prussian agent — Karl Marx.

In Russia, where *Capital* is more read and appreciated than anywhere else, our success is even greater. On the one hand, we have the *critics* (mostly young university professors, some of them personal friends of mine, as well as some writers for the reviews), and, on the other, *the terrorist central committee,* whose *program,* secretly printed and issued in Petersburg recently, has provoked great fury among the anarchist Russians in *Switzerland,* who publish *The Black Redistribution* [1] (this is the literal translation from the Russian) in Geneva. These persons — most (not all) of them people who left Russia *voluntarily* — constitute the so-called party of propaganda as opposed to the terrorists who risk their lives. (In order to carry on *propaganda in Russia* — they move *to Geneva!* What a *quid pro quo* [exchange]!) These gentlemen are against all political-revolutionary action. Russia is to leap into the anarchist-communist-atheist millennium in one breakneck jump! In the meantime they are preparing for this leap by a tiresome doctrinairism whose so-called *principes courent la rue depuis feu Bakounine* [principles have been commonplaces ever since the late Bakunin].

And now enough for this time. Let me hear from you soon. Best regards from my wife.

Totus tuus [entirely yours],

Karl Marx

I should be very much pleased if you could find me something good (meaty) on economic conditions in *California,* of course at my expense. California is very important for me because nowhere else has the upheaval most shamelessly caused by capitalist centralization taken place with such speed.

---

[1] *Cherny Peredel,* published for a few months in 1881 by a group headed by Plekhanov, Zasulich, and Axelrod during the period of their transition from the Narodnik (Populist) movement to Marxism.

MARX TO SWINTON [1]

London N. W., June 2, 1881

Dear Mr. Swinton:

I need hardly recommend you the bearer of these lines, my excellent friend Mr. Hartmann. I send you through him a photogram of mine; it is rather bad, but the only one left to me.

As to the book of Mr. Henry George, I consider it as a last attempt — to save the capitalistic regime. Of course, this is not the meaning of the author, but the older disciples of Ricardo — the radical ones — fancied already that by the public appropriation of the rent of land everything would be righted. I have referred to this doctrine in the *Misère de la Philosophie* [The Poverty of Philosophy] (published in 1847, against Proudhon).

Mrs. Marx sends you her best compliments. Unfortunately her illness assumes more and more a fatal character.

Believe me, dear Sir,

Yours most sincerely,

Karl Marx

The "Viereck" [Louis Viereck] was so stultified at his arrival in the U.S. that he confounded my friend Engels with myself, and transformed my compliments to you in those of Engels; he did the same with regard to another American friend of mine by whose letter I was informed of the *quid pro quo* [exchange].

MARX TO SORGE

London, June 20, 1881

Dear Sorge:

. . . Before I received your copy of Henry George [2] I had gotten two others, one from Swinton and one from Willard Brown; I therefore gave one to Engels and one to Lafargue. Today I must confine myself to a very brief formulation of my opinion of the book. Theoretically the man is *total arrière* [utterly backward]! He understands nothing about the nature of *surplus value,* and so wanders about in speculations that follow the English pattern, but are even behind the English, about the portions of surplus value that have attained independent existence, *i.e.,* the relationships of profit, rent, interest, etc. His fundamental dogma is that *everything would be all right* if land rent were paid to the state. (You will also

[1] This letter was written in English.

[2] Henry George, *Progress and Poverty*, 1879.

find payment of this kind among the *transition measures* included in the *Communist Manifesto*.) This idea originally belonged to the bourgeois economists; it was first put forward (apart from a similar demand at the end of the eighteenth century) by the earliest *radical* disciples of Ricardo, just after his death. I said of it in 1847, in my book against Proudhon: "Nous concevons que des économistes tels que Mill (der ältere, nicht sein Sohn John Stuart, der dies auch etwas modifiziert wiederholt), Cherbuliez, Hilditch et autres, ont demandé que la rente soit attribuée à l'Etat pour servir à l'acquittement des impôts. C'est là la franche expression de la haine que le *capitaliste industriel* voue au *propriétaire foncier*, qui lui parait une inutilité, une superfétation, dans l'ensemble de la production bourgeoise." ["We understand such economists as Mill (the elder, not his son John Stuart, who also repeats this in a somewhat modified form), Cherbuliez, Hilditch, and others demanding that rent should be handed over to the state to serve in place of taxes. That is a frank expression of the hatred the *industrial capitalist* bears toward the *landed proprietor*, who seems to him a useless thing, an excrescence upon the general body of bourgeois production."][1]

We ourselves, as I have already mentioned, adopted this appropriation of land rent by the state among numerous other *transitional measures*, which, as is likewise stated in the *Manifesto*, are and must be contradictory in themselves.

But the first person to turn this *desideratum* [requirement] of the *radical* English bourgeois economists into *the socialist panacea*, to declare this procedure to be the solution of the antagonisms involved in the present mode of production, was *Colins*, an old ex-officer of Napoleon's Hussars, born in Belgium, who in the latter days of Guizot and the early days of Napoleon the Little [Napoleon III], favored the world with bulky volumes from Paris about this "discovery" of his. Like the other discovery he made, that though there is no God there is an *"immortal"* human soul, and that animals have "no feelings." For if they had feelings, that is souls, we should be cannibals and a kingdom of righteousness could never be established on earth. His "anti-landownership theory" together with his theory of the soul, etc., has been preached every month for years in the Paris *Philosophie de l'Avenir* by his few remaining followers, mostly Belgians. They call themselves *"collectivistes rationels"* [rational collectivists], and have praised Henry George. After them and besides them, among others, the Prussian banker and former

[1] Karl Marx, *The Poverty of Philosophy*, International Publishers, New York, 1936, p. 136.

lottery collector Samter of East Prussia, a shallow-brained fellow, has eked out this "socialism" into a thick volume.

All these "socialists" since Colins have this much in common, that they leave *wage labor* and hence *capitalist production* in existence and try to bamboozle themselves or the world into believing that through the transformation of land rent into a state tax *all the evils* of capitalist production would vanish of themselves. The whole thing is thus simply an attempt, trimmed with socialism, *to save capitalist rule* and indeed to *re-establish* it on *an even wider basis* than its present one.

This cloven hoof (at the same time ass's hoof) also peeps out unmistakably from the declamations of Henry George. It is the more unpardonable in him because he on the contrary, ought to have asked himself: How did it happen that in the United States, where, relatively, that is, compared with civilized Europe, the land was accessible to the great masses of the people and still is to a certain degree (again relatively), capitalist economy and the corresponding enslavement of the working class have developed *more rapidly* and more *shamelessly* than in any other country!

On the other hand, George's book, like the sensation it has made among you, is significant because it is a first, though unsuccessful, effort at emancipation from orthodox political economy.

H. George does not seem, moreover, to know anything about the history of the early *American anti-renters*,[1] who were practical men rather than theoretical. Otherwise he is a writer with talent (with a talent for Yankee advertising too), as his article on California in the *Atlantic* proves, for example. He also has the repulsive presumption and arrogance that distinguish all such panacea-mongers without exception. . . .

Salut fraternel,
Yours,
K. Marx

---

[1] The Anti-Rent Party, a movement of rebellious tenant farmers during the early 1840's, grew out of the discontent with the survival of old manorial land rights in the "patroonships" along the Hudson River in New York. These farmers refused to pay rent for their land claimed by the heirs of the old patroons and shot down the deputy sheriffs who came to enforce payment. Branded as outlaws by Governor Wright of New York, they resorted to political action for relief. The Anti-Renters controlled the votes of about ten counties and held the balance of power for two years.

MARX TO SORGE

[London] December 15, 1881

Dear Sorge:

. . . Your Henry George is revealing himself as more and more of a humbug. . . .

Yours,

K. Marx

The English have recently begun to occupy themselves more with *Capital,* etc. Thus in the last *October* (or November, I am not quite sure) number of the *Contemporary* there is an article by *John Rae* on German socialism. (Very inadequate, full of mistakes, but "fair," as one of my English friends told me the day before yesterday.) And why fair? Because [1] John Rae does *not suppose* that for the forty years I am spreading my pernicious theories I was being instigated by *"bad"* motives. *"Seine Grossmut muss ich loben!"* [I must praise his magnanimity!] The fairness of making yourself at least sufficiently acquainted with the subject of your criticism seems a thing quite unknown to the penmen of British philistinism.

Before this, in the beginning of June, there was published by a certain *Hyndman* a little book: *England for All.* It pretends to be written as an exposé of the program of the *"Democratic Federation"* — a recently formed association of different English and Scotch radical societies, half bourgeois, half *prolétaires* [proletarians]. The chapters on Labor and Capital are only literal extracts from or circumlocutions of the *Capital,* but the fellow does neither quote the book, nor its author, but to shield himself from exposure remarks at the end of his preface: "For the ideas and much of the matter contained in Chapters II and III, I am indebted to the work of a great thinker and original writer, etc., etc." Vis-á-vis myself, the fellow wrote stupid letters of excuse, for instance, that "the English don't like to be taught by foreigners," that "my name was so much detested, etc." With all that his little book — so far as it pilfers the *Capital* — makes good propaganda, although the man is a "weak" vessel, and very far from having even the patience — the first condition of learning anything — of studying a matter thoroughly. All these amiable middle-class writers — if not specialists — have an itching to make money or name or political capital *immediately* out of any new thoughts they may have got at by any favorable windfall. Many evenings this fellow has pilfered from me, in order to take me out and to learn in the easiest way.

[1] From here on this letter was written in English.

Lastly, there was published on the first December last (I shall send you a copy of it) in the monthly review *Modern Thought* an article: "Leaders of Modern Thought: No. XXIII — Karl Marx. By Ernest Belfort Bax."

Now that is the first English publication of that kind which is pervaded by a real enthusiasm for the new ideas themselves and boldly stands up against British philistinism. This does not prevent that the biographical notices the author gives of me are mostly wrong, etc. In the exposition of my economic principles and in his translations (*i.e.*, quotations of the *Capital*) much is wrong and confused, but with all that the appearance of this article, announced in large letters by placards on the walls of West End London, has produced a great sensation. What was most important for me, I received the said number of *Modern Thought* already on the 30th of November, so that my dear wife had the last days of her life still cheered up. You know the passionate interest she took in all such affairs.

ENGELS TO SORGE

London, June 20, 1882

Dear Sorge:

. . . Marx was in Algiers for about two months, where he suffered a relapse of pleurisy, as I think I wrote you. After this was cured, he went to Monte Carlo in Monaco and suffered another, but this time a mild one. From there he went to Paris about three weeks ago and is now with his daughter, Mrs. Longuet [Jenny Marx], in Argenteuil near Paris, traveling to Enghien every day to take the sulphur springs there for his chronic bronchial catarrh and cough. His general health is very good; as for his further movements, they depend entirely upon the doctors.

The English translation of the *Manifesto* [*Communist Manifesto*] sent us is quite unprintable without complete revision. But you will understand that this is out of the question under the present circumstances. . . .

The presumption of the Lassalleans after their arrival in America was inevitable. People who carried the only true gospel with them in their bag could not speak unpretentiously to the Americans, still languishing in spiritual darkness. What was at stake, moreover, was finding a new footing in America to take the place of the one that was disappearing more and more under their feet in Germany. To make up for it we are happily rid of them in Germany; in America, where everything proceeds ten times as fast, they will soon be disposed of. . . .

In Germany things are going ahead excellently on the whole. To be sure, Messrs. Literati of the party have tried to turn it toward reactionary, tame-bourgeois education, but this failed utterly. The infamies to which the Social-Democratic workers are everywhere subjected have made them everywhere much more revolutionary than they were even three years ago. You will have read the details in the *Sozialdemokrat*. Of the leaders, Bebel is the one who has behaved best in this affair too. Liebknecht wavered somewhat, since not only does he welcome every halfway, so-called democratic, "eddicated man" with open arms and without looking him over carefully, but his son-in-law, the fat sleepyhead Bruno Geiser, is one of the biggest whiners. These people would like to beg off the Socialist Law at any price by mildness, meekness, toadying, and tameness, because it makes short work of their literary earnings. As soon as the law is abolished (even the bourgeois do not count upon its prolongation by the present Reichstag or any other possible Reichstag, because it has proved to be totally ineffective), the split will probably become an open one, and the Vierecks, Höchbergs, Geisers, Blos and Co. will form a separate Right wing, where we can negotiate with them from case to case until they finally collapse. We said this immediately after the passage of the Socialist Law, when Höchberg and Schramm published in the *Jahrbuch* what was under the circumstances a quite infamous estimate of the party's activity up to that time and demanded of the party more "eddicated," respectable, Sunday-best manners. . . .

Best regards,

Yours

F. Engels

Tell Adolph that Pumps [nickname of Mary Ellen Burns, Engels' niece] has a little girl.

ENGELS TO HEPNER

London, July 25, 1882

Dear Mr. Hepner:

The delay in my reply was caused by Marx's illness and his many changes of residence. Only recently was I able to correspond with him about business matters. Our opinion regarding your projected undertaking [1] is as follows:

Since, legally, you are wholly within your rights in reprinting over there anything published in Europe, in our opinion it would be best for you to make use of this right without further ado and without asking anyone about it. If you wish to reprint the *Communist Manifesto,* we cannot have the slightest objection to your so doing, and we would not think of protesting against it so long as no changes and omissions, which are inadmissible in a historical document anyhow, or improper notes, compel us to do so. We cannot write a preface if for no other reason than that we are not together,[2] and even more so because we should thus be establishing a certain solidarity with an undertaking which we are neither in a position nor desire to supervise and control. On this basis you are entirely free to reprint whatever you please without our ever having occasion to complain about the company in which our books appear.

The same applies to my *Condition of the Working Class.* If you reprint it as it stands, I can have no objections. But should I give you special permission to do so, I should also be obliged to make the additions and notes that link the book with the present day, and that would be a six months' task. Moreover, I should then want to have guarantees in advances that the undertaking, once begun, would be carried out.

I hope that I have convinced you that it would be in your own best interests to proceed entirely upon your own. Without being compelled to do so we shall place no obstacle in the path of the undertaking, rather the contrary.

As for a new abridgment of *Capital,* Marx has had so many unpleasant experiences with that sort of thing that one cannot approach him with such proposals any more, especially now. But (this *confidentially!*) Marx eliminated the worst mistakes from the *second* edition of *Most's* abridgment and made a few additions, so that this abridgment still has some advantages and could be reprinted.

There is not much else that I could recommend to you for reprinting. The Leipzig literature comprises chiefly socialism of the future and doctoral dissertations of parliamentary candidates. The

[1] Hepner had written Engels from New York regarding his plan to issue a "workers' library" in German, and requested permission to republish the *Manifesto of the Communist Party* with a new preface by Marx and Engels. He also asked Engels for suggestions regarding books by other writers that were worth translating or republishing.

[2] Marx was in Argenteuil near Paris. See p. 131.

French writings of Jules Guesde are good in most cases, but they are written too much with an eye to French conditions.[1] Bracke's *Down With Socialism* is perhaps not suited for use over there. Bebel's parliamentary speeches are by far the best that Germany has produced in our line, but they are, of course, occasional pieces — Lassalle swarms with economic errors, and his whole viewpoint was superseded long ago. Bracke's *Lassallean Proposal* is quite good criticism, but not exhaustive.

Well, you have to choose. Best wishes for your undertaking.

Yours,

Fr. E.

ENGELS TO SORGE

LONDON MCH 14 1883
CABLE SORGE 135 BLOOMFIELD ST. HOBOKEN
NEW JERSEY

MARX DIED TODAY

ENGELS LONDON

ENGELS TO SORGE

London, March 15, 1883, 11:45 P.M.

Dear Sorge:

Your telegram arrived tonight. Heartfelt thanks!

It was not possible to keep you regularly informed about Marx's state of health because it was constantly changing. Here, briefly, are the main facts:

Shortly before his wife's death he had an attack of pleurisy, in October '81. After he recovered, he was sent to Algiers in February '82; he encountered cold, wet weather on the journey and arrived with another attack of pleurisy. The atrocious weather continued, and when he got better, he was sent to Monte Carlo (Monaco) to avoid the heat of the approaching summer. Again he arrived with a milder attack of pleurisy. Again abominable weather. Cured at last, he went to Argenteuil near Paris to stay with his daughter, Mme. Longuet. He took the sulphur springs near by at

[1] Guesde's first writings were: *La république et les grèves* [*The Republic and Strikes*], Paris 1878; *Essai de catéchisme socialiste* [*Essay of Socialist Catechism*], Brussels, 1878; and *Collectivisme et revolution* [*Collectivism and Revolution*], Paris, 1879.

Enghien for the bronchitis he had had for so long. Here again the weather was frightful, but the treatment did some good. Then he went to Vevey for six weeks and came back in September, apparently almost fully recovered. He was allowed to spend the winter on the south coast of England, and he himself was so tired of wandering about with nothing to do that another period of exile to the south of Europe would probably have harmed him in spirit as much as it would have benefited him in health. When the foggy season commenced in London, he was sent to the Isle of Wight. There it did nothing but rain; he caught another cold. Schorlemmer and I were planning to pay him a visit on New Year's Day when news came that made it necessary for Tussy to join him at once. Then followed the death of Jenny [Marx's daughter], and he came back with another attack of bronchitis. After all that had gone before, and at his age, this was dangerous. A number of complications set in, particularly an abscess of the lung and a terribly rapid loss of strength. Despite this the general course of the illness was progressing favorably, and last Friday the chief physician in attendance on him, one of the foremost young doctors in London and specially recommended to him by Ray Lankester, gave us the most brilliant hope for his recovery. Yet anyone who has ever examined lung tissue under the microscope knows how great is the danger of a blood vessel being broken through in a suppurating lung. And that is why I had a deathly fear, every morning for the past six weeks, of finding the shades down when I turned the corner of the street. Yesterday afternoon at 2:30, the best time for visiting him, I arrived to find the house in tears. It seemed that the end was near. I asked what had happened, tried to get at the bottom of the matter, to offer comfort. There had been a slight hemorrhage, but suddenly he had begun to sink rapidly. Our good old Lenchen, [Helene Demuth] who had looked after him better than any mother cares for her child, went upstairs and came down again. He was half-asleep, she said, I might come in. When we entered the room he lay there asleep, but never to wake again. His pulse and breathing had stopped. In those two minutes he had passed away, peacefully and without pain.

All events occurring with natural necessity bring their own consolation with them, however dreadful they may be. So in this case. Medical skill might have been able to assure him a few more years of vegetative existence, the life of a helpless being, dying — to the triumph of the doctors' art — not suddenly, but inch by inch. But our Marx would never have borne that. To live, with all the unfinished works before him, tantalized by the desire to complete them and unable to do so, would have been a thousand times more bitter than the gentle death that overtook him. "Death is not a misfortune for him who dies, but for him who survives," he used to say, quoting Epicurus. And to see this mighty genius lingering on as a physical wreck for the greater glory of medicine and the mockery of the philistines whom he had so often annihilated in the prime of his strength — no, it is a thousand times better as it is, a thousand times better that we bear him, the day after tomorrow, to the grave where his wife lies at rest.

And after what had gone before, and what even the doctors do not know as well as I do, there was in my opinion no other alternative.

Be that as it may. Mankind is shorter by a head, and the greatest head of our time. The movement of the proletariat goes on, but gone is the central point to which Frenchmen, Russians, Americans, and Germans spontaneously turned at decisive moments to receive always that clear incontestable counsel which only genius and a perfect knowledge of the situation could give. Local lights and small talents, if not the humbugs, obtain a free hand. The final victory is certain, but the detours, the temporary and local errors — even now so unavoidable — will grow more than ever. Well, we must see it through; what else are we here for? And we are far from losing courage because of it.

Yours,

F. Engels

ENGELS TO CUNO

London, March 29, 1883

Dear Cuno:

Your letter gave rise to universal laughter here last night. Everyone who knew the Moor in his home life and in intimate circles knows that he was never called Marx or even Karl, but only the Moor, as each of us had his nickname, and they stopped using one's nickname only when a relationship of close intimacy ceased. The Moor was Marx's nickname from his university days; at the *Neue Rheinische Zeitung* they likewise always called him Moor. If I had ever called him by some other name, he would have thought some misunderstanding had arisen between us that had to be cleared up.

Yours,

F. Engels

ENGELS TO VAN PATTEN [1]

London, April 18, 1883

Dear Comrade:

My reply to your inquiry of April 2 regarding Karl Marx's attitude toward the anarchists in general and toward Johann Most in particular will be brief and to the point.

Since 1845 Marx and I have held the view that one of the ultimate results of the future proletarian revolution will be the gradual dissolution of the political organizations known by the name of *state*. The main object of this organization has always been to secure, by armed force, the economic oppression of the laboring majority by the minority which alone possesses wealth. With the disappearance of an exclusive wealth-possessing minority there also disappears the need for an armed force of suppression, or state power. At the same time, however, it was always our opinion that in order to attain this and the other far more important aims of the future social revolution, the working class must first take possession of the organized political power of the state and by its aid crush the resistance of the capitalist class and organize society anew. This is to be found as early as the *Communist Manifesto* of 1847, Chapter II, conclusion.

The anarchists stand the thing on its head. They declare that the proletarian revolution must *begin* by abolishing the political organization of the state. But the only organization that the proletariat finds ready to hand after its victory is precisely the state. This state may require very considerable alterations before it can fulfil its new functions. But to destroy it at such a moment would mean to destroy the only organism by means of which the victorious proletariat can assert its newly conquered power, hold down its capitalist adversaries, and carry out that economic revolution of society without which the whole victory must end in a new defeat and in

---

[1] This letter, written in English, was in answer to a communication from the Secretary of the Central Labor Union of New York, Philip Van Patten, who had written Engels on April 2, 1883:

"When all parties were united in connection with the recent memorial celebration in honor of Karl Marx, many loud declarations were made on the part of Johann Most and his friends that Most had stood in close relation to Marx and had popularized his work, *Capital*, in Germany and that Marx had been in agreement with the propaganda which Most had conducted. We have a very high opinion of the capacities and the activity of Karl Marx, but we cannot believe that he was in sympathy with the anarchistic and disorganizing methods of Most, and I should like to hear your opinion as to the attitude of Karl Marx on the question of anarchism versus socialism. Most's ill-advised, stupid chatter has already done us too much harm here, and it is very unpleasant for us to hear that such a great authority as Marx approved of such tactics."

a mass slaughter of the workers similar to that after the Paris Commune.

Does it require my express assurance that Marx opposed this anarchist nonsense from the first day it was put forward in its present form by Bakunin? The whole internal history of the International Workingmen's Association proves it. Ever since 1867 the anarchists tried, by the most infamous methods, to seize the leadership of the International; the main hindrance in their way was Marx. The five-year struggle ended, at the Hague Congress in September 1872, with the expulsion of the anarchists from the International; and the man who did most to effect this expulsion was Marx. Our old friend, Friedrich Anton Sorge, in Hoboken, who was present as a delegate, can give you further details if you wish.

And now for Johann Most.

If anyone asserts that Most, since he became an anarchist, has had any relations with Marx whatever or has received any assistance from Marx, he has been deceived or he is deliberately lying. After the publication of the first number of the London *Freiheit*, Most did not visit Marx or me more than once, or at most twice. Just as little did we visit him — we did not even meet him by chance anywhere or at any time. In the end we did not even subscribe to his paper any more, because there was "really nothing" in it. We had the same contempt for his anarchism and his anarchist tactics as for the people from whom he had learned them both.

While he was still in Germany Most published a "popular" summary of Marx's *Capital*. Marx was asked to look through it for a second edition. I did this work together with Marx. We found that it was impossible to do more than strike out the very worst of Most's blunders unless we were to rewrite the whole thing from beginning to end. Moreover, Marx allowed his corrections to be inserted only on the express condition that his name should never be brought into any connection even with this corrected edition of Johann Most's compilation.

You are at liberty to publish this letter in the *Voice of the People* if you wish.

With fraternal greetings,

F. E.

ENGELS TO SORGE

London, April 24, 1883

Dear Sorge:

Enclosed a few lines for Hartmann from his friend Brocher, a confused anarchist but honest to the core. Please transmit them.

The *Volkszeitung* has made enough blunders, but still not as many as I expected. And all of them have done their part — Schewitsch, Cuno, Douai, Hepner. They were a know-better quartet of people who know damned little, jointly and severally. Still I felt obliged to write a few lines to the editors; they had printed my cable to you as one addressed to *them,* and merely falsified the second one, to *them,* to the effect that Marx died in Argenteuil. We wrote that we here refused to put up with that; in doing this they would make it impossible for me to send them any more communications, and if they again permitted themselves to misuse my name in such a manner they would compel me to ask you at once to state publicly that the whole thing was a forgery on their part. The gentlemen should practice their Yankee humbug among themselves. Moreover, the Americans are much more decent: according to the *Volkszeitung* a telegram had been sent to me, which I never received, and almost believed the gentlemen of the *Volkszeitung* had pocketed the money themselves. Now Van Patten writes that no money at all had been available. Now I am compelled to publish this here, otherwise it would be said that I had kept the telegram from the Paris press and the *Sozialdemokrat*. The answer regarding Most that I sent Van Patten in reply to his inquiry will no doubt have been published before this letter arrives.

At the Copenhagen Congress it was decided that Liebknecht and Bebel visit America next spring. It is a question of money for the election campaigns of 1884-85 (all this *between the two of us*). Liebknecht has suggested that Tussy [Eleanor Marx] go along as his secretary, and she would very much like to do so; thus you are very likely to see her there soon. We haven't made any plans at all as yet. Literary work (third edition of *Capital,* Vol. I, publication of Volume II — the manuscript has been found, but we still do not know how ready it is for the press or in need of additions — the biography based on the voluminous correspondence, etc.) absorbs all our free time, and Tussy has a number of literary engagements to fill besides.

You have a perfect right, of course, to print the passages of Marx's letters dealing with Henry George. The question is, however, whether it wouldn't be better to wait until I can send you Marx's marginal notes in his copy of George's book and then print them all together. Theoretically acute but brief and unexemplified summaries, such as Marx gives, are still too difficult for the everyday American, nor is there any hurry. As soon as I have time I shall look the things over. If you send me the passage in question from Marx's letter [1] in the meantime, that will simplify the job.

Yours,

F. E.

ENGELS TO SORGE

London, June 29, 1883

Dear Sorge:

My evening at work has been ruined by visitors, and that gives me some free time to write you.

The criticism of Henry George that Marx sent you [2] is such a masterpiece in content and so homogeneous in style that it would be a pity to weaken it by adding the desultory marginal notes written in English in Marx's copy. These will always remain for eventual use later. The whole letter to you was written with a view to subsequent publication verbatim, as Marx usually did in such cases. Thus you are not committing any indiscretion in having it printed. If it is to be printed in English, I'll translate it for you, since the translation of the *Manifesto* again shows that there doesn't seem to be anyone over there who can translate *our* German, at least, into literary, grammatical English. That requires training as a writer in both languages, and training not merely in the daily press. It is dreadfully hard to translate the *Manifesto;* the Russian translations are still by far the best I have seen.

The third edition of *Capital* is giving me a tremendous amount of work. We have a copy in which Marx notes the changes and additions to be made according to the French edition, but all the detail work is yet to be done. I have finished it as far as "Accumulation," but here this involves almost a total re-working of the whole theoretical section.[3] Then there is the responsibility. For the French translation is in part a simplification of the German, and Marx would never have written like that in German. Moreover, the bookseller is pressing me.

Before I finish with it I cannot think of undertaking Volume II. There exist at least four versions of the beginning; that is how

[1] See p. 127.
[2] See pp. 127-29.
[3] See p. 108.

often Marx began it, always being interrupted by illness in editing the definitive text. I cannot say as yet how the arrangement and the conclusion of the last one, dated 1878, will agree with the first, dating from 1870.

Almost everything dating from the period before 1848 has been saved: Not only the manuscripts composed by him and me at the time almost completely (except for those gnawed away by mice), but the correspondence, too. Everything since 1849 is complete, of course, and the material after 1862 is even classified to some degree. There is also very extensive written material on the International, enough, I think, for its whole history, but I haven't yet been able to examine it more closely.

There are three to four mathematical manuscripts, too. I once showed your Adolph [Sorge's son] an example of Marx's new foundation of the differential calculus.

If not for the voluminous American and Russian material (more than two cubic meters of books on Russian statistics alone), Volume II [of *Capital*] would have been printed long ago. These detailed studies detained him for years. As always, everything was to be complete down to the present day, and now all that has come to nought, with the exception of his excerpts, which I hope will contain, as was his custom, many critical remarks that can be used for the notes of Volume II. . . .

I have already read five sheets of the final proofs of the third edition; the man promises to deliver three sheets a week.

Yours,

F. E.

I simply haven't the time to answer the many long letters sent me by little Hepner. His reports always interest me, though mixed with much personal gossip and written with the superiority of one who has just landed. You must therefore convey my excuses to him for the present.

Schewitsch has replied to me "dignifiedly," regretting my "pettiness." Dignity sits well on him. He'll get no answer.

Nor will Most, who must confirm everything I assert, and for that very reason is so furious. I believe he will find support in that sectarian land, America, and cause trouble for some time. But that is just the character of the American movement: that all mistakes must be experienced in practice. If American energy and vitality were backed by European theoretical clarity, the thing would be finished over there in ten years. But that is impossible historically.

ENGELS TO SORGE

London, March 7, 1884

Dear Sorge:

. . . I shall hardly have the time to enter into a debate with Stiebeling. Such little gods can safely be left to themselves. Besides, sectarianism cannot be prevented in America for years to come. And so the great Most will also end up as Karl Heinzen the Second, no doubt. I am getting the *Wochen [Weekly] -Volkszeitung*, but there isn't much in it.

I do not know how matters stand with the trip of Bebel, Liebknecht, or someone else to America. In reply to their inquiry I told them that, in my opinion, it would not do to tap America [financially] every three years for the elections. The situation in Germany, moreover, is very good. Our boys are standing up to it famously. The Socialist Law is involving them in a local struggle with the police everywhere, which entails lots of cleverness and trickery and usually ends victoriously for us, providing the best propaganda in the world. All the bourgeois papers utter sighs from time to time over the enormous progress of our people, and they are all afraid of the coming elections. Two weeks ago I had one of my nephews from Barmen here, a Liberal Conservative, and I told him: "In Germany we are now so far advanced that we can fold our hands in our laps and let our enemies work for us. Whether you abolish, extend, or modify the Socialist Law, or make it more rigorous, makes no difference; whatever you do plays into our hands." "Yes," he said, "conditions are working for you remarkably." "To be sure," I said, "but they wouldn't be if we hadn't understood them correctly as early as forty years ago and acted accordingly." He made no answer.

Things are going better in France, too, since Lafargue, Guesde, and Dormoy have come out of prison. They are very active, visit the provinces often, where most of their strength is concentrated, luckily enough, and have papers in Reims and St. Pierre-les-Calais; they are holding their Congress in Roubaix a month from now. Then they have a very well-attended lecture in Paris every Sunday: Lafargue on the materialist conception of history, Deville on *Capital.* I shall write them to send you the lectures, all of which are printed. It is fortunate that they haven't a daily paper in Paris at present; it is much too early for that. A new edition of the *Poverty of Philosophy* is being published in Paris. It is also being printed in German in Zurich, and in Russian in Geneva. I believe I still haven't sent you a copy of my *Socialism Utopian and Scientific,* because I myself have received but one or two copies. (The louts!)

The thing has now appeared in its third edition in German, as well as in French, Italian, Russian, and Polish. Aveling wants to translate it into English; this young man is also very good, but has too many irons in the fire and now is engaged in a wearisome struggle with his ex-friend Bradlaugh. As a result of the socialist movement here the latter is losing ground and with it his — means of subsistence. He has to protect himself, but it is not easy for the narrow-minded and rascally fellow. . . .

In two weeks' time I shall at last be able to begin on the second volume of *Capital* — that is still a tremendous job, but I look forward to it with pleasure.

Read Morgan (Lewis H.), *Ancient Society,* published in America in 1877. It discloses primeval times and their communism in masterly fashion. *He independently discovered Marx's theory of history anew* and closes with communist conclusions for the present day. Cordial regards to Adolf.

Yours,

F. E.

ENGELS TO SORGE

London, December 31, 1884

Dear Sorge:

. . . *Capital,* Volume II (about 600 printed pages), will go to press in January. The editing will be finished in about ten days, leaving only the revision of the final text to be done. It has cost enough labor — there were two complete versions and six fragmentary ones!

Volume III comes next, after I have taken care of some urgent intervening work. There are two versions and a notebook of equations; it will also come to some 600-700 pages.

Lastly, Volume IV, *Theories of Surplus Value,* from the oldest manuscript dating from 1859-1861. That is still shrouded in total darkness; it can be undertaken only after everything else is completed. It comprises some thousand closely written quarto pages.

I am completely revising my *Peasant War.* It will become the pivotal point of all German history. That too means work. But the preliminary studies are practically completed.

The English translation of *Capital* is going forward slowly. More than half is finished. Tussy's husband, Aveling, is helping, but is not as thorough as Sam Moore, who is doing the principal sections. . . .

The Democratic Federation here was split apart last Sunday. The adventurer Hyndman, who had gotten control of the whole thing, was exposed as having incited the members against one another, intercepted correspondence for the Council, and founded bogus branches in the provinces to plant his creatures in the conferences and congresses. He received a vote of no confidence, but the majority seceded, chiefly because, they asserted, the whole organization is nothing but a *swindle*. That is true; they haven't 400 dues-paying members and their reading public is the sentimental bourgeoisie. Now they want to found a new organization [1] (Morris, Bax, Aveling, etc.), leaving *Justice* and *To-day* to Hyndman and his men (Fitzgerald, Champion, Burrows, etc.). They themselves, at last realizing their weak forces, will begin with only a little monthly. As the capitalist financial backers also resigned (they noticed most how Hyndman exploited them), Hyndman will have to pay for his unprofitable papers himself, or else sell the whole party, so far as it follows him (which will be apparent in about a week), to the highest bidder. And as he is trying to get into Parliament in the next elections, he must hurry.

There are all sorts of petty-bourgeois prejudices among the German deputies: for example, the majority wants to vote for the steamship subsidy "in the interests of industry." This also makes for plenty of correspondence. Luckily there is Bebel, who always grasps the decisive point correctly, and thus I hope that it will be settled without disgrace. Since I have been carrying on the "official" correspondence with Bebel instead of with Liebknecht, not only is everything handled smoothly, but things get done, and my opinion reaches them intact. Bebel is quite a splendid fellow; I hope he doesn't ruin his shaky health.

Well now, Happy New Year and better health—Regards to Adolf.

Yours,

F. E.

ENGELS TO MRS. [FLORENCE KELLEY] WISCHNEWETZKY[2]

London, February 10, 1885

Dear Madam:

I herewith return Mr. Putnam's [3] letter — of course it would be a splendid success if we could secure publication [4] by that firm —

---

[1] The seceding group founded the Socialist League.

[2] This letter and all following letters to Florence Kelley were written in English.

[3] G. H. Putnam, of the New York publishing firm.

[4] Of Engels' *The Condition of the Working Class in England in 1844.*

but I am afraid Mr. P. will stick to his objections, the great strength of which, from a publisher's standpoint, I fully recognize. Perhaps the fact that a new German edition of my work is in actual preparation may shake him a little. My friends in Germany say that the book is important to them just now because it describes a state of things which is almost exactly reproduced at the present moment in Germany; and as the development of manufacturing industry, steam and machinery, and their social outcrop in the creation of a proletariat, in America corresponds at the present moment as nearly as possible to the English status of 1844 (though your go-ahead people are sure to outstrip the old world in the next 15-20 years altogether), the comparison of industrial England of 1844 with industrial America of 1885 might have its interest too.

Of course in the new preface to the English translation I shall refer as fully as space will permit to the change in the condition of the British working class which has taken place in the interval; to the improved position of a more or less privileged minority, to the certainly not alleviated misery of the great body, and especially to the impending change for the worse which must necessarily follow the breakdown of the industrial monopoly of England in consequence of the increasing competition, in the markets of the world, of Continental Europe and especially of America.

Very sincerely yours,

F. Engels

ENGELS TO SCHLUETER

London, May 15, 1885

Dear Mr. Schlüter:

As for the poems:

The *Marseillaise* of the Peasant War was: *Eine feste Burg ist unser Gott* [*A Mighty Fortress is Our God*], and conscious of victory as the text and melody of this song are, it cannot and need not be taken in this sense today. Other songs of the time are to be found in collections of folksongs: *Des Knaben Wunderhorn,* and the like. More may perhaps be found there. But the mercenary soldier largely pre-empted our folk poetry even then.

Of foreign songs I know only the pretty Danish song of *Herr Tidmann,* which I translated in the Berlin *Social-Demokrat* [No. 18, February 5, 1865] in 1865.

There were all sorts of Chartist songs, but they aren't to be had any more. One began:

> *Britannia's sons, though slaves you be,*
> *God your creator made you free;*
> *To all he life and freedom gave,*
> *But never, never made a slave.*

I don't know any others.
All that has vanished, nor was this poetry worth much.
In 1848 there were two songs sung to the same melody:
  1. "Schleswig-Holstein."
  2. "The Hecker Song":

> *Hecker, hoch dein Name schalle*
> *An dem ganzen deutschen Rhein.*
> *Deine Grossmut, ja dein Auge*
> *Flössen schon Vertrauen ein.*
> *Hecker, der als deutscher Mann*
> *Vor der Freiheit sterben kann.*

I think that's enough. Then the variant:

> *Hecker, Struve, Blenker, Zitz und Blum,*
> *Bringt die deitsche Ferschte um!*

In general, the poetry of past revolutions (the *Marseillaise* always excepted) rarely has a revolutionary effect for later times because it must also reproduce the mass prejudices of the period in order to affect the masses. Hence the religious nonsense even among the Chartists. . . .

Yours,
F. Engels

ENGELS TO SORGE

London, June 3, 1885

Dear Sorge:
  . . . Thanks for the Grönlund and Ely, as well as for the newspapers. Ely is a well-meaning philistine and at least takes more pains than his German companions in adversity and stupidity, which is always to be appreciated. Grönlund, on the other hand, makes a strongly speculative impression on me; his pushing of our views, to the extent that he understands them or not, obviously serves to push

his own utopianisms as real live German socialism. In any event, a symptom. . . .

You had the same correct forebodings about the Reichstag fellows that I did — they let tremendous petty-bourgeois desires come to light in connection with the steamship subsidy. It almost resulted in a split, which is not desirable at the present time, as long as the Socialist Law is in force. But as soon as we have some more elbow-room in Germany, the split will doubtless occur and then it cannot but be helpful. A petty-bourgeois Socialist fraction is unavoidable in a country like Germany, where philistinism, even more than historical law, "ain't got no beginning." It is also useful as soon as it has constituted itself apart from the proletarian party. But this separation now would be merely harmful, if it were provoked by *us*. If they themselves disavow the program in practice, however, so much the better, and we can seize upon it.

You in America also suffer from all sorts of great scholars such as Germany's petty-bourgeois socialists possess in Geiser, Frohme, Blos, etc. The historical digressions of the Stiebelings, Douais, etc., on migrations in the *Sozialist* amused me very much, since these people have studied all that much better and much more thoroughly than I have. Douai, in particular, gives himself extraordinary airs. Thus, in No. 13 of the *Sozialist* he says: In the German conquests in Italy, etc., the king received one-third of the land, two-thirds going to the soldiers and officers, of which in turn two-thirds went to the former slaves, etc. *"As can be read in Jornandes and Cassiodorus."* I was dumbfounded when I read all that. *"The same is reported regarding the Visigoths." "Nor was it otherwise* in France." Now all that is invented from A to Z, and *neither in Jornandes nor in Cassiodorus nor in any other contemporary source is there a word of it*. It is both colossal ignorance and impudence to throw such nonsense up to me and to tell me I am "demonstrably wrong." The sources, practically all of which I know, state exactly the contrary. I have let it pass this time because it happened in America, where one can hardly fight such a matter out; let Monsieur Douai take care in the future — I might lose patience sometime. . . .

Yours,

F. E.

ENGELS TO MRS. [FLORENCE KELLEY] WISCHNEWETZKY

London, January 7, 1886

Dear Mrs. Wischnewetzky:

I have received your Ms. but have not as yet been able to look at it, so cannot say how long it will take me. Anyhow I shall lose no time, you may be sure. As to those wise Americans who think their country exempt from the consequences of fully expanded capitalist production, they seem to live in blissful ignorance of the fact that sundry states, Massachusetts, New Jersey, Pennsylvania, Ohio, etc., have such an institution as a Labor Bureau, from the reports of which they might learn something to the contrary.

Yours very truly,

F. Engels

ENGELS TO SORGE

London, January 29, 1886

Dear Sorge:

. . . An American woman [Florence Kelley Wischnewetzky] has translated my book on the working class in England and has also sent me the manuscript for revision — some passages of which will take some time. Publication in America is assured, but I can't understand what this person now finds in the old thing. . . . Give Dietzgen my regards. He has a hard row to hoe, but it will come out all right. After all, the movement in America is making fine progress. It was not to be expected that the Anglo-Americans go at the thing other than in *their* way, contemptuous of reason and science, but they are coming closer none the less. And, finally, they will come over altogether. Capitalist centralization is proceeding there with seven-league boots, quite otherwise than over here.

I trust your health is again fully restored; I am quite well, on the whole, else I could never get through with my work.

I am persuading Bebel to go over there together with Liebknecht. Perhaps Tussy and Aveling will go along. But that is still far off.

Best regards to Adolf.

Yours,

F. Engels

ENGELS TO MRS. [FLORENCE KELLEY] WISCHNEWETZKY

London, February 3, 1886

My dear Mrs. Wischnewetzky:

Today I forwarded to you, registered, the first portion of the Ms. up to your page 70, inclusive. I am sorry I could not possibly send it sooner. But I had a job on my hand which must be finished before I could start with your Ms. Now I shall get on swimmingly; as I proceed I find we get better acquainted with each other, you with my peculiar old-fashioned German, I with your American. And indeed, I learn a good deal at it. Never before did the difference between British and American English strike me so vividly as in this *experimentum in proprio corpore vili* [experiment on my own poor body]. What a splendid future must there be in store for a language which gets enriched and developed on two sides of an ocean, and which may expect further additions from Australia and India!

I do not know whether this portion of the Ms. will arrive in time to reach Miss Foster [1] before her sailing, but I hope you will not be put to any particular inconvenience through my delay, which was indeed unavoidable. I cannot be grateful enough to all the friends who wish to translate both Marx's and my writings into the various civilized languages and who show their confidence in me by asking me to look over their translations. And I am willing enough to do it, but for me as well as for others the day has but 24 hours, and so I cannot possibly always arrange to please everybody and to chime in with all arrangements made.

If I am not too often interrupted in the evenings, I hope to be able to send you the remainder of the Ms. and possibly also the introduction in a fortnight. This latter may be printed either as a preface or as an appendix. As to the length of it I am utterly incapable of giving you any idea. I shall try to make it as short as possible, especially as it will be useless for me to try to combat arguments of the American press with which I am not even superficially acquainted. Of course, if American workingmen will not read their own states' Labor Reports, but trust to politicians' extracts, nobody can help them. But it strikes me that the present chronic depression, which seems endless so far, will tell its tale in America as well as in England. America will smash up England's industrial monopoly — whatever there is left of it — but America cannot herself succeed to that monopoly. And unless *one* country has the monopoly of the markets of the world, at least in the decisive

---

[1] A friend of Florence Kelley, who was arranging for publication of her translation of Engels' book.

branches of the trade, the conditions — relatively favorable — which existed here in England from 1848 to 1870 cannot anywhere be reproduced, and even in America the condition of the working class must gradually sink lower and lower. For if there are three countries (say England, America, and Germany) competing on comparatively equal terms for the possession of the *Weltmarkt* [world market], there is no chance but chronic overproduction, one of the three being capable of supplying the whole quantity required. That is the reason why I am watching the development of the present crisis with greater interest than ever and why I believe it will mark an epoch in the mental and political history of the American and English working classes — the very two whose assistance is as absolutely necessary as it is desirable.

Yours very truly,

F. Engels

ENGELS TO SORGE

February 9, 1886

D[ear] S[orge]:

You will have received my letter of January 30, as well as *To-day,* and the new edition of the *Kom[munisten] prozess.*[1] N[ew] Y[ork] *Volks [zeitung] — Wochenbl[att]* of January 23 received, *nothing else.* You will also have received the September issue of *To-day.*

Yesterday the gentlemen of the S[ocial] D[emocratic] F[ederation] again committed the most horrible idiocy in the streets — it will have been telegraphed to you already. Let's hope they are now played out.

How is Adolf getting along in his business?

Yours,

F. E.

ENGELS TO MRS. [FLORENCE KELLEY] WISCHNEWETZKY

London, February 25, 1886

Dear Mrs. Wischnewetzky:

To-day I mailed to you, *registered,* the rest of the Ms. with my — introduction or postscript — according to where it may suit you to place it. I believe the title had better be a simple translation: *The Condition of the Working Class in England in 1844,* etc.

---

[1] Karl Marx, *Enthüllungen über den Kommunistenprozess zu Köln* [*Revelations of the Communist Trial in Cologne*].

I am glad that all obstacles to publication have been successfully overcome. Only I am sorry that Miss Foster has applied to the Executive of the Sozialistische Arbeiterpartei in New York, as appears from their report of meeting in *Der Sozialist*, New York, February 13. Neither Marx nor myself has ever committed the least act which might be interpreted into asking any workingmen's organization to do us any personal favor — and this was necessary not only for the sake of our own independence but also on account of the constant bourgeois denunciations of "demagogues who coax the workingmen out of their hard-earned pennies in order to spend them for their own purposes." I shall therefore be compelled to inform that Executive that this application was made entirely without my knowledge or authority. Miss F. no doubt acted in what she thought the best way, and this step of hers is in itself no doubt perfectly admissible; still, if I could have foreseen it, I would have been compelled to do everything in my power to prevent it.

The revision of your translation has delayed that of the English translation of *Das Kapital* by three weeks — and at a most critical period of the year too. I shall set about it tonight and it may take me several months. After that, the German third volume must be taken in hand; you see, therefore, that for some time it will be impossible for me to undertake the revision of other translations, unless few and far between and of small volume. I have at this moment waiting here an Italian translation of Marx's *Lohnarbeit und Kapital* [*Wage Labor and Capital*], which must wait some weeks at least. But if you will translate that into English (it was recently republished in Zurich) and will not be too pressing for time, I shall be glad to revise it, and you cannot have a better popular pamphlet than that. My *Entwicklung* [*Socialism: Utopian and Scientific*] Aveling intends to translate, and as the subject is in part rather difficult, I could not well give it to anyone except he be here on the spot, accessible to verbal explanation. As to my *Anti-Dühring*, I hardly think the English-speaking public would swallow that controversy and the hostility to religion which pervades the book. However, we may discuss that later on, if you are of a different opinion. At present Marx's posthumous manuscripts must be dealt with before anything else.

The semi-Hegelian language of a good many passages of my old book is not only untranslatable but has lost the greater part of its meaning even in German. I have therefore modernized it as much as possible.

Yours very truly,

F. Engels

ENGELS TO MRS. [FLORENCE KELLEY] WISCHNEWETZKY

London, March 12, 1886

Dear Mrs. Wischnewetzky:

Deeply buried as I am in the English *Capital,* I have only the time to write a few lines in haste. It did not require all your exposition of the circumstances to convince me that you were perfectly innocent of what had been done in America with your translation. The thing is done and can't be helped, though we both are convinced that it was a mistake.

I thank you for pointing out to me a passage in the appendix which indeed is far from clear. The gradation from the Polish Jew to the Hamburger, and from the Hamburger again to the Manchester merchant, does not at all come out to the front. I have tried to alter it in a way which may meet both your and my objections to it and hope I have succeeded.

And now I cannot conclude without expressing to you my most sincere thanks to you for the very great trouble you have taken to revive, in English, a book of mine which is half-forgotten in the original German.

Ever at your service as far as my time and powers allow, believe me, dear Mrs. Wischnewetzky,

Yours very faithfully,

F. Engels

The dedication to the English Workingmen should be left out. It has no meaning today.

ENGELS TO SORGE

London, April 29, 1886

Dear Sorge:

... The manuscript[1] contains largely the same things that Marx noted in his copy for the third edition. In other passages, which provide for more insertions from the French, I am not binding myself to these unconditionally (1) because the work for the third edition was done much later and hence is decisive for me, and (2) because, for a translation to be made in America, far away from him, Marx would rather have had many a difficult passage correctly translated from the French simplification than incorrectly from the German, and this consideration now vanishes. Nevertheless, it has given me many useful hints, which will, in time, find appli-

[1] Marx's instructions for a proposed English translation of *Capital* in America.

cation in the German edition too. As soon as I am through with it, I shall return it to you by registered mail. . . .

The Broadhouse-Hyndman translation of *Capital* is nothing but a farce. The first chapter was translated from the German, full of mistakes to the point of ridiculousness. Now it is being translated from the French—the mistakes are the same. At the present rate of speed the thing won't be finished by 1900.

Thanks for the calendar. To be sure, I had not suspected that Douai was so terribly underrated as a great man. May he take with him into the grave the consciousness of his greatness, together with all of its underrating, without seeing it lessened by sugar-coating. But he was the right man for America, and if he had remained an ordinary democrat, I would have wished him the best of luck. But as it is, he got into the wrong pew. As for the purist,[1] who declaims against our style and punctuation: he knows neither German nor English, else he wouldn't find Anglicisms where there aren't any. The German he admires, which was drilled into us in school, with its horrible periodic structure and the verb at the very end — separated from the subject by ten miles of intervening matter — it took me thirty years to *un*learn that German again. That bureaucratic schoolmaster's German, for which Lessing doesn't exist at all, is on the decline even in Germany. What would this good fellow say if he heard the deputies speaking in the Reichstag, who have abolished this horrible construction because they always got tangled up in it and spoke like the Jews: *"Als der Bismarck ist gekommen vor die Zwangswahl, hat er lieber den Papst geküsst auf den Hintern als die Revolution auf den Mund."* [When Bismarck was faced with the alternative, he kissed the Pope's behind rather than the Revolution's lips]. This advance was first introduced by little Lasker; it is the only good thing he did. If Mr. Purist comes to Germany with his schoolmaster's German, they will tell him he talks American. "You know how petty the learned German philistine is" — he seems to be particularly so in America. German sentence structure together with its punctuation as taught in the schools forty or fifty years ago deserves only to be thrown on the scrap heap, and that is happening to it in Germany at last.

I think I have already written you that an American lady, married to a Russian, has gotten it into her head to translate my old book. I looked over the translation, which required considerable work. But she wrote that publication was assured and that it had to be done at once, and so I had to go at it. Now it turns out that she

---

[1] An old German-American party member had sent Sorge a commentary on the style and punctuation of Volume II of *Capital*, which Sorge had sent to Engels.

turned the negotiations over to a Miss Foster, the secretary of a women's rights society, and the latter committed the blunder of giving it to the Socialist Labor Party. I told the translator what I thought of this, but it was too late. Moreover, I am glad that the gentlemen over there do not translate anything of mine; it would turn out beautifully. Their German is enough, and then their English!

The gentlemen of the *Volkszeitung* must be satisfied. They have gained control of the whole movement among the Germans, and their business must be flourishing. It is a matter of course that a man like Dietzgen is pushed to the rear there. Playing with the boycott and with little strikes is, of course, much more important than theoretical education. But with all that the cause is moving ahead mightily in America. A real mass movement exists among the English-speaking workers for the first time.[1] That it proceeds gropingly at first, clumsy, unclear, unknowing, is unavoidable. All that will be cleared up; the movement will and must develop through its own mistakes. Theoretical ignorance is a characteristic of all young peoples, but so is rapidity of practical development. As in England, all the preaching is of no use in America until the actual necessity exists. And this is present in America now, and they are becoming conscious of it. The entrance of masses of native-born workers into the movement in America is for me one of the greatest events of 1886. As for the Germans over there, let the sort now flourishing join the Americans gradually; they will still be somewhat ahead of them. And, lastly, there still is a core among the Germans over there which retains theoretical insight into the nature and the course of the whole movement, keeps the process of fermentation going, and finally rises to the top again.

The second great event of 1886 is the formation of a workers' party in the French Chamber by Basly and Camélinat, two hand-picked "worker" deputies, nominated and elected by the Radicals, but who, contrary to all the regulations, did not become servants of their Radical masters but spoke as workers. The Decazeville strike[2] brought the split between them and the Radicals to a head — five other deputies joined them. The Radicals had to come out in the open with their policy toward the workers, and, as the government exists only with the Radicals' support, that was dreadful, for they

---

[1] It was a period of great ferment among the American workers; strikes were in preparation to win the eight-hour day, and the Knights of Labor was growing tremendously.

[2] A strike of the coal miners in the south of France in January 1886, suppressed by government troops.

were justifiably held accountable by the workers for every act of the government. In short, the Radicals, Clemenceau and all the others, behaved wretchedly, and then there took place what no preacher had succeeded in accomplishing up to then: *the French workers' defection from the Radicals.* And the second result was: the union of all the socialist fractions for joint action. Only the miserable possibilists[1] kept apart, and consequently they are disintegrating more and more every day. The government helped this new departure tremendously by its blunders. For it wants to float a loan of 900,000,000 francs and needs high finance for this purpose, but the latter are also stockholders in Decazeville and refuse to lend the money unless the government breaks the strike. Hence the arrest of Duc and Roche. The workers' reply is: Roche's candidacy in Paris for next Sunday (elections to the Chamber) and Duc's (Quercy's) candidacy for the Municipal Council, where he is certain of election. In brief, a splendid movement is merrily under way in France again, and the best thing about it is that our people, Guesde, Lafargue, Deville, are the theoretical leaders.

The reaction upon Germany did not fail to make its appearance. The revolutionary language and action of the Frenchmen made the whining of Geiser, Viereck, Auer and Co. appear feebler than ever, and thus only Bebel and Liebknecht spoke in the last debate on the Socialist Law, both of them very good. With this debate we can show our faces in respectable society again, which was by no means the case with all of them. In general, it is good for the Germans to have their leadership disputed somewhat, especially since they have elected so many philistine elements (which was unavoidable, to be sure). In Germany everything becomes philistine in quiet periods; the spur of French competition then becomes absolutely necessary, nor will it be lacking. French socialism has suddenly grown from a sect into a party, and only now and only thereby is the mass affiliation of the workers possible, for the latter are sick and tired of sectarianism, and that was the secret of their following the extremist bourgeois party, the Radicals. Next Sunday will show considerable progress in the elections, though it is scarcely to be expected that Roche will win.

I think the printing of the English translation of *Capital*, Volume

[1] Possibilists: the petty-bourgeois, reformist wing of the French *Parti Ouvrier*, which split off from the party in 1882. The possibilists confined the activity of the working class within the framework of what is "possible" under capitalism. In 1902, they organized the opportunist French Socialist Party, together with other reformist groups as a counterpoise to the Socialist Party of France. The two parties merged in 1905.

I, will begin in two to three weeks. I am far from through with revision, but three hundred pages are entirely ready and another hundred nearly ready for the printer. Another thing. A Mr. J. T. McEnnis interviewed me a few days ago under the pretext of getting advice on labor legislation for the State of Missouri. I soon discovered that newspaper business was behind it, and he confessed that he was working for the leading democratic paper of St. Louis, but gave me his word of honor that he would submit every word to me in advance for revision. The man was sent to me by the Russian Stepniak. Nearly two weeks have passed, and I am afraid he did not keep his promise. I have forgotten the name of the St. Louis paper. Therefore, if anything is printed regarding the interview, please have the enclosed statement printed in *Der Sozialist,* the *Volkszeitung,* and anywhere else you think necessary. If the man does come and keep his promise, I shall, of course, let you know at once, and you can then tear up the statement. Here the movement is not progressing at all, luckily enough. Hyndman and Co. are political careerists who spoil everything, while the anarchists are making rapid progress in the Socialist League. Morris and Bax — one as an emotional socialist and the other as a chaser after philosophical paradoxes — are wholly under their control for the present and must now undergo this experience *in corpore vili* [on their own poor bodies]. You will note from the *Commonweal* that Aveling, largely thanks to Tussy's energy, no longer shares the responsibility for this swindle, and that is good. And these muddleheads want to lead the British working class! Fortunately the latter wants to have absolutely nothing to do with them.

    Best regards.

Yours,
F. Engels

ENCLOSURE

To the Editor, etc.:

    If the St. Louis .... should print an interview of one of that paper's correspondents with me, I have the following remarks to make:

    A Mr. McEnnis did visit me as a representative of that paper, questioning me regarding various topics, but under his promise upon *his word of honor* that he would not send off a line without having shown it to me beforehand. Instead of doing so, he has not let me hear from him again. I therefore state herewith that I must refuse any and all responsibility for his publication, especially as I had an opportunity to convince myself that Mr. McEnnis, for lack of the necessary rudimentary knowledge, would hardly be able, even with the best of intentions, to understand my remarks correctly.

Frederick Engels

London, April 29, 1886.

ENGELS TO MRS. [FLORENCE KELLEY] WISCHNEWETZKY

[London] June 3, 1886

Dear Mrs. Wischnewetzky:

I have looked over the proofs and corrected in pencil a few additional mistakes.

That the get-up of the work would be anything but elegant I foresaw as soon as I knew who had it in charge, and am therefore not much surprised; I am afraid there is no help now, so it's no use grumbling.

Whatever the mistakes and the *Borniertheit* [narrow-mindedness] of the leaders of the movement, and partly of the newly-awakening masses too, one thing is certain: the American working class is moving, and no mistake. And after a few false starts, they will get into the right track soon enough. This appearance of the Americans upon the scene I consider one of the greatest events of the year.

What the downbreak of Russian Czarism would be for the great military monarchies of Europe — the snapping of their mainstay — that is for the bourgeois of the whole world the breaking out of class war in America. For America after all is the ideal of all bourgeois: a country rich, vast, expanding, with purely bourgeois institutions unleavened by feudal remnants of monarchical traditions, and without a permanent and hereditary proletariat. Here every one could become, if not a capitalist, at all events an independent man, producing or trading, with his own means, for his own account. And because there were not, *as yet,* classes with opposing interests, our — and your — bourgeois thought that America stood *above* class antagonisms and struggles. That delusion has now broken down, the last Bourgeois Paradise on earth is fast changing into a Purgatorio, and can only be prevented from becoming, like Europe, an Inferno by the go-ahead pace at which the development of the newly fledged proletariat of America will take place. The way in which they have made their appearance on the scene is quite extraordinary: six months ago nobody suspected anything and now they appear all of a sudden in such organized masses as to strike terror into the whole capitalist class. I only wish Marx could have lived to see it!

I am in doubt whether to send this to Zurich or to the address in Paris you give at foot of your letter. But as in case of mistake Zurich is safest, I forward this and the proofs to Mr. Schlüter, who no doubt will forward them wherever it may be necessary.

Ever sincerely yours,

F. Engels

ENGELS TO MRS. [FLORENCE KELLEY] WISCHNEWETZKY

Eastbourne, August 13, 1886

Dear Mrs. Wischnewetzky:

My reply to your kind letter of the 9th June was delayed for the simple reason that overwork compelled me to suspend *all* my correspondence (such as did not command immediate despatch) until the Ms. of the translation of *Das Kapital* was finally ready for the printer. Such is now the case and I can at last attend to the heap of unanswered letters before me; and you shall have the first chance. Had you told me in the above letter that you had spare time on your hand for party work, I should at once have sent you a short reply; I am sorry if through my fault you were prevented from doing some useful work.

I quite forgot, when proposing to you *Lohnarbeit und Kapital* [*Wage Labor and Capital*], that an English translation had already appeared in London. As this is offered for sale in New York, it would be useless to translate it over again.

Now about *Der Ursprung* [*The Origin of the Family*]. The thing is more difficult to translate than *Die Lage* [*The Condition of the Working Class in England in 1844*] and would require comparatively greater attention and more time per page on your part. But if I had time left to me for the looking it over, that would be no obstacle provided you could devote that time and attention to it, and leave me a larger margin of blank paper to suggest alterations. There is, however, another matter to consider. If the thing is to come out in English at all, it ought to be published in such a way that the public can get hold of it through the regular book trade. That will *not* be the case, as far as I can see, with *Die Lage*. Unless the trade arrangements are very different in America from those in Europe, the booksellers will not deal in works published by outside establishments belonging to a workingmen's party. This is why Chartist and Owenite publications are nowhere preserved and nowhere to be had, *not even in the British Museum,* and why all our German party publications are — and were, long before the Socialist Law — not to be had through the trade, and remained unknown to the public outside the party. That is a state of things which sometimes cannot be avoided but ought to be avoided wherever possible. And you will not blame me if I wish to avoid it for the English translations of my writings, having suffered from it in Germany for more than forty years. The state of things in England is such that publishers can be got — either now or in the near future — for socialist works, and I have no doubt that in the course of next year I can have an English translation published here and the translator paid; and as I have moreover long since promised Dr. Aveling the translation of the *Entwicklung* [*Socialism: Utopian and Scientific*] and the *Ursprung,* if he can make it pay for *himself,* you see that an American edition, brought out outside the regular book trade, would only spoil the chance of a London edition to be brought out in the way of the regular trade and therefore accessible to the public generally and everywhere.

Moreover, I do not think that this book is exactly what is wanted at the present moment by the American workingman. *Das Kapital* will be at their service before the year is out; that will serve them for a *pièce de résistance* [main dish]. For lighter, more popular literature, for real propaganda, my booklet will scarcely serve. In the present undeveloped state of the movement, I think perhaps some of the French popularizations would answer best. Deville and Lafargue have published two series of lectures, *Cours d'économie sociale* [Course of Social Economy], about two years ago, Deville taking the economic and Lafargue the more general historic side of the Marxian theory. No doubt Bernstein can let you look at a copy, and get one from Paris, and then you might judge for yourself. Of course I do not mean Deville's larger work, the extract from *Das Kapital,* which in the latter half of it is very misleading.

August 14th. To return to the *Ursprung.* I do not mean to say that I have absolutely promised Aveling to let him have it, but I consider myself bound to him in case a translation is to come out in *London.* The final decision then would depend very much upon the nature of the publishing arrangements you can make in America. To a repetition of what Miss Foster has done with *Die Lage* I decidedly object. When I see my way to an English edition, brought out by a firm known in the bourgeois trade, and not only of this book, but probably of a collection of various other writings, with the advantage of having the translation done here (which saves me a deal of time), you will admit that I ought to look twice before sanctioning the bringing out, in America, of this little book alone and thereby spoiling the whole arrangement. And with the present anti-socialist scare [1] in America, I doubt whether you will find regular publishers very willing to associate their name with socialist works.

A very good bit of work would be a series of pamphlets stating in popular language the contents of *Das Kapital*. The theory of surplus value, No. 1; the history of the various forms of surplus value (cooperation, manufacture, modern industry), No. 2; accumulation and the history of primitive accumulation, No. 3; the development of surplus value making in colonies (last chapter), No. 4 — this would be specially instructive in America, as it would give the economic history of that country, from a land of independent peasants to a centre of modern industry and might be completed by specially American facts.

In the meantime you may be sure that it will take some time yet before the *mass* of the American working people will begin to *read* socialist literature. And for those that *do* read and will read, there is matter enough being provided, and least of all will *Der Ursprung* be missed by them. With the Anglo-Saxon mind, and especially with the eminently practical development it has taken in America, theory counts for nothing until imposed by dire necessity, and I count above all things upon the teaching our friends will receive by the consequences of their own blunders to prepare them for theoretical schooling.

Yours very sincerely,

F. Engels

I shall be in this place until the 27th instant; after that, in London.

ENGELS TO SORGE

London, September 16, 1886

Dear Sorge:

I am taking an hour off by sheer force to write you. After the (triple) proofs of the *Capital* translation kept me in such suspense that I was prevented from doing other work for weeks, they are now coming in bunches. Six signatures are to be delivered each week (that means 18 signatures to be corrected weekly), and everything is to be finished in a month. Let's wait and see. But this makes for a lively time for me, since old man Becker is coming from Geneva

[1] After the Haymarket massacre in Chicago on May 4, 1886.

to visit me tomorrow, next week Schorlemmer is coming and probably the Lafargues, while other people also want to come here from Switzerland. So if I don't get a letter off today, I know I won't be able to do so later.

Many thanks for your efforts regarding the interviewer.[1] He was the last. Now that he broke his word of honor I have a reason for letting them cool their heels, unless we ourselves are interested in spreading something through such a liar. You are right — on the whole I cannot complain. The man tries to be at least personally decent, and not he, but the American bourgeoisie, is responsible for his stupidity.

A fine gang seems to be at the head of the party in New York; the *Sozialist* is a model of what a paper should *not* be. But neither can I support Dietzgen in his article on the anarchists [2] — he has a peculiar way of dealing with things. If a person has a perhaps somewhat narrow opinion on a certain point, Dietzgen cannot emphasize enough (and often too much) that the matter has two sides. But now, because the New Yorkers are behaving contemptibly, he suddenly takes the other side and wants to picture us all as anarchists. The moment may excuse this, but he shouldn't forget all his dialectics at the decisive moment. However, he has gotten over it by now, no doubt, and is certainly back on the right track; I have no worries on that score.

In a country as untouched as America, which has developed in a purely bourgeois fashion without any feudal past, but has unwittingly taken over from England a whole store of ideology from feudal times, such as the English common law, religion, and sectarianism, and where the exigencies of practical labor and the concentrating of capital have produced a contempt for all theory, which is only now disappearing in the educated circles of scholars — in such a country the people must become conscious of their own *social* interests by making blunder after blunder. Nor will that be spared the workers; the confusion of the trade unions, socialists, Knights of Labor, etc., will persist for some time to come, and they will learn only by their own mistakes. But the main thing is that they have started moving, that things are going ahead generally, that the spell is broken; and they will go fast, too, faster than anywhere else, even though on a singular road, which seems, from the theoretical standpoint, to be an almost insane road. . . .

I hope your health is better; I am *apparently* still robust enough,

[1] See pp. 156-57.

[2] In an article in the Chicago *Vorbote*, Dietzgen had proposed that no distinction should be made, for the time being, between anarchists, socialists, and communists.

but, because of an internal ailment, I have constantly suffered for the past three years from a somewhat limited freedom of movement, which now and then is very limited indeed, so that I am no longer fit for military service, unfortunately.

As soon as the translation is finished I must first of all get rid of the minor work pressed upon me — revision of other people's work, particularly translations — *and not let any others be forced on me* so that I can at last get back to Volume III. It lies there all dictated, but there is still a good six months of hard work in it. This damned English translation has cost me nearly a year. But it was absolutely necessary, and I do not regret it.

September 17
. . . The movement here remains in the hands of adventurers (Democratic Federation) on the one hand, and of faddists and emotional socialists (Socialist League) [1] on the other. The masses still stand aloof, though the *beginning* of a movement is also noticeable. But it will still take some time before the masses get under way, and that is good, so that time will be left to develop real leaders. In Germany the *bourgeoisie,* whose cowardly stagnation is beginning to harm us, will finally start moving somewhat again; on the one hand, the impending change of sovereigns will start everything tottering, and, on the other, Bismarck's obeisance to the Tsar is arousing even the drowsiest sleepyheads. In France the situation is excellent. The people are learning discipline, in the provinces through the strikes, and in Paris through opposition to the Radicals.

Best regards,   Yours,

F. E.

ENGELS TO SORGE

London, November 29, 1886
Dear Sorge:
. . . The Henry George boom has of course brought to light a colossal mass of fraud, and I am glad I was not there. But in spite of it all it was an epoch-making day. The Germans have not under-

---

1 The Socialist League, an organization headed by William Morris, Belfort Bax, and the Avelings, that split off from the opportunist Social Democratic Federation in 1884. The *Commonweal* was its official organ. Shortly after the formation of the League anarchists made their way into it and, with the aid of Morris, gradually gained control. The League's founders left it and, in 1889, the *Commonweal* likewise fell into the anarchists' hands.

stood how to use their theory as a lever which could set the American masses in motion; they do not understand the theory themselves for the most part and treat it in a doctrinaire and dogmatic way as something that has to be learned by heart, which then will satisfy all requirements forthwith. To them it is a credo and not a guide to action. What is more, they learn no English on principle. Hence the American masses had to seek out their own path and seem to have found it for the time being in the K[nights] of L[abor], whose confused principles and ludicrous organization seem to correspond to their own confusion. But from all I hear, the K. of L. are a real power, especially in New England and the West, and are becoming more so every day owing to the brutal opposition of the capitalists. I think it is necessary to work inside them, to form within this still quite plastic mass a core of people who understand the movement and its aims and will therefore take over the leadership, at least of a section, when the inevitably impending breakup of the present "order" takes place. The rottenest side of the K. of L. was their political neutrality, which has resulted in sheer trickery on the part of the Powderlys, etc.; but the edge of this has been taken off by the behavior of the masses in the November elections, especially in New York. The first great step of importance for every country newly entering into the movement is always the constitution of the workers as an independent political party, no matter how, so long as it is a distinct workers' party. And this step has been taken, much more rapidly than we had a right to expect, and that is the main thing. That the first program of this party is still confused and extremely deficient, that it has raised the banner of Henry George, these are unavoidable evils but also merely transitory ones. The masses must have time and opportunity to develop, and they can have the opportunity only when they have a movement of their own — no matter in what form so long as it is *their own* movement — in which they are driven further by their own mistakes and learn through their mistakes. The movement in America is at the same stage as it was with us before 1848; the really intelligent people there will first have to play the part played by the Communist League among the workers' associations before 1848. Except that in America now things will proceed infinitely faster; for the movement to have gained such election successes after scarcely eight months of existence is wholly unprecedented. And what is still lacking will be set going by the bourgeoisie; nowhere in the whole world do they come out so shamelessly and tyrannically as over there, and your judges brilliantly outshine Bismarck's pettifoggers in the Reich. Where the bourgeoisie wages the struggle by such methods, the struggle comes to a decision rapidly, and if we in Europe do not hurry up the Americans will soon outdistance us. But just now it is doubly necessary to have a few people on our side there who are thoroughly versed in theory and well-tested tactics and can also speak and write English; because, for good historical reasons, the Americans are worlds behind in all theoretical questions, and while they did not bring over any medieval institutions from Europe, they did bring over masses of medieval traditions, religion, English common (feudal) law, superstition, spiritualism, in short, every kind of imbecility which was not directly harmful to business and which is now very serviceable for stupefying the masses. If there are people at hand there whose minds are theoretically clear, who can tell them the consequences of their own mistakes beforehand and make clear to them that every movement which does not keep the destruction of the wage system constantly in view as the final goal is bound to go astray and fail — then much nonsense can be avoided and the process considerably shortened. But it must be done in English; the specific German character must be laid aside, and for that the gentlemen of the *Sozialist* hardly have the qualifications, while those of the *Volkszeitung* are cleverer only where *business* is involved.

In Europe the effect of the American elections in November was tremendous. That England, and America in particular, had no labor movement up to now was the big trump card of the radical republicans everywhere, especially in France. Now these gentlemen have been utterly contradicted; on November 2nd the whole foundation, especially of Mr. Clemenceau's policy, collapsed. "Look at America," was his eternal motto; "where there is a real republic, there is no poverty and no labor movement!" And the same thing is happening to the liberals and "democrats" in Germany and here — where they are also witnessing the beginnings of their own movement. The very fact that the movement is so sharply accentuated as a labor movement and has sprung up so suddenly and forcefully has stunned the people completely.

Here the lack of any competition, on the one hand, and the government's stupidity, on the other, has enabled the gentlemen of the Social Democratic Federation to occupy a position which they did not dare to dream of three months ago. The hubbub about the plan — never seriously intended — of a parade behind the Lord Mayor's procession on November 9, and later the same hubbub about the Trafalgar Square meeting on November 21, when the setting-up of artillery was talked of, and the government finally backed down — all this forced the gentlemen of the S.D.F. to hold a very ordinary meeting at last on the 21st, without empty rodomontades and pseudorevolutionary demonstrations with *obbligato* mob accompaniment — and the philistines suddenly gained respect for the people who had stirred up such a fuss and yet behaved so respectably. And since, except for the S.D.F., nobody concerns himself with the unemployed, who constitute a great mass each winter during the chronic stagnation of business and suffer very acute hardships, the S.D.F. has the game won in advance. The labor movement is beginning here and no mistake, and if the S.D.F. is the first to reap the harvest, it is the result of the cowardice of the radicals and the stupidity of the Socialist League, which is quarreling with the anarchists and cannot get rid of them, and hence has no time to concern itself with the living movement that is taking place outside in front of its face. Moreover, how long Hyndman and Co. will persist in their present, comparatively rational mode of action is problematical. I expect that they will soon commit colossal blunders again; they're in too much of a hurry. And then they will see that this can't be done in a serious movement.

Things are getting prettier all the time in Germany. In Leipzig sentences of as much as four years at hard labor for "sedition"! They want to provoke a riot at all costs. . . .

Your old

F. E.

ENGELS TO MRS. [FLORENCE KELLEY] WISCHNEWETZKY

London, December 28, 1886

Dear Mrs. Wischnewetzky:

Your letter of November 13th never reached me, for which I am very sorry; it would have suited me much better to write a preface *then,* and moreover would have left me more time.

But let me first congratulate you on the happy family event in which you have been the principal actor and add my best wishes for your own health and that of the little one newly arrived.

Of course the appendix is now a little out of date, and as I anticipated something of the kind, I proposed that it should be written when the book was ready through the press. Now a preface will be much wanted, and I will write you one; but before, I must await the return of the Avelings to have a full report of the state of things in America; and it seems to me that my preface will not be exactly what you desire.

First, you seem to me to treat New York a little as the Paris of

America, and to overrate the importance, for the country at large, of the local New York movement with its local features. No doubt it has a great importance, but then the Northwest, with its background of a numerous farming population and its independent movement, will hardly accept blindly the George theory.

Secondly, the preface of *this* book is hardly the place for a thoroughgoing criticism of that theory, and does not even offer the necessary space for it.

Thirdly, I should have to study thoroughly Henry George's various writings and speeches (most of which I have not got) so as to render impossible all replies based on subterfuges and side-issues.

My preface will of course turn entirely on the immense stride made by the American workingman in the last ten months, and naturally also touch H.G. and his land scheme. But it cannot pretend to deal extensively with it. Nor do I think the time for that has come. It is far more important that the movement should spread, proceed harmoniously, take root, and embrace as much as possible the whole American proletariat, than that it should start and proceed from the beginning on theoretically perfectly correct lines. There is no better road to theoretical clearness of comprehension than to learn by one's own mistakes, *"durch Schaden klug werden."* And for a whole large class, there is no other road, especially for a nation so eminently practical and so contemptuous of theory as the Americans. The great thing is to get the working class to move *as a class;* that once obtained, they will soon find the right direction, and all who resist, H.G. or Powderly, will be left out in the cold with small sects of their own. Therefore I think also the K. of L. a most important factor in the movement which ought not to be pooh-poohed from without but to be revolutionized from within, and I consider that many of the Germans there have made a grievous mistake when they tried, in the face of a mighty and glorious movement not of their own creation, to make of their imported and not always understood theory a kind of *alleinseligmachendes* [it alone bringing salvation] dogma, and to keep aloof from any movement which did not accept that dogma. Our theory is not a dogma but the exposition of a process of evolution, and that process involves successive phases. To expect that the Americans will start with the full consciousness of the theory worked out in older industrial countries is to expect the impossible. What the Germans ought to do is to act up to their own theory — if they understand it, as we did in 1845 and 1848 — to go in for any real general working-class movement, accept its *faktische* [actual] starting point as such and work it gradually up to the theoretical level by pointing out how every mistake made, every reverse suffered, was a necessary consequence of mistaken theoretical orders in the original program; they ought, in the words of the *Communist Manifesto: in der Gegenwart der Bewegung die Zukunft der Bewegung repräsentieren* [To represent the future of the movement in the present of the movement]. But above all give the movement time to consolidate; do not make the inevitable confusion of the first start worse confounded by forcing down people's throats things which, at present, they cannot properly understand but which they soon will learn. A million or two of workingmen's votes next November for a *bona fide* workingmen's party is worth infinitely more at present than a hundred thousand votes for a doctrinally perfect platform. The very first attempt — soon to be made if the movement progresses — to consolidate the moving masses on a national basis will bring them all face to face, Georgeites, K. of L., trade unionists, and all; and if our German friends by that time have learnt enough of the language of the country to go in for a discussion, then will be the time for them to criticize the views of the others and thus, by showing up the inconsistencies of the various standpoints, to bring them gradually to understand their own actual position, the position made for them by the correlation of capital and wage labor. But anything that might delay or prevent that national consolidation of the workingmen's party — on no matter what platform — I should consider a great mistake, and therefore I do not think the time has arrived to speak out fully and exhaustively either with regard to H.G. or the K. of L. . . .

As to the title: *I* cannot omit the 1844, because the omission would give an entirely false idea of what the reader has to expect. And as I, by the preface and appendix, take a certain responsibility, I cannot consent to its being left out. You may add: "With preface and appendix by the author," if you think proper.

The proofs I return corrected by the same mail.

Yours very faithfully,

F. Engels

ENGELS TO MRS. [FLORENCE KELLEY] WISCHNEWETZKY

London, January 27, 1887

Dear Mrs. Wischnewetzky:

Herewith I send you, at last, the Preface. No sooner had the Avelings returned when I was seized with a slight conjunctivitis

which was, however, sufficient to prevent all regular work, especially as the short time I could devote each day to writing was
unavoidably taken up by urgent correspondence. Although my eye
is not yet quite free from inflammation, yet I have managed to get
through the preface and hope the delay will not have inconvenienced
you too much.

As I have not been able to keep a copy, I must request you to
return the Ms. when done with. I suppose you will be good enough
to see it through the press.

I hope Dr. Wischnewetzky has arrived safe after a good passage.
I regret that I could not have him all to myself for a couple of hours,
but he just dropped in at an evening when, for the time being, the
old "International" was made to undergo a practical revival.

The movement in America, just at this moment, is I believe best
seen from across the ocean. On the spot personal bickering and local
disputes must obscure much of the grandeur of it. And the only
thing that could really delay its march would be the consolidation
of these differences into established sects. To some extent that will
be unavoidable, but the less of it the better. And the Germans have
most to guard against this. Our theory is a theory of evolution, not
a dogma to be learnt by heart and to be repeated mechanically.
*Je weniger sie den Amerikanern von aussen eingepaukt wird und je
mehr sie sie durch eigene Erfahrung — unter dem Beistand der
Deutschen — erproben, desto tiefer geht sie ihnen in Fleisch und
Blut über* [The less it is drilled into the Americans from the outside
and the more they test it through their own experience — with the
help of the Germans — the deeper will it pass into their flesh and
blood.] When we returned to Germany, in Spring 1848, we joined the
Democratic Party as the only possible means of gaining the ear of
the working class; we were the most advanced wing of that party,
but still a wing of it. When Marx founded the International, he
drew up the General Rules in such a way that *all* working-class
socialists of that period could join it — Proudhonists, Pierre Leroux-
ists, and even the more advanced section of the English trade unions:
and it was only through this latitude that the International became
what it was, the means of gradually dissolving and absorbing all
these minor sects, with the exception of the anarchists, whose sudden appearance in various countries was but the effect of the violent
bourgeois reaction after the Commune and could therefore safely
be left by us to die out of itself, which it did. Had we from 1864 to
1873 insisted on working together only with those who openly
adopted our platform, where should we be today? I think all our
practice has shown that it is possible to work along with the general

movement of the working class at every one of its stages without giving up or hiding our own distinct position and even organization, and I am afraid that if the German-Americans choose a different line they will commit a great mistake.

I hope you are by this time perfectly restored to health and that your husband and children are well too. Kind regards to Dr. W[ischnewetzky].

Very truly yours,

F. Engels

ENGELS TO MRS. [FLORENCE KELLEY] WISCHNEWETZKY

London, February 9, 1887

Dear Mrs. Wischnewetzky:

I reply at once to your letter, January 28th postmark. The preface was sent on January 27th, and your telegram received Sunday, February 6th. I replied immediately per cable:

"Sent registered 27th January."

As to the distorted passage from my letter which the irrepressible Eaton could not refrain from publishing, it is no use for Rosenberg and Co. to saddle Aveling with it. The passage about the hundred thousands and millions occurred in my letter to you[1] and in no *other* letter. So you will know who is responsible for this indiscretion and for putting this nonsense into my mouth. As far as I am concerned I have no objection to your publishing the whole passage and indeed the whole letter.

Your fear as to my being unduly influenced by Aveling in my view of the American movement is groundless. As soon as there was a national American working-class movement, independent of the Germans, my standpoint was clearly indicated by the facts of the case. That great national movement, no matter what its first form, is the real starting point of American working-class development. If the Germans join it, in order to help it or to hasten its development in the right direction, they may do a great deal of good and play a decisive part in it. If they stand aloof, they will dwindle down into a dogmatic sect and be brushed aside as people who do not understand their own principles. Mrs. Aveling, who has seen her father at work, understood this quite as well from the beginning, and if Aveling saw it too, all the better. And all my letters to America, to Sorge, to yourself, to the Avelings, from the very beginning, have repeated this view over and over again. Still I was glad to see

---

[1] See pp. 166-67.

the Avelings before writing my preface, because they gave me some new facts about the inner mysteries of the German party in New York.

You appear to take it for granted that Aveling has behaved in America as a swindler, and not only that: you call upon me, upon the strength of assertions and allusions contained in your letter, to treat him as such and to do all in my power to have him excluded from the literary organs of the party. Now for all these assertions you *cannot* have any proof because you have not been able to hear any defense. Still you are better off than we here; you have at least heard *one* side, while we do not even know what the distinct charge is!

In the early hole-and-corner stages of the working-class movement, when the workingmen are still under the influence of traditional prejudices, woe be to the man who, being of bourgeois origin or superior education, goes into the movement and is rash enough to enter into money relations with the working-class element. There is sure to be a dispute upon the cash account, and this is at once enlarged into an attempt at exploitation. Especially so if the "bourgeois" happens to have views on theoretical or tactical points that disagree with those of the majority or even of a minority. This I have constantly seen for more than forty years. The worst of all were the Germans; in Germany the growth of the movement has long since swept that failing away, but it has not died out with the Germans outside Germany. For that reason Marx and I have always tried to avoid having any money dealings with the party, no matter in what country.

And when the Avelings went to America I had very strong misgivings on that point. Only when it was arranged that the tour should be made together with Liebknecht, I felt more at rest, because Liebknecht, as an old hand, would know how to deal with such complaints, and because any charges brought against him on that score would merely make the complainants ridiculous in Germany and in Europe generally. Well, the tour was arranged differently afterwards, and here is the result.

From this you will see that I look upon this matter a great deal cooler than what people seem to do in New York. But moreover, I have known Aveling for four years; I know that he has twice sacrificed his social and economic position to his convictions, and might be, had he refrained from doing so, a professor in an English university and a distinguished physiologist instead of an overworked journalist with a very uncertain income. I have had occasion to observe his capacities by working with him, and his character by seeing him pass through rather trying circumstances more than once, and it will take a good deal (more than mere assertions and innuendos) before I believe what some people tell about him now in New York.

But then, had he tried to swindle the party, how could he do that during all his tour without his wife being cognizant of it? And in that case the charge includes her too. And then it becomes utterly absurd, in my eyes at least. Her I have known from a child, and for the last seventeen years she has been constantly about me. And more than that, I have inherited from Marx the obligation to stand by his children as he would have done himself, and to see, as far as lies in my power, that they are not wronged. And that I shall do, in spite of fifty Executives. The daughter of Marx swindling the working class — too rich indeed!

Then you say: "No one here imagines that Dr. Aveling put the money in his pocket, *or spent it as the bills indicate.* They believe that he merely tried to cover his wife's expenses." That is a distinct charge of forgery, and this you give as an extenuating charitable supposition. What then, if this be the attenuated charge, what is the full charge? And on what ground is this charge made? "The ridiculous bills which Dr. Aveling sent in." I should like to see a few of these "ridiculous" bills. For fifteen weeks they were sent every Sunday to the Executive who gave no sign of disapproval. Nor did they budge when the Avelings, Dec. 19, returned to New York. It was only on the 23rd, when they were on the point of leaving, when they could no longer defend themselves against charges, real or trumped-up, that the Executive discovered these bills, to which, *singly,* they had never objected, were ridiculous when *added up!* That is to say they object, not to the bills, but to the rules of addition. Why, then, did the Executive, instead of shortening the tour, try to extend it, and just at the close of it plan a second visit of the Avelings to Chicago, which fortunately did not come off? It strikes me that in all this it is not the bills which are ridiculous but the Executive.

Well, at the meeting of December 23rd, the Avelings hear for the first time that these bills are ridiculous, and the Executive lays before them a statement of account drawn up by themselves. As soon as his statement is objected to Dr. Aveling at once accepts that of the Executive, according to which — as I have seen myself in Rosenberg's handwriting — a balance is due to him of $176.00. Then, being again bullied by Walther, he refuses that balance, returns $76.00 at once, and sends the rest from London. And then you say that "Dr. Aveling's returning the $100.00 has not helped matters at all." Why, what in the name of goodness do these people want then?

Is Aveling to be treated as a swindler because the Executive appropriate $176.00 which, *on their own showing,* belong to *him?*

Then the mystery with which the Executive envelop this matter becomes darker and darker. When the article in the *New York Herald* appeared and was cabled across, the Avelings sent the enclosed circular to the sections, and at the same time, to the *Executive.* That circular — unless I take Aveling to be a liar and a swindler, which I decline doing until further conclusive evidence — is in my eyes conclusive against the Executive, at least until I see their reply. But what do the Executive do? They get infamous attacks into the *Volkszeitung,* they spread rumors and reports behind Aveling's back, they call meetings of the sections and lay *their* version before them, and get them to vote resolutions in a matter which cannot be judged without an impartial audit of the whole accounts and a full defense of the absent accused. And having, as it appears, succeeded in their New York circle to slander Aveling, not as a man who has spent their money extravagantly (for such, rightly or wrongly, might be their honest conviction), but as a swindler and forger of accounts, they rise to the level of the occasion created by their own inventive genius, and promise a circular proclaiming Aveling a swindler and forger to the working class of the whole world! And all this, mind you, behind the back of, and unknown to the man whom they charge, and who can, not only not defend himself, but not even make out the precise facts on which the charge is based! If this is the way people are to be judged in our party, then give me the *Leipzig Reichsgericht* [Supreme Court of Germany] and the Chicago jury.[1]

Fortunately we have passed that stage in the older parties in Europe. We have seen Executives rise and fall by the dozen; we know they are as fallible as any pope, and have even known more than one that lived sumptuously on the pence of the workingmen, and had swindlers and forgers of accounts in their midst. In their circular, the Executive will not only have to define their charge — which perhaps will thus at last become known to us — but also to prove it. People on this side do not take the word of their own Executives for gospel, much less that of Mr. Walther and Mr. Rosenberg, be it ever so "official."

In my opinion, the Executive have placed themselves in a very uncomfortable position. Had they grumbled at the accounts as merely extravagant, they might have secured a hearing outside their own circle, for that is more or less a matter of opinion. But having never objected to the accounts sent in, they felt they had cut the

---

[1] The hand-picked jury that convicted eight militant workers of murder after the Haymarket massacre of May 4, 1886.

ground from under their own feet, and, as weak people do under the circumstances, exaggerated the charge in order to cover themselves. Thus they came to the fresh charge of swindling and forgery which they can never prove and must be content to insinuate. But an infamy insinuated to cover mere weakness remains neither more nor less an infamy. And having swelled what was originally a mere trifling matter of disputed accounts into a criminal offense, they actually feel bound to go before the various working-class parties with it. And naturally, they do it in a sneaking underhand way, preventing the accused from even hearing the charge. One mistaken step leads to another, and at last they arrive in a complete mess and are caught in their own net. And all that not out of inborn malice, but sheer weakness.

You will now see that I must distinctly decline following your advice as to "giving Kautsky a hint, not to let the letters appear which are advertised in the name of Aveling," because the Executive are going to launch "an official circular" against Aveling, and "his name as one of the staff can only injure any organ." Neither Kautsky nor myself has, I believe, ever given any ground for anyone to suppose that we would treat thus the friends we have worked with for years, upon the strength of mere assertions and innuendos. And if I were to say anything of the kind to Kautsky, I should simply drive him to the conclusion that I was either falling rapidly into dotage or that I was no longer to be trusted across the road. Indeed I feel certain you regretted having written this passage as soon as the letter had gone.

I see very well that you wrote your letter in what you considered the interests of the party, and thus were led to represent to me the case of Aveling as hopeless and judged without appeal. But so far he is judged by nobody but the Executive who are themselves parties, accusers, judges, and jury all in one, for the resolution of the New York sections, whatever it may be, counts for nothing. What the other sections may say remains to be seen, but even they, if impartial, can only declare themselves incompetent until they have the full facts and until the accused has been heard. And I for one consider it utterly ruinous to the party to introduce into it, and even to outdo, the kind of justice practised by Bismarck and the American bourgeois, who do at least respect forms and give the prisoner at the bar a hearing — and for us to act thus at the very moment we protest against these infamous proceedings.

No doubt it may suit the Executive, under the pretense of avoiding public scandal, to shirk publicity. But that will not do. Either they must retract the dishonoring charge, reduce the case to its simple dimensions of a dispute about accounts, and settle that honorably and straightforwardly, or they must come out publicly with the charge and have it fought out. There has already too much of it been allowed to leak out, and it cannot remain where it is, nor is Aveling the man to leave it there. And as I cannot allow the Avelings to be accused of infamies behind their back, it was my duty to communicate your letter to Mrs. Aveling (he being too ill at present) and to read her my reply. And if at any time circumstances should require the publication of this my letter, you are at liberty to publish it *in full*, while I reserve to myself the same right, of course without dragging in your name, unless the people should have done so previously.

I am, dear Mrs. Wischnewetzky,

Very truly yours,

F. Engels

ENGELS TO SORGE

London, February 12, 1887

Dear Sorge:

Received your letter of January 30th yesterday, and sent off various things to you the day before yesterday. More is to follow in a few days. The English *Capital* is selling very well; the jackass of a publisher, who had no idea of what he had got hold of, is quite astonished.

I hope your health is better; abstinence is also becoming obligatory for me. Every day brings some little bodily ailment which demands consideration and interferes with the customary devil-may-care mode of life. Well, there's no remedy for that.

Lafargue promised me, when he was here at Christmas, to send you the *Socialiste* regularly. Only *after* his return did I get a few extra copies of the article "situation, etc."![1] It opened the Frenchmen's eyes to the fact that for them war means the downfall of the republic — unless *quite* extraordinarily favorable circumstances cause a European revolution to result from it, which, however, the bourgeois, the petty bourgeois, and the peasants also do not want. Nobody had thought of that before, but now all of them are saying it. I am now reading the article in Rumanian in a confused *Revista Sociale* published in Jassy and am learning the language in the process.

---

[1] Engels' article *"Situation politique de l'Europe"* in *Le Socialiste*, No. 63, November 6, 1886.

The gentlemen of the Executive of the Socialist Labor Party are behaving quite abominably towards the Avelings. After the *Herald* article was published through their indiscretion, if not inspiration, a quite infamous article appeared in the *Volkszeitung*, for which I can only hold Mr. Douai responsible for the present. The Avelings answered the *Herald* scandal with the enclosed circular, which was sent out from here around January 18th to all the sections as well as to the Executive. Well, on January 28th the latter had a person whom I may not name for the present, but whom you must therefore guess, write me an embarrassed letter in which it is asserted as a fact, an undisputed fact, that Aveling tried to cheat them. He sent in false accounts — so it is assumed out of Christian charity — in order to cover his wife's hotel expenses (the party paid only the railroad fare for Tussy), and returning the $176.00 does not change matters, for that isn't the point at issue at all, etc. Nothing but insinuations, not a single fact, not even a *definite charge*. And then it is said: they have already had the New York sections pass a resolution on the matter in order to issue a circular to all the European parties to brand Aveling. And I am called upon to warn Kautsky not to print anything any more by such a blackguard as Aveling, who is to be expelled from all party organs!

You can imagine how I replied to these dirty tricks. If I can find anyone to make a copy of the letter I shall send you it — with my inflamed eye I cannot copy it for the third time. The gentlemen haven't the slightest pretext. For when Aveling first heard on December 23rd, through a letter from Rosenberg, that the Executive would object to some items in his statement of account, he answered Rosenberg at once, sending the letter by special messenger: "I cannot discuss money matters with the party, and am ready to accept anything without discussion that the National Executive of the S.L.P. thinks right!" And that was before he knew what they would say and offer him! And now these fellows go ahead, pocket $176.00, which belong to the Avelings according to their own reckoning, and declare *for that very reason* that Aveling, and not they themselves, is a swindler!

Now we shall have to go through with the affair. Unfortunately, however, we here know no one in New York except yourself who can be relied on, ever since the *Volkszeitung*, too, has behaved so vulgarly. I should be pleased if you could let us know how Schewitsch and others stand, whether or not they have already let themselves be duped by the Executive's lies. We would at least know whom to turn to in New York without bothering you. But one must marvel at the fact that the very people in New York who are indignant about the Chicago jury[1] outdo the disgracefulness of that jury in this case and damn people without even giving them a hearing, without even telling them what the charges against them are.

Yours,

F. E.

ENGELS TO SORGE

London, March 3, 1887

Dear Sorge:

. . . We can be quite satisfied with the elections in Germany. The increase in votes is splendid, especially under the prevailing pressure not only of the government, but of the manufacturers as well, who, wherever possible, placed before the workers the alternative of voting for the Bismarckians or being discharged. I fear this will have occurred again during the runoff balloting, the results of which are not known here as yet. The Pope is forbidding the Catholics to vote for us, the liberal gentlemen voluntarily prefer Bismarck to the Socialists, and the manufacturers are exercising direct compulsion — if we win a couple of seats under these conditions they are well deserved. But it is not at all a question of the number of seats, but solely of the statistical record of the irresistible growth of the party.

You think the people disgraced themselves by electing Geiser, Frohme, Viereck, etc. That can't be helped. They must take the candidates where they find them and as they find them. That is the general lot of all workers' parties in unremunerated parliaments. Nor does it mean anything. The people are under no illusions at all regarding their representatives; the best proof of this was the complete defeat of the "fraction" in its conflict with the *Sozialdemokrat*.[2] And Messrs. Deputies know it too; the gentlemen of the Right wing know that they are being tolerated merely because of the Socialist Law, and will be thrown out at once the day the party regains its freedom of action. Then, too, matters will still be wretched enough with our representatives, but I think I prefer the party to be better than its parliamentary heroes — rather than the other way round. . . .

Yours,

F. Engels

[1] See footnote, p. 172.
[2] Regarding the steamship subsidy which the German government tried to put through the Reichstag.

ENGELS TO SORGE

London, March 10, 1887

Dear Sorge:

Postcard and letter of February 21 received. You guessed right. It would be useless to send a copy of the long letter, as the formulation of the complaints in the Executive's circular is considerably different and milder, and up to now all the rest is only private gossip. How the people in Europe see the thing is shown by Singer's reply to the circular sent him: "It is the old story; it's only a pity that the Avelings have to suffer for it." No doubt you have received this circular, which I sent you in four English and four German copies, as well as my letter of about a week ago.

W[ischnewetzky] is not able to translate the *Manifesto*. Only one man can do that, Sam Moore, and he is working on it now; I already have the first section in ms. But it should be remembered that the *Manifesto*, like almost all the shorter works of Marx and myself, is far too difficult for America at the present time. The workers over there are only beginning to enter the movement . . . they are still quite crude, tremendously backward theoretically, in particular, as a result of their general Anglo-Saxon and special American nature and previous training — the lever must be applied directly in practice, and for that a whole new literature is necessary. I suggested to W[ischnewetzky] some time ago that she embody the main points of *Capital* in popularly written independent little pamphlets. Once the people are somewhat on the right road, the *Manifesto* will not fail to make its impression, whereas now it would be effective only among a few.

I communicated your comments on the English *Capital* to the publisher, who made the very practical reply: a favorable article in the *North American Review* would suffice to bring about an American reprint,[1] and he wants to skim the cream off first. Moreover, the thing is selling very well in America, too; in addition to Bordelli, another big bookseller has placed a standing order, while the sale here has been so rapid that the whole first edition is gone, except for 50 copies, and the second printing — still at the same price — is on the press. And all that in spite of very little advertising, and before a single big newspaper has mentioned it! The first serious article on it was in the *Athenaeum* of March 5 — very favorable. The others will now follow and help us sell the second printing, after which the cheap third edition can be issued.

[1] *The North American Review* was long regarded as the leading monthly magazine in the United States.

The Socialist Labor Party may be what it likes,[1] and claim for itself the results of its predecessors' work as much as it likes, but it is the sole workers' organization in America wholly standing on our platform. It has more than 70 sections throughout the North and West, and as such, and only as such, have I recognized it. I have expressly said that it is a party only in name. And I am convinced that the gentlemen of the Executive were very much disappointed with my preface and would have preferred not to have it. For they themselves belong to the wing which I say will ruin the party if it gains the upper hand. And it seems to be aiming at that. In the local *Justice* Rosenberg attacks the K. of L. because of the longshoremen's strike;[2] he may not be entirely wrong about the individual facts, but he displays a lack of insight into the course of the movement that will soon destroy the party if these people continue to rule. The very blunders of the careerist leaders of the K. of L. and their inevitable conflicts with the Central Labor Unions in the big Eastern cities must lead to a crisis within the K. of L. and bring it to a head, but the blockhead doesn't realize that. Over here the unemployed agitation of the Social-Democratic Federation has also collapsed without result. The church parade in St. Paul's was a clumsy aping of the Chartists and likewise without result; in short, nothing is happening here as yet. Perhaps things will be better next fall; it would be desirable for the rogues at the head of the S.D.F. to have worn themselves out and vanished before then.

Yours,

F. E.

ENGELS TO SORGE

London, March 16, 1887

Dear Sorge:

Many thanks for your letters of February 28th and March 2nd, with the enclosures, and for your many efforts. I am returning the Exec[utive]'s circular herewith, as we have it. We sent the enclosed letter to J[onas] at once in reply to the *Volkszeitung* article (so the pretty Jonas kept Aveling's reply for a whole month before deciding to print it). If he should not print it and you can exert any pressure

[1] Engels had received complaints regarding the comments on the Socialist Labor Party made in his preface to the American edition of *The Condition of the Working Class in England in 1844*.

[2] The great strike of nearly 30,000 longshoremen and other workers in the port of New York in January and February 1887.

upon him, it would be excellent. But his article seems to indicate a certain retreat already.

The great point in dispute regarding the objectionable items in A[veling]'s account will doubtless have been solved by our circular of February 26th. It is extraordinary that people who make a fuss about such details, which cannot be understood at all out of their context, do not say to themselves that the other side of this context must be heard before one takes it upon oneself to sit in judgment. But these expenses would also have been found in Liebk[necht]'s account if the latter had handed in his accounts at all. He said, however, that the party must bear all my expenses, and so I'll not write anything down. And they were satisfied with that. The Ex[ecutive] then says nothing about the fact that Aveling, in Boston, for instance, paid almost all the expenses, not only for L[iebknecht], but for his daughter as well, although it is set forth in the accounts and we were decent enough not to mention it in the circular. L[iebknecht] let all the wine, etc., be brought to A[veling]'s room and thus charged to A[veling]'s account during their trip. The Executive knows all that and suppresses it. But the meanest of all is that it sent out its circular over there on *January 7th,* but sent it to us only on *February 3rd,* so that it gained a whole month's unhampered headstart in its calumnies before we even learned what A[veling] was really accused of.

I do not believe without further proof that the resol[ution] has been adopted by most of the sections. The way in which the Knights of Labor are being treated is, if I am to base myself upon A[veling]'s and Tussy's reports, diametrically opposed to the views of all the sec[tions] in the West. But if that is the case, the whole "party" can bury itself alive.

It is really fortunate that you sent me the *Soz[ialist]*. Up to now I was able to give Kautsky or the Avelings the second copy received from the Executive, so that it had its uses. This week the fine gang no longer sent me the paper. I take that to mean that the next numbers will again contain contemptible slanders of A[veling]. We wrote to Müller in St. Paul, asking him also to print the second circular of February 26. While the Ex[ecutive] exploits secret journalism in its own way as it pleases, it apparently wants to place the onus upon A[veling] if he is the first to publish.

It seemed to us here to be a matter of course that A[veling] did not answer the *New York Herald*. The art[icle] was so weirdly absurd and, what is more, both of them said it wasn't customary in America to answer such farces seriously. From what I know of the *Herald* they would hardly have printed it either. Only after the art[icle] was reprinted here did A[veling] reply at once. But even if A[veling] had answered the *Herald* art[icle], *how would that have helped him against the Ex[ecutive]?* Thus this seems to me to be a lame excuse of Schewitsch's. In general, I am astounded at the enormous flabbiness of most of the New Yorkers that has come to light in this connection. The Ex[ecutive] disseminates lies as big as your fist and everyone believes it — from Jonas to Schewitsch and to the Wischnewetzkys! The Ex[ecutive] does seem to be a great authority in New York after all.

No more time, unfortunately, to send you various papers today — they shall go off tomorrow — mails are closing.   Yours,

F. E.

ENGELS TO SORGE

London, April, 6, 1887

Dear Sorge:

Postcard with Dietzgen clipping of March 24th and letter of the 25th received. Hepner will hardly be in a position to judge from a few isolated facts whether Aveling should have been "franker." I myself do not dare to decide it, but I merely know that in money matters Aveling is just as much of an unlucky fellow as Hepner himself. Both of them have an enviable talent for getting themselves innocently involved in differences regarding money.

Whoever told you that Kautsky has grown reserved is either lying himself or has been deceived. I trust Kautsky as I trust myself; like most young people, he can act somewhat precociously at times, but if he had any doubts he would have communicated them to me first. At any rate, I shall ask him tonight to tell me what, if anything, the report can refer to.

Wilhelm [Wilhelm Liebknecht], who cloaked himself in silence at first, is suddenly all afire. Here is what he writes me on March 28th (between the two of us — please do not transmit to others the literal text, but only whatever part of the content you consider fitting):

"The New Yorkers will probably come around. I wrote them in a very sharp tone weeks ago — that under no circumstances will I allow myself to be played off against Aveling and Tussy. I categorically *demanded an apology*, and as I have said, I think they will submit. It is a great pity that Aveling did not write me at once when he returned" (this is an empty excuse, as I informed him of the principal charges, as far as we knew them then, as early as January 20th). "I learnt of the whole affair only through you, and the election campaign, which naturally took all of my time, was in progress then. And so much time has been lost. But everything will be straightened out. If the New Yorkers are stubborn, I shall proceed *against them* publicly. Tell that to Aveling and Tussy."

In general the paper takes a strong stand against the gentlemen of the Executive. Aveling has received sympathetic letters from many private sources in New York. The Am[erican] Section in Rochester declares that it continues to have confidence in him, while the German Sect[ion] in *Cleveland* (or *Buffalo,* I forget) takes his side completely. And a month ago the Ex[ecutive] — without waiting for the Sections' vote — sent all the documentary material to the auditing commission for a decision, thus again appealing to a new tribunal! Of course we wrote the commission at once, sent them documents, and demanded access to certain letters, etc.

You will have received a copy of A[veling]'s reply to the second *Volkszeitung* article, which is indeed even more scurrilous.

Our Parisians have gotten themselves into a mess again. They lost the *Cri du Peuple,* and now the *Socialiste* is also dead for lack of funds. For fifty years, the Paris workers have spoiled their stomachs so much with their sectarian and phrasemongering socialism that they cannot stand any healthy food at the present time. *Paris, le centre du lumière, la ville de l'idée, est dégoutée d'idées* [Paris, the center of enlightenment, the city of ideas, is disgusted with ideas].

On the other hand, the crisis in Russia seems to be impending. The last assassinations have fairly capped the climax; everything is in a state of turmoil, and in addition general military service, under the well-known Russian conditions, has ruined the Russian Army, as I maintained was inevitable as much as ten years ago.

Best regards.

Yours,
F. Engels

ENGELS TO SORGE

London, April 9, 1887

Dear Sorge:

I wrote you on the 6th and received your letter of March 29th. Thanks for your efforts with regard to Jonas. I think they will bear fruit.

So the Ex[ecutive] wants to reply. That will mean a new concealment of facts. But this resolve to reply itself proves how absurd and shabby it was to try to cheat the sect[ions] into rendering judgment upon its initial allegations. First the sect[ions] are to decide. Then, even before the period agreed on has expired, the Ex[ecutive] begs the auditing commission for a verdict. And now it itself confesses that further light is required before a decision can be rendered!

In any event the gentlemen have ruined themselves. And if the Wischnewetzkys, who have behaved rather like Washragskys in the whole affair, have been constrained to call them liars, things must have reached a pretty pass. The very fact that Mrs. W[ischnewetzky] decided to show you my letter proves the dilemma the two of them are in. I was "humane" enough to judge the Ex[ecutive] to be real German louts as much as a year ago.

This pleases me in so far as I now hope to be relieved of Mrs. W[ischnewetzky]'s harassing about translations. First of all, she translates like a factory, leaving the real work to me; second, she neglected its publishing miserably, letting these louts get hold of it. We are no longer so badly off that we have to go begging with our manuscripts. And now, after I wrote an additional preface for her, things are at a standstill, evidently just because this preface is not to the taste of the Ex[ecutive]!

The A[veling]s have also received sympathetic letters and section resolutions from Springfield, Mass.; others will probably arrive in the next few days from the West.

According to English *Conservative* reports the Swiss government seems to be preparing to take steps against the Zurich *Sozialdemo-krat*. I have expected that ever since the war scare began; when Swiss neutrality is endangered the Swiss become villainous. It may blow over, however.

On the other hand, everything seems to indicate that the last two assassinations in Russia have capped the climax. Confidence in the government had vanished long ago; now confidence in the Tsar has gone, too. The army is full of discontented, conspiring officers. The Pan-Slavists want to place the half-brother of the present Tsar, the eldest son of Alexander II and the Dolgoruki woman, on the throne. And the police is powerless against the nihilists. According to the *Frankfurter Zeitung* 482 officers have been sent into exile from Moscow via Odessa to the penal colony on Sakhalin in the Pacific. I do not believe it will last out this year, if a war does not create a way out. But even that will probably come too late. And if it but starts in Russia, then hurrah!

Aveling's campaign among the Radical clubs in the East End here is making good progress. The relative election victories in Chicago and Cincinnati now in America [1] are helping him a lot — John Bull doesn't want to be outdone by those other fellows; it is the *only* foreign influence that has any drawing power here. In the great coercion meeting [2] in Hyde Park the day after tomorrow Aveling will speak from two of the fifteen platforms and Tussy from one of them. It promises to become one of the great meetings through which the London workers demonstrate a turning point in English politics. Moreover, the German elections have not been without effect here, too. . . .

Yours,

F. Engels

ENGELS TO SORGE

London, April 23, 1887

Dear Sorge:

I wrote you on the 9th. Thanks for the postcard and the things you sent. The publication of my preface in the *Volkszeitung* in a translation made over there is effrontery twice over. First, because I want to have nothing to do with the paper so long as it behaves so scurrilously towards Aveling. And, second, because I cannot put up with any outsider's translation of my English writings into German, and especially such a translation, which is full of mistakes and misunderstands the most important points. This woman has had my preface ever since the beginning of February (sent on January 27th), and in the only letter I have received from her since then, dated March 19th (postmarked *April 8th*), she merely mentions the plan of a German edition, for which she asked my consent — she knew that I had no copy of it here. I wrote her at once to return the original to me so that I might translate it. There are things in it where each word must be weighed. And then she connives behind my back with Jonas and Co.!

I protested at once. Let her show you my letters. This is the last straw. It is impossible for me to work with a person who continually commits such silliness.

But she'll hear from me. Her last long letter on the Aveling affair can be characterized by one word alone: filth. The endeavor of a

---

[1] The Union Labor Party had won several election victories in the spring municipal elections in Illinois, Wisconsin, Ohio, and other states, mostly in the Middle West.

[2] A mass meeting protesting against the coercion laws and repressive measures in Ireland.

weak person, influenced by every gust of wind, to justify herself in a wrong cause, which she herself must consider wrong. I shall answer her next week *con amore* [with love]. This kind of person must not think that she can bamboozle me like a baby.

Hyndman's correspondence in the *Standard* is pitiable and cowardly. He wants to maintain contact with George, while the latter grows more and more set on his land fad, and therefore must suppress all that is socialist. Things are going badly with him here, too. The sensational effects have vanished and new ones can't be had every day. But without them Hyndman cannot maintain himself in his role. The Avelings, on the other hand, have begun very effective agitation in the Radical clubs of the East End, laying special emphasis on the American example of an independent labor party. And the American example is the only thing that has an effect here — besides the German elections. The cause is making good progress and — if things continue in America as they have been going — can cost the Liberals the whole East End of London in a year.

Things are gradually approaching a crisis in the Socialist League as well. A delegates' conference is to be held at Whitsuntide, and it is hoped that the struggle with the anarchist elements that have crept in and are being supported by Morris will be decided there.

In Germany one persecution after another. It seems that Bismarck wants to have everything ready, so that when the revolution breaks out in Russia, which is probably only a question of months, it can immediately be started in Germany too.   Yours,

F. E.

ENGELS TO SORGE

London, May 4, 1887

Dear Sorge:

What you write on April 28th regarding the New York louts is certainly quite true, but you must not forget that I can answer only the points that you emphasize yourself, and not those about which you say nothing.

The *Manifesto* has been translated, and only my accursed eyes prevent me from looking over the work. In addition, a French, an Italian, and a Danish manuscript are in my desk, waiting to be looked through! What is more, forty years ago you were Germans,[1]

1 Sorge had urged that the *Communist Manifesto* be translated into English, and when Engels hesitated, declared that the *Manifesto* "had had an effect on us boys even forty years ago."

with a German aptitude for theory, and that is why the *Manifesto* had an effect at the time, whereas, though translated into French, English, Flemish, Danish, etc., it had absolutely no effect upon the other peoples. And for the untheoretical, matter-of-fact Americans I believe simpler fare is all the more digestible since *we* experienced the story told in the *Manifesto,* while they did not.

The affair with my book has been simply bungled by Mrs. Wischn[ewetzky], who gave Miss Foster *plein pouvoir* [full powers], which Miss Foster then turned over to the Ex[ecutive]. I protested immediately, but it had been done already. Up to the present Mrs. Wischnewetzky has bungled everything she has handled; I shall never give her anything again. She can do what she wants, and I shall be glad if she accomplishes something; but I have enough, and let her leave me in peace in the future. I answered her last letter a week ago.[1]

I sent the copy of the circular received from you to Liebknecht, at his request, but upon condition that he return it. He promises to send us what we require for publication.

Aveling is carrying on splendid agitation in the East End of London. The American example is having an effect; the Radical clubs — to whom the Liberals owe their 12 seats out of the 69 in London — have approached [Aveling] for lectures on the American movement, and Tussy and he are actively at work. It is an immediate question of founding an English workers' party with an independent class program. If this turns out well, it will force both the Social Democratic Federation and the Socialist League into the background, which would be the best solution of the current squabbles. Hyndman sees that his existence is menaced, especially as he has fallen out with almost all his followers. He has therefore reprinted the Executive's charges against Aveling in *Justice.* This is very good, for it puts an end to the gossip behind one's back and gives Aveling a chance to discuss the matter everywhere. Let's hope that the position of the Socialist League is also cleared up at Whitsuntide; the anarchists must be expelled or we'll drop the whole mess.

The Avelings have sent you *Time* with their articles on America; I take it you have received it? (March, April, May numbers.) Even the Tory *Standard* praises them! At the present moment the Avelings are doing more than all the others here and are much more useful — and then I'm supposed to answer Mother Wischnewetzky's childish misgivings regarding the grave charge under which Dr. A[veling] will stand until he has *disproved* the circ[ular] of the Ex[ecutive]!

[1] This letter has not been found.

The madam seems to have quite forgotten, among her gossipy German sisters, that it is not A[veling] who has to disprove, but the Ex[ecutive] that has to prove!

Commonweal, Gleichheit, and *To-day* are being sent you by today's steamer. De Paepe's bragging about the Belgian socialists in the *Gleichheit* will have amused you. The movement there is going ahead very well, ever since the Flemish took matters out of the hands of the Walloons, and the people of Ghent took them away from those in Brussels, but the little fellow cannot avoid boasting. What is funniest is that, while the men of Brussels would gladly found a new international, in which *they* would be the General Council, Powderly has asked them to join the K. of L. Thus Pope Powderly competing with Pope de Paepe!

Cordial regards and wishes for your recovery. Yesterday I was in America with the Avelings, that is to say, in Buffalo Bill's Camp — very fine.   Yours,

                                                                      F. E.

ENGELS TO SORGE

                                                    London, May 7, 1887
Dear Sorge:

I wrote you on the 4th and received yours of April 26th. Many thanks for the reports, which were doubtless written under severe physical tribulations. I can only take the passage regarding Mrs. Wischnewetzky and her regretting having written her denunciatory letter to mean that it was written with her consent to spare her a direct *pater peccavi* [Father, I have sinned]. I had to write her today and I told her "if that, as I must suppose, was written with her consent, I was perfectly satisfied and had no longer any reason to revert to that subject in a spirit of controversy." You see, I want to make it as easy for her as possible. But she is awkward and, besides, a luckless person of the first water. She writes me that she wants to publish my preface [1] in German. I have no objections, naturally. But she knows that I kept no copy, and yet she does not send me the Ms. so that I can translate it. Nor do I receive the book itself or even a single galley proof of the preface. Instead, the preface is turned over to the *Volkszeitung* for a thoroughly dull translation, containing errors, to boot, which almost lead me to conclude that she even copied my English Ms. incorrectly. Well, now she writes me that

1 Engels had written the preface to the American edition of *The Condition of the Working Class in England in 1844* in English.

she has sent the Ms. off to me at last (not   a word about the V[olks] z[eitung] trans[lation]) — but what doesn't arrive is the Ms.!

I am especially pleased to hear that Mr. Jonas has had to climb down a peg. In view of his business jealousy of the Ex[ecutive] he was the last one to have any reason for zeal in this affair on the Ex[ecutive's] behalf; throughout this whole period he has behaved as scurrilously as possible, just *because* he realized that he had burned his fingers.

Our friend Liebkn[echt], too, suddenly does not want "to break with the Executive." I have put a pistol to the head of the good-hearted L[iebknecht], who doesn't want to spoil his relations with either side, and he'll come around all right. If he hadn't made fools of us in that manner, our reply to Circular II [1] would have been finished already. But it is hardly so pressing, and it should be a crushing answer. We have won, thanks to your support and activity, without which we should be far from where we are now. It is good that we old fellows can still rely upon one another.

Yours,

F. Engels

ENGELS TO MRS. [FLORENCE KELLEY] WISCHNEWETZKY
London, May 7, 1887

Dear Mrs. Wischnewetzky:

I have received your note of April 25th with thanks, but no *preface;* if I receive it per next steamer on Monday I shall send you word at once. In the meantime as I received no copy of the book as yet, will you please see that I get at least *something* to work upon, a proofsheet or whatever it is, as the *V[olks]z[eitung]* translation cannot pass under any circumstances. I shall work at the translation as fast as my inflamed eye will allow; I am only sorry you did not send me the Ms. or a proof as soon as the idea of a German edition occurred to you.

Sorge writes to me: "The Wischnewetzkys greatly regret that the dissimulations and suppressions of the Executive led them to send you that letter, and they have made all conceivable efforts to obtain justice for Aveling in the New York section." [2] If this, as I must suppose, was written with your consent, then I am perfectly satisfied, and have no desire whatever to return to that subject in a spirit of controversy.

[1] See p. 179.

[2] The quoted passage was written in German.

Nobody was more rejoiced than I when I learnt that the book was finally out of the hands of that despicable Executive and of the S.L.P. generally. Forty years' experience has shown me how useless and literally thrown away are all those publications by small cliques, that by their very mode of publication are excluded from the general book market, and thereby from literary cognizance. It was the same thing even with the party publications in Germany up to 1878; and only since the *Sozialistengesetz* [Anti-Socialist Law] which forced our people to organize a book trade of their own, in opposition both to the government and to the officially organized Leipzig book trade, has this been overcome. And I do not see why in America, where the movement begins with such gigantic and imposing force, the same mistakes, with the same drawbacks in their wake, should be quite unnecessarily gone through over again. The whole socialist and, in England, Chartist literature has thereby been made so extinct that even the British Museum cannot now procure copies at any price!

I remain, dear Mrs. Wischnewetzky, very sincerely yours,

F. Engels

ENGELS TO SORGE

London, June 30, 1887

Dear Sorge:

Letters, etc., up to June 16th received.

I am writing to the Wischnewetzkys [1] to phrase the footnote as follows: "to repudiate the absurd slanders which Aveling has been exposed to in consequence of his agitational tour of America." If they don't want that either, they can turn to you, and then you can, if necessary, authorize them *to delete the whole footnote*. For I cannot quote Aveling without saying a word about the stuff as well.

The story of Scribner's announcement of *Capital* looks like deliberate piracy. Thanks for the information; I shall turn it over to Sonnenschein. As far as I know, Scribner is *not* Sonnenschein's agent in New York.

That the men of the Ex[ecutive] believed they had purchased Liebk[necht]'s silence with the election funds was to be expected and was not unjustified. Fortunately, I had L[iebknecht] completely under my thumb as a result of his first bragging letter and made very resolute use of it when he tried to withdraw.

1 This letter has not been found.

Hyndman continues to gossip about A[veling] here too, and has been greatly aided by A[veling]'s bashfulness in speaking about the affair. If we could only get hold of the fellow once, he would have cause to remember it, but in the meantime he himself is ruining his position more and more. He is so miserably envious that he cannot tolerate any competitor, and is living in open or concealed warfare with everyone. And A[veling] has become zealous for battle at last, and Tussy will see to it that he remains so. . . .

I am fed up with Father McGlynn, and George has turned into a real founder of a sect. Nor did I expect anything else, but this experience was hard to avoid in view of the newness of the movement. Such people must have the length of their tether, but the masses learn only from the consequences of their own mistakes. . . .

Yours,

F. Engels

ENGELS TO MRS. [FLORENCE KELLEY] WISCHNEWETZKY
July 20, 1887

Dear Mrs. Wischnewetzky:

I have returned to you by this mail the whole of the two sets of reviews you sent me, with sincere thanks. They have greatly amused me. Criticism is almost on the same level everywhere, from Stockholm and London to New York and San Francisco, and since the rapid rise of a shoddy bourgeoisie in Russia I am afraid that even there the reviews will soon sink to the common level.

Yours sincerely,

F. Engels

ENGELS TO SORGE
Eastbourne, August 8, 1887

Dear Sorge:

. . . The story about the Wischnewetzkys is becoming more and more entertaining.[1] Such an Executive would have been deposed long ago in Germany. These people must think everything is permitted them, and that the party will follow them through thick and thin as a reward for their expecting the Americans to place them-

1 In meetings of the New York Section the Wischnewetzkys had bitterly attacked the Executive for its stand in the Aveling affair, and had been expelled for so doing.

selves under the command of a German group, in which the purest louts seem to be getting more and more of an upper hand. If Messrs. Germans make that the condition for their participation over there, the movement will soon stride over them. History is on the move over there at last, and I must know my Americans badly if they do not astonish us all by the vastness of their movement, but also by the gigantic nature of the mistakes they make, through which they will finally work out their way to clarity. Ahead of everyone else in practice and still in swaddling clothes in theory — that's how they are, nor can it be otherwise. But it is a land without tradition (except for the religious), which has begun with the democratic republic, and a people full of energy as no other. The course of the movement will by no means follow the classic straight line, but travel in tremendous zigzags and seem to be moving backward at times, but that is of much less importance there than with us. Henry George was an unavoidable evil, but he will soon be obliterated, like Powderly or even McGlynn, whose popularity at the moment is quite understandable in that God-fearing country. In autumn much will be — I won't say cleared up, but more and more complicated, and the crisis will come closer. The annual elections, which force the masses to unite over and over again, are really most fortunate. . . .

Yours,

F. Engels

ENGELS TO MRS. [FLORENCE KELLEY] WISCHNEWETZKY

London, September 15, 1887

Dear Mrs. Wischnewetzky:

I have received your letter of August 28th.

I am glad the pamphlet [1] sells so well. The copies I received I shall hand over to Aveling, who has just returned from the country, to be distributed partly among the socialist periodicals, partly at his East End meetings at his lectures on the American movements. I shall also try through him to get an agent for its sale and let you know the result.

What I wrote about Trübner [London bookseller] has come true more than I expected. Yesterday Dr. Baernreither, Austrian M. P., told me that he had asked Trübner — with whom he dealt regularly — to procure him a copy of our book. Tr[übner] said *he had none,*

---

[1] The preface to the American edition of *The Condition of the Working Class in England in 1844.*

and that Dr. B[aernreither] *had better order it through an American agency, whose address he gave to* B[aernreither], and through which B[aernreither] ordered the book. Thus Tr[übner] not only boycotts but actually burkes the book.

As to the copies sent to Kautsky, he could hardly act otherwise than he did. Neither Lovell nor yourself ever wrote him a line of instruction. I myself never heard whether any copies had been sent to the press here and to what papers. We were completely in the dark, and if the book has not got into the hands of the English press and not been noticed, that is entirely the fault committed on your side of the water. Had I been informed of what had been done in that respect, or had I been told that that was left to me, I could have acted. There is no doubt of a sale for it here, but not while it is in Trübner's hands; and if I was authorized to find an agent here I have no doubt of being able to do so: of course you would have to send a limited number of copies as a consignment.

The repudiation of the socialists by George[1] is in my opinion an unmerited piece of good luck which will redeem to a great extent the — unavoidable — blunder of placing George at the head of a movement he did not even understand. George as the standard-bearer of the whole working-class movement was a dupe; George as the chief of the Georgites will soon be a thing of the past, the leader of a sect, like the thousands of other sects in America.

Your pamphlet on philanthropy has not yet come to hand.

Your translation of Marx's free trade speech I shall look over with pleasure and compare it with the French original, of which I have perhaps the only copy extant. We will see about the preface later on. The Seventh *Bemerkung* [observation] from the *Misère de la Philosophie* [*Poverty of Philosophy*] would fit in very well. As to the chapter on rent, that seems more doubtful, as there is a good deal of reference to Proudhon's notions in it and I doubt whether Mr. Tucker's lucubrations[2] deserve any attention.

The reply of the Executive to my footnote[3] is in itself so deprecatory and meaningless that to reply to it would be a work of supererogation. I cannot reply in time for the congress,[4] and the fact remains that I have openly taken sides against the Executive in this matter. A fresh controversy across the Atlantic can lead to

[1] At the Syracuse convention of the United Labor Party and in Henry George's weekly, *The Standard.*

[2] Tucker was the publisher of a philosophical anarchist paper, *Liberty,* in New York and Boston, in which he defended and disseminated Proudhon's doctrines.

[3] The footnote to Engels' preface referred to on p. 187.

[4] The national convention of the Socialist Labor Party, which met in Buffalo in September 1887.

nothing. As to the *Socialist* and *Volkszeitung* boycotting me, I am sorry for it on account of the book and pamphlet, otherwise it is a matter of perfect indifference to me; I have got over such chicanery too often by simply waiting and looking on.

Your expulsion I read in the *Volkszeitung* at the time; it was what I expected. I hope your pamphlet will come in time for the congress; it would have been well if it had been out a month ago so as to come into the hands of the sections before they sent delegates. I am curious what the congress will do, but do not hope for too much.

Faithfully yours,
F. Engels

Fortunately the movement in America has now got such a start that neither George, nor Powderly, nor the German intriguers can spoil or stop it. Only it will take unexpected forms. The real movement always looks different to what it ought to have done in the eyes of those who were tools in preparing it.

ENGELS TO SORGE

London, September 16, 1887

Dear Sorge:

. . . I shall be able to look for and find Marx's letter on George only when I begin putting things in order, that is, as soon as some new bookcases I have ordered to give me more space arrive. Then you'll get a translation at once. There's no hurry — George must still compromise himself some more. His repudiation of the socialists is the greatest good fortune that could happen to us. Making him the standard-bearer last November was an unavoidable mistake for which we had to pay. For the masses are to be set in motion only along the road that fits each country and the prevailing circumstances, which is usually a roundabout road. Everything else is of subordinate importance, if only the actual arousing takes place. But the mistakes unavoidably made in doing this are paid for every time. And in this case it was to be feared that making the founder of a sect the standard-bearer would burden the movement with the follies of the sect for years to come. By expelling the founders of the movement, establishing his sect as the special, orthodox, George sect, and proclaiming his narrow-mindedness as the *borne* [boundary] of the whole movement, George saves the latter and ruins himself.

The movement itself will, of course, still go through many and disagreeable phases, disagreeable particularly for those who live in the country and have to suffer them. But I am firmly convinced that things are now going ahead over there, and perhaps more rapidly than with us, notwithstanding the fact that the Americans, for the time being, will learn almost exclusively from practice and not so much from theory.

The reply of the New York Executive to my footnote is pitiful. Nor do I hope for much from their convention. The people in the East — the sections — do not seem to be worth much, while a shift in the center of gravity of the Social-Democratic Party to the West is rather unlikely. . . .

I shall write you about Germany as soon as I have talked with Bebel here.

In general politics everyone is preparing for the death of old [Kaiser] Wilhelm [I], after which the Russians will take greater liberties in the Orient, and Bismarck will encourage them to do so in order to hold on to his job. But I hardly think it will end in war. The uncertainty regarding what a war will turn into is so great, the intentions of the Cabinets to betray each other are so definite, and the certainty that the war will have to be fiercer, bloodier, more costly, and more exhausting than any previous one (ten to twelve million soldiers facing one another) is so positive that all are making threats but no one has the courage to begin. But in this game it can start *without* their wanting it to, and that is the danger. . . .

Yours,

F. E.

ENGELS TO MRS. [FLORENCE KELLEY] WISCHNEWETZKY

London, December 3, 1887

Dear Mrs. Wischnewetzky:

. . . Your translation of *Free Trade* shall have attention as soon as ever possible. I shall also write a preface, only I am sure it will not in any case be *what you want*. It is impossible for me to answer the probable arguments of American protectionists beforehand. I do not know that sort of literature and have no time to go into it. My reasoning in nine cases out of ten would miss the mark, and moreover, whatever we may say, they will always find a way out, and have something to say that we cannot foresee. To enter into polemics with them directly, one must be in America. And I have always found that a good book makes its way and has its effect whatever the penny-a-liners of the day may say.

Yours faithfully,

F. Engels

ENGELS TO SORGE

London, January 7, 1888

Dear Sorge:

First of all, Happy New Year and the prospect that you will soon begin to feel at home in the new locality, and that you are again fully cured of all the ills of the summer.

... Let's hope the war cloud blows away — everything apart from that is going along so well according to our wishes that we can very well dispense with a general war, which would be more colossal than any heretofore, although even this would have to end to our advantage. Bismarck's policy is driving the masses of workers and petty bourgeois into our camp in droves. The pitifulness of the social reform, announced so pompously, which is a sheer pretext for coercive measures against the workers (Puttkamer's strike edict[1], the proposed reintroduction of labor books, the theft of trade-union and mutual benefit funds), is having a tremendous effect. The new Socialist Law will do little harm; the exile provision will scarcely pass *this time,* and if it does pass, its duration is questionable. For if old Wilhelm perished soon, and the Crown Prince came to the helm for only six months — which would be the best for us — everything would probably be in confusion. Bismarck has worked so hard to eliminate the Crown Prince altogether and to establish a regency of *young* Wilhelm [the Crown Prince's son, later Kaiser Wilhelm II] a swaggering lieutenant of the guards, that he would doubtless be eliminated himself if this happened, a brief illusory liberal regime taking his place. That would suffice to shatter the philistine's confidence in the stability of Bismarck's management; and even if Bismarck again took over the reins under the young fellow, the philistine's faith would be gone, and the youngster is not quite the old man. For the false Bonapartes of today are nothing if one doesn't believe in them and in their invincibility. And if the youngster and his mentor Bismarck then grew fresh and proposed even more insolent measures than we have now, matters would rapidly approach the critical point.

A war, on the other hand, would throw us back for years. Chauvinism would swamp everything, for it would be a fight for existence. Germany would put about five million armed men into the field, or ten per cent of the population, the others about four to five per cent, Russia relatively less. But there would be ten to fifteen million combatants. I should like to see how they would be fed; there would be devastation like that in the Thirty Years'

---

[1] The decree of April 11, 1886 on the employment of repressive measures against striking workmen.

War. And nothing could be settled quickly, despite the colossal fighting forces. For France is protected on the northeast and the southeast by very extensive fortifications along the frontier, and the new works around Paris are exemplary. So it will last a long time, nor is Russia to be taken by storm either. If, therefore, everything goes as Bismarck wishes, more will be demanded of the nation than ever before, and it is possible enough that postponement of the decisive victory and partial defeats will produce an internal upheaval. But if the Germans were defeated from the outset or forced into a permanent defensive, things would certainly start. If the war were fought out to the end without internal disturbances, a state of exhaustion would ensue such as Europe has not experienced for two hundred years. American industry would then win out all along the line and would place all of us before the alternative: either a relapse to pure agriculture for *self-consumption* (American grain prohibits anything else) or — social transformation. I imagine, therefore, that the plan is not to push matters to the extreme, to more than a sham war. But once the first shot is fired, control ceases, the horse may bolt.

Thus everything is driving towards a decision, war or peace, and I must hasten to finish Volume III. But events demand that I remain *au courant* [well-informed], and that takes away much time, particularly the military side of it; and yet I must still take care of my eyes. If I could retire to the life of a secluded scholar! For all that, it must be done; I am starting on it next month at the latest. . . .

Your old

F. E.

ENGELS TO SORGE

London, February 22, 1888

Dear Sorge:

. . . I hope it doesn't come to war, although then my military studies, which I had to resume because of the war scare, will be of no use. The chances are as follows: Germany, thanks to the long-existing general compulsory military service and universal elementary education, can mobilize 2,500,000 to 3,000,000 trained men and provide them with officers and non-coms. France cannot mobilize more than 1,250,000 to 1,500,000, and Russia scarcely 1,000,000. At worst, Germany is capable of defending itself against the two of them. Italy can raise and maintain 300,000 men, while Austria can raise about 1,000,000. Thus the German-Austrian-Italian chances are good for a war on land, while England's attitude decides the war at sea. It would be very amusing if Bismarck had to cut down his own chief support, Russian tsarism!

Everything is approaching a crisis, war or no war! Affairs in Russia cannot remain as they are for long. The Hohenzollerns are through: the Crown Prince mortally ill and his son a cripple, a swaggering lieutenant of the guards. In France the downfall of the bourgeois republic, of the exploiters, is coming closer and closer; the scandals, like those in 1847, are threatening a *révolution du mépris* [revolution caused by contempt for the existing authorities]. And here an instinctive socialism, which fortunately resists any definite formulation according to the dogma of one or another socialist organization and hence will accept it all the more easily from a decisive event, is getting more and more of a hold on the masses. It need only start somewhere or other and the bourgeois will marvel at the latent socialism that will break out and be manifest then.

Your old
F. Engels

ENGELS TO MRS. [FLORENCE KELLEY] WISCHNEWETZKY

London, February 22, 1888

Dear Mrs. Wischnewetzky:

I have duly received your letters December 21st and January 8th and return Lovell's letter with thanks.

I am not astonished at Grönlund's proceedings. I was rather glad he did not call on me here. From all I hear he is full of vanity and self-conceit. . . . *Es muss auch solche Käuze geben* [it takes all sorts to make a world]. In America not less than in England all these self-announced *grands hommes* [great men] will find their own level as soon as the masses begin to stir — and will then find themselves shifted to that level of their own with a velocity that will astonish them. We have had all that in Germany, and in France, and in the International, too. . . .

Your remarks about my books being boycotted by the official German Socialists of New York are quite correct, but I am used to that sort of thing, and so the efforts of these gents amuse me. Better so than to have to undergo their patronage. With them the movement is a business, and "business is business." This kind of

thing won't last very long; their efforts to boss the American movement as they have done with the German-American one must fail
miserably. The masses will set all that right when once they move.

Here things go slowly but well. The various little organizations
have found their level and are willing to co-operate without bickering. The police brutalities in Trafalgar Square have done wonders
in helping to widen the gap between the workingmen Radicals and
the middle-class Liberals and Radicals; the latter have behaved
cowardly in and out of Parliament. The Law and Liberty League —
a body gaining ground every day — is the first organization in which
Socialist delegates, *as such,* sit aside of Radical delegates. The stupidity of the present Tory government is appalling — if old Disraeli
were alive, he would box their ears right and left. But this stupidity
helps on matters wonderfully. Home Rule for Ireland *and for
London* is now the cry here, the latter a thing which the Liberals
fear even more than the Tories do. The working-class element is
getting more and more exasperated, through the stupid Tory
provocations, is getting daily more conscious of its strength at the
ballot-box, and more penetrated by the Socialist leaven. The
American example has opened their eyes, and if next autumn there
were to be a repetition, in any large American town, of the New
York election campaign of 1886, the effect here would be instan-
taneous. The two great Anglo-Saxon nations are sure to set up
competition in Socialism, as well as in other matters, and then it
will be a race with ever-accelerated velocity.

Can you let me have the American customs tariff, and the list of
internal taxes upon American industrial and other products? And
if possible, some information as to how the latter are balanced by
the former with regard to cost of production? That is, for instance,
if the inland duty on cigars is 20 per cent, an import duty of 20
per cent would balance it as far as foreign competition is concerned.
That is what I should like to have some information about before
I write my preface to *Free Trade.*[1]

Reciprocating your kind wishes, I remain

Yours very truly,
F. Engels

---

[1] "Speech on Free Trade," delivered by Marx on January 9, 1848, at an open
meeting of the Democratic Society in Brussels. See pp. 191, 199. The English
translation, revised by Engels, was published by Lee and Shephard, Boston, in
1888.

ENGELS TO SCHLUETER

London, March 17, 1888

Dear Mr. Schlüter:

. . . The younger Lehmann [Kaiser Frederick III] writes an abominable, affected German. He gives one every ground for a warning against the half-educated, a horrible example of which he proved himself to be in his confused Liberal-Conservative-Manchesterian manifesto [Frederick III's speech from the throne]. Moreover, it isn't easy to play the emperor while breathing one's last. In any event, if he lasts another six months, it will contribute some instability and uncertainty to politics, and that is just what we need. As soon as the philistine begins to suspect that the existing order is not eternal, but on the contrary, is just about tottering, it will be the beginning of the end. Lehmann [Kaiser Wilhelm I] was the cornerstone of the edifice; this stone has fallen out, and we shall soon see how far all this rubbish has rotted away. This may represent a temporary relief for us, but depending on the circumstance, it may also mean a temporary change for the worse or even war. In any case — things are getting lively again.

Best wishes to Ede and Liebknecht, if the latter is with you, as I assume.

Yours,

F. E.

ENGELS TO MRS. [FLORENCE KELLEY] WISCHNEWETZKY

London, April 11, 1888

Dear Mrs. Wischnewetzky:

Your call for the ms.[1] comes upon me very suddenly and I am afraid I shall not be able to oblige you. I am allowed to write two hours a day, no more, have a large correspondence to attend to, find that at the end of the two hours am only just getting warm in harness, and then, just then, must stop. Under these circumstances I am quite unable to do *articles de saison* [seasonal articles] to order, especially for a distant market, and do not see my way to having the pamphlet ready in ms. by May 15th, much less have it ready printed in New York by that time. Still I will set about it at once, after clearing off urgent letters, and do my best. I interrupt an important piece of business on purpose, to clear this matter off.

Still in my opinion you need not fear of losing your opportunity.

[1] The preface to Marx's "Speech on Free Trade."

The free trade question will not disappear from the American horizon until settled. I am sure that protection has done its duty for the United States and is now an obstacle, and whatever may be the fate of the Mills bill,[1] the struggle will not end until either free trade enables the United States manufacturers to take the leading part in the world market to which they are entitled in many branches of trade, or until both protectionists and free traders are shoved aside by those behind them. Economic facts are stronger than politics, especially if the politics are so much mixed up with corruption as in America. I should not wonder if during the next few years one set of American manufacturers after the other passed over to the free traders — if they understand their interests they *must*.

Thanks for the official publications [2] — I think they will be just what I want.

I am glad of your success against the Executive as far is it goes [3] — from *Volkszeitung Weekly* March 31st I see they won't give in yet — there you see what an advantage it is to be on the spot. The non-resisting weakness which went straight against the Avelings because they were absent — that weakness you could work around to your favor because you were not absent; and thus the hostility to you is reduced to mere local *klatsch* [gossip], which with perseverance you are sure to overcome and live down. . . .

Yours faithfully,
F. Engels

ENGELS TO MRS. [FLORENCE KELLEY] WISCHNEWETZKY

London, May 2, 1888

Dear Mrs. Wischnewetzky:

By this mail I send you *registered* the ms.,[4] that is to say, the copy Mrs. Aveling made of it when she found that with your close handwriting and absence of margin it was impossible to insert in pencil legibly the suggested alterations. There were many, arising from the fact that you translated from a German translation and we had the original to work upon. Many alterations have therefore no other

---

[1] A tariff bill before Congress at the time.

[2] See p. 197.

[3] Mrs. Wischnewetzky had attacked the Executive Committee of the S. L. P. for its careless publication of Engels' *The Condition of the Working Class in England in 1844*. For this she was expelled from the party, but reinstated in August, 1888.

[4] Marx's *Speech on Free Trade*.

purpose than to bring the English text nearer to the French original. In others, I have for the sake of clearness taken more liberties.

The preface is nearly done in the rough, but as you will require a German translation, I shall have to keep it a little longer on that account. Anyhow I will hurry on as much as the two hours a day will allow me to do — my doctor has again last week bound me strictly to that limit.

Please tell Sorge that according to present arrangements the *Sozialdemokrat* is going to be removed to London.[1] But it will be well to keep this quiet for the present; when our friends intend this to be talked about and to get it into the news-hunting press, they will no doubt arrange that themselves.

I am boycotted here almost as much as you are in New York — the various socialist cliques here are dissatisfied at my absolute neutrality with regard to them, and being all of them agreed as to that point, try to pay me out by not mentioning any of my writings. Neither *Our Corner* (Mrs. Besant) nor *To-day* nor the *Christian Socialist* (of this latter monthly, however, I am not quite certain) has mentioned the *Condition of the Working Class* though I sent them copies myself. I fully expected this but did not like to say so to you until the proof was there. I don't blame them, because I have seriously offended them by saying that so far there is no real working-class movement here, and that, as soon as that comes, all the great men and women who now make themselves busy as officers of an army without soldiers will soon find their level, and a rather lower one than they expect. But if they think their needle-pricks can pierce my old well-tanned and pachydermatous skin, they are mistaken.

Yours very truly,

F. Engels

ENGELS TO SORGE

London, July 11, 1888

Dear Sorge:

In all haste, information which you must, however, keep *absolutely secret*. You must not be surprised if you see me over there around the middle of August or a few days later — I shall perhaps

---

[1] The offices of the *Sozialdemokrat*, central organ of the Social-Democratic Party of Germany, were moved to London after the expulsion of the editorial board — Bernstein, Motteler, Schlüter, and Tauscher — from Switzerland.

make a short pleasure trip across the ocean.[1] Be so good as to tell me *at once* where you live so that I can look you up, and in case you shouldn't be there at that time, *where* I can find you. Also whether the Wischnewetzkys will be in New York around that time. I shall see nobody else upon my arrival, for I do not want to fall into the hands of the Messrs. German Socialists — that is why the thing must be kept secret. If I come, I shall not come alone — with the Avelings who have business to transact over there. More soon.

Yours,

F. E.

ENGELS TO SORGE

London, August 4, 1888

Dear Sorge:

Thanks for your two letters, and I thank you for the hospitality offered me. Whether I shall be able to avail myself of it, however, is somewhat doubtful, as the following will show.

For, if everything goes well, Schorlemmer will also come along — he is in Germany and not quite well, but wires that he is arriving on Monday. And as we shall have to stay together — at least Schorlemmer and I — Aveling has already reserved rooms for all of us in a hotel, and so I shall have to go there, at least at first. How it will be arranged later will be decided then. At any rate Schorlemmer and I will stay in the city only a couple of days and tour the country as soon as possible, for he must lecture again at the beginning of October and we want to see as much as possible.

I expect that little Cuno will be lying in wait for me, but I think I have a magic spell to make him tractable. When I return, shortly before we sail, I shall have to see various people at the *Volkszeitung*. That can't be avoided, nor does it do any harm, but at the beginning I want a rest.

We are leaving on the 8th on the *City of Berlin*. Aveling has shifted to the dramatic field with success and is to produce four plays over there in four cities (three and a half written by him).

As Monday is Bank Holiday, when nothing can be done because all the shops are closed, and we must leave on Tuesday, I have all sorts of things still to be done — I must also meet Lenchen and Pumps (who has been married for seven years now and has two

---

[1] Engels was fatigued, and his eyes troubled him a great deal. In order to rest, he decided to take a trip to the United States accompanied by the chemist Schorlemmer and the Avelings.

children) at 5:40 at Charing Cross on their arrival from Germany and Paris respectively, and therefore must close. I, too, am mighty glad at the prospect of meeting again. All the rest verbally.

Yours,

F. E.

ENGELS TO SORGE

Boston, August 28, 1888

Dear old chap:

Arrived here yesterday morning, received your letters to Schorlemmer and me this morning — many thanks. I left the cough medicine in Hoboken, and Schorlemmer is also cured of his complaint. We have just visited Mrs. Harney; she says Harney will come to London in October where I shall then see him. I have not been able to locate my nephew [Willie Burns] as yet; I think I'll find him tomorrow here in the hotel or in Roxbury. This Boston is badly scattered, but more human than New York City. Cambridge, in fact, is very pretty, quite Continental European in appearance. Cordial greetings to you and your wife; without you we still wouldn't be restored to health! We are remaining here until Saturday. Letters will be sure to reach us here until Friday evening.

Yours,

F. E.

ENGELS TO SORGE

Boston, August 31, 1888

Dear Sorge:

Received the newspaper the day before yesterday and your letters today. Thanks! But I am sorry that your throat is not in good shape yet, and, it seems, has even taken over my cough. If our visit has made us well and you sick, it is a very unpleasant business.

Yesterday we were in Concord, visiting the reformatory and the town. We liked both of them very much. A prison in which the prisoners read novels and scientific books, establish clubs, assemble and discuss without warders present, eat meat and fish twice daily with bread *ad libitum* [at will], with ice water in every workroom and fresh running water in every cell, the cells decorated with pictures, etc., where the inmates, dressed like ordinary workers, look one straight in the eye without the hangdog look of the usual criminal prisoner — that isn't to be seen in all Europe; for that the Europeans, as I told the superintendent, are not bold enough. And he answered in true American fashion, "Well, we try to make it pay, and it does pay." I gained great respect for the Americans there.

Concord is exceedingly beautiful, graceful, as one wouldn't have expected after New York and even after Boston, but it's a splendid hamlet to be buried in, but not alive! Four weeks there, and I should perish or go crazy.

My nephew Willie Burns is a splendid fellow, clever, energetic, in the movement body and soul. He is getting along well; he works on the Boston and Providence R.R. (now the Old Colony), earns $12.00 a week, and has a nice wife (brought along from Manchester), and three children. He wouldn't go back to England for any money; he is exactly the youngster for a country like America.

Rosenberg's resignation and the strange debate on the *Sozialist* in the *Volkszeitung* seem to be symptoms of collapse.[1]

We hear but little and seldom of Europe here, merely through the New York *World* and *Herald*.

Today Aveling will have finished all his work in America. The rest of the time is his own. Whether we'll go to Chicago is still uncertain; we have plenty of time for the rest of the program.[2]

Cordial greetings to your wife and to you from all of us, and especially from your

F. Engels

ENGELS TO SORGE

Montreal, September 10, 1888

Dear Sorge:

We arrived here yesterday, after having had to turn about between Toronto and Kingston because of a storm (it was quite a nasty breeze) and tie up in Port Hope. Thus the two days from Toronto to here turned into *three*. The St. Lawrence and the rapids are very pretty. Canada is richer in ruined houses than any other country but Ireland. We are trying to understand the Canadian French here — that language beats Yankee English holler.[3] This evening we leave for Plattsburg and then into the Adirondacks and possibly to the Catskills, so that we can hardly be back in New

[1] The collapse (of the Socialist Labor Party) came one year later. See pp. 220, 224.

[2] Engels had had Sorge draw up a sort of program for his tour.

[3] The last phrase was written in English.

York by Sunday. As we must board our ship Tuesday evening and still have to see various sights in New York, and must also be together during these last few days more than would otherwise be necessary, Schorlemmer and I will not be able to join you in Hoboken this time, much as we regret it, but must go to the St. Nicholas [a hotel in downtown New York] with the Avelings. In any event we are coming out to visit you as soon as we get there.

It is a strange transition from the States to Canada. First one imagines that one is in Europe again, and then one thinks one is in a positively retrogressing and decaying country. Here one sees how necessary the feverish speculative spirit of the Americans is for the rapid development of a new country (presupposing capitalist production as a basis); and in ten years this sleepy Canada will be ripe for annexation — the farmers in Manitoba, etc., will demand it themselves. Besides, the country is half-annexed already socially — hotels, newspapers, advertising, etc., all on the American pattern. And they may tug and resist as much as they like; the economic necessity of an infusion of Yankee blood will have its way and abolish this ridiculous boundary line — and when the time comes, John Bull will say "Yea and Amen" to it.

Yours,

F. E.

ENGELS TO SORGE

Plattsburg, N. Y.

Tuesday, September 11, 1888

Dear Sorge:

Landed here safely. At 1 p.m. we leave for the Adirondacks, back tomorrow night, and then through the lakes to the Hudson. Saturday night New York, we hope.

Should you have received letters for me, please send them to me at Albany — Narragansett Hotel — but they must reach there Friday evening at the latest.

I take it you have received my letter from Montreal. Your throat is in order again, isn't it?

Shall we see your son before we leave New York?

All of us are well and in good spirits. Best regards from all to you and your wife.

Yours,

F. Engels

ENGELS TO SORGE

Plattsburg, N. Y.
Wednesday, September 12, 1888

Dear Sorge:

Returned this evening from Lake Placid. Tomorrow down Lake Champlain.

I think I forgot to ask you in my last letter to get us 150 of those cigars; we are all out of them. Best regards.

Your

F. Engels

ENGELS TO MRS. [FLORENCE KELLEY] WISCHNEWETZKY

New York, September 18, 1888

Dear Mrs. Wischnewetzky:

We returned on Saturday evening from our trip to Boston, Niagara, the St. Lawrence, Adirondacks, Lakes Champlain and George, down the Hudson to New York City. We enjoyed ourselves very much and, all of us, brought home a stock of invigorated health which I hope will see us through the winter. Tomorrow afternoon we are leaving per *City of New York* and look forward to a little excitement, breakdowns of machinery and suchlike things, but hope to arrive, in spite of all, in 8-10 days in London. I cannot leave America without again expressing my regret that unfortunate circumstances prevented me from seeing you more than once and but for a few moments. There are so many things that we should have talked over together, but it cannot be helped and I shall have to go on board without taking leave of you personally. Anyhow, I do hope that the troubles you have gone through lately will be the last, that your own health and that of Dr. Wischnewetzky and the children will be all you can wish for. I shall be glad to hear soon again from you, and all your wishes shall have my best attention.

I have some copies of the pamphlet from Mr. Sorge; it is very creditably got up and, so far, I have discovered only two misprints. Please let me know how many copies you are sending me to England and how many I may distribute to the press; I believe it ought to be sent to *all* the chief dailies and weeklies in London and some in the provinces, also the monthlies. Of course, unless instructed to the contrary, I shall entrust the sale to Reeves. As he has accepted the agency for your American publications generally, his name might have been put on the title page; he will have to print a new title page and send in a bill for that.

Hoping to see Dr. Wischnewetzky in London on his return, I remain, dear Mrs. Wischnewetzky,

Ever yours faithfully,

F. Engels

ENGELS TO SORGE

London, October 10, 1888

Dear Sorge:

At last we got back — a week ago last Saturday, and since then I have sent you two *To-days,* a pile of *Commonweals,* and today a pile of *Gleichheits,* together with two more *Commonweals.* One *Gleichheit* is missing; Eduard Bernstein took it and I haven't got it back yet.

Little change here — the next number of the *Sozialdemokrat* will be printed here. Otherwise nothing seems to have happened.

The *City of New York* is a humbug, quiet in calm weather, of course, but once she starts rolling no one can get her out of it so soon. And the machinery is in a miserable state — one engine runs at hardly half-power and the other threatened to break down any moment owing to overexertion. We didn't do over 390 knots in any one day, and once we did only 313.

As far as the political situation can be surveyed, we judged it quite correctly over there. For so long a time Bismarck has drummed it into the stupid youngster Wilhelm that he is a greater Old Fritz that the fellow now begins to take it seriously and wants to be both Kaiser and Chancellor in one. Bismarck is letting him do as he pleases now, so that he may compromise himself seriously, in order that the former can jump in as the saving genius. In the meanwhile he has placed his son Herbert alongside the insolent youngster as a spy and guard. The conflict between the two won't be long in coming, and then the fun begins.

In France the Radicals are compromising themselves in the government more than was to be hoped for. As against the workers, they are disavowing the whole old program of their own and are behaving like pure opportunists, pulling the chestnuts out of the fire for the opportunists and doing their dirty work. That would be quite excellent if it weren't for Boulanger and if they weren't driving the masses into his arms almost forcibly. The man is not very dangerous personally, but this mass popularity is driving the army towards him completely, and therein lies a grave danger — a momentary rise of this adventurer, with war as the salvation from his embarrassment.

So Jonas has extricated himself from the trap very cleverly and fabricated an interview in a way that I cannot easily repudiate.[1]

Mother Wischnewetzky is furious because I "was in New York for ten days and did not find the time to undertake the two hours' easy railway journey to her; she had so much to talk over with me." Well, if I hadn't caught cold and weren't plagued with indigestion, and if I had been in New York for ten days on end at all!

Cordial regards to your wife.

Your old
F. Engels

ENGELS TO SORGE

December 15, 1888

Dear Sorge:

. . . Volume III involves more than I thought. I have had to rework a chapter completely from the material, while I myself must construct another one, only the title of which exists. Yet the work is going ahead, and it will astonish Messrs. economists considerably. My eyes are better, and I am still five years younger than I was in July. Regard to your wife.

Yours,
F. E.

ENGELS TO MRS. [FLORENCE KELLEY] WISCHNEWETZKY

London, January 12, 1889

Dear Mrs. Wischnewetzky:

No doubt you feel disappointed at my having left America without coming to see you at your seaside retreat. But I was really too unwell, while in New York, to attempt an excursion of any kind. As you are aware, I arrived with a severe cold which Dr. Wischnewetzky declared to be bronchitis. This got worse instead of better, and moreover I got a severe indigestion which made me feel on shore the seasickness I had not felt on the ocean. Under these circumstances, and with a long journey over unknown ground before me, I felt I was bound to get cured at once and to subordinate everything else to this consideration. I therefore placed myself under the motherly care of Mrs. Sorge, did not leave Hoboken for

[1] This refers to an article in the New York *Volkszeitung* on Engels' visit to the United States.

days together, and at last got right again — about the time when we had to leave New York. Had it not been for this, I should certainly have come to pass a day with you; as it was, I had to choose between perfect rest at Hoboken and an excursion which was almost sure to have upset me for the whole of the journey and maybe laid me up somewhere far out in the country.

The 500 copies from Lee and Shephard [1] have arrived — but too late to be sent out before the Christmas holidays, when nothing but holiday literature is noticed. I have therefore kept them back until now. On Monday the copies to the press will go out and the rest be forwarded to Reeves. As the boycott of the London Socialists against Marx and myself (exactly like that of English prehistoric old fogies against Morgan) seems still in force, I am curious what the effect will be.

With best wishes for the New Year,

Yours faithfully,
F. Engels

ENGELS TO SORGE

London, January 12, 1889

Dear Sorge:

. . . What characterizes European socialism at the present moment is discord. In France the possibilists have sold out to the government and are supporting their papers, which have no sale, from the secret funds. In the election on the 27th they are voting for the bourgeois Jacques, while our people and the Blanquists have nominated Boulé, who, Lafargue thinks, will get only ten to twenty thousand votes, which they regard as a defeat. In the provinces, on the other hand, things are going better. The possibilists had set *their* congress for Troyes, but let it drop when the organizers invited *all* Socialists. Thus only our people came, and they demonstrated there that if the possibilists dominate in Paris, the provinces belong to us. Now there will be two congresses (international ones) in Paris this year, that of our people and that of the possibilists. The Germans will probably attend neither one.

Here in London the farce of the army of officers without soldiers continues. It is the Robert Blum column of '49: [2] a colonel, 11 offi-

---

[1] See footnote, p. 197.

[2] One of the many volunteer detachments in the Baden campaign of 1849. See Engels' *Germany: Revolution and Counter-Revolution.*

cers, 1 bugler, and 1 private. In public they agree with one another outwardly, but the hidden cliques are all the greater. From time to time there are squabbles in public again. Thus Champion has been thrown out of the Social Democratic Federation; he founded a newspaper (a copy of which is being sent you this week) and is attacking Hyndman, and particularly the latter's ally, Adolphe Smith-Headingley, a Franco-Englishman who swears by the possibilists and is the chief intermediary in the alliance between Hyndman and the possibilists. In the period after the Commune the fellow was one of the loafers of the French branch[1] here, which reviled and lied about us. Then he belonged to the pseudo-General Council of Jung, Hales and Co., and is still lying about us now, of which I have proof. During the International Trades Congress this scoundrel-translator had the impudence to enter my house one Sunday under the protection of Anseele and van Beveren. When Schlüter comes he can tell you how I threw him out.

As soon as the working class here, which is only twitching as yet, really gets into motion, each of these gentlemen here will be put on his level and in his proper place — partly within and partly outside the movement. This is the stage of infantile diseases.

There are also squabbles in the office of the *Sozialdemokrat*. Schlüter can tell you about it. What is more, he is somewhat involved too, and knows how to conceal what doesn't suit him. When I see how wrong things are managed here at the center of the paper, I admire our workers all the more, who are able to adjust and neutralize all that.

Mother Wischnewetzky is very much hurt because I did not visit her in Long Branch instead of getting well in your home and putting myself in shape for the trip. She seems to be hurt by a breach of etiquette and lack of gallantry towards ladies. But I do not allow the little women's-rights ladies to demand gallantry from us; if they want men's rights, they should also let themselves be treated as men. She will doubtless calm down.

Bismarck received two pretty rebukes from Geffcken and Morier.[2] That the Reich Supreme Court is still not ready to accept his

---

[1] A "French Section of 1871" was formed by the Communard exiles. This section was connected with Bakunin's Alliance of Socialist Democracy. Most of the French exiles broke with this section of anarchists and police spies and established a new section, acting in full concord with the General Council. See p. 86.

[2] Geffcken, a leading Conservative, had attacked Bismarck's policies. At the end of 1888 Morier, secretary of the British Legation in Darmstadt, was accused of espionage on behalf of France during the Franco-Prussian War. Bismarck's son Herbert obliquely confirmed the charge. In reply, Morier published his correspondence with Marshal Bazaine, which refuted the charges against him.

corps-student's interpretation of the criminal code is, however, the result of the fact that young Wilhelm recently adorned these gentlemen in Leipzig with his special contempt.

Diplomatic intrigue is at its peak. The Russians have received twenty million pounds. In April the Prussians are getting their new 8 mm. magazine rifle (the 11 mm. one — a remodeled Mauser — was absolutely unfit for use in war). The Austrians are wildly boasting that they are *prêts et archiprêts* [ready and more than ready], which shows that they want a beating again, and in France Boulanger *can* take power. The only purpose of Bismarck's maneuvers with Salisbury in East Africa is to involve England so deeply in joint operations with Germany that it cannot withdraw even under Gladstone. Hence the Morier affair was staged by Wilhelm quite against his [Bismarck's] wishes, but he has to bear it. In short, the situation is growing tense, and it *can* lead to war in the spring. . . .

Yours,

F. E.

[*Marginal note.*] Section I of Volume III [of *Capital*] finished; Sections II and III in work. Seven sections in all.

ENGELS TO SORGE

London, February 23, 1889

Dear Sorge:

Postcard of January 19th and letter of February 10th received. I get the *Labor Standard* [1] and am giving Wischnewetzky's articles to Tussy, who will use them if a new edition of the *Labor Movement* is issued. They contain material that is characteristic of America. Such neglect of safety measures against fire and the like would simply not pay in Europe. But over there it is like the railways and everything else: if they only *exist,* no matter how, it suffices.

Thanks for the Appleton announcement. [2] Upon inquiry Sonnenschein states that he has sold 500 copies of the cheaper edition to Appleton.

I do not see *Der arme Teufel* [*The Poor Devil*]. It is Motteler's favorite reading material, nor does anyone begrudge him it. What it says about Aveling is simply a lie, no matter what it may be. I shall write Kautsky what you say about Rappap[ort]: lack of material and the desire for comprehensiveness brings many a person

---

[1] A paper published by J. P. McDonnell in Paterson, N. J.

[2] Appleton, the New York publishing firm, had advertised the English translation of *Capital.*

in who doesn't belong there [in the columns of *Die Neue Zeit*]. Kautsky has been in Vienna since July and won't return here before July.

I have sent you a *registered* book packet, containing the *Holy Family* in addition to some French things. *But you mustn't tell Schlüter that I sent it to you;* I had half-promised him my spare copy for the archives before I left for America — but you take precedence. It will probably arrive in March or April.

Furthermore — all by today's mail — another package of French things in addition to the *Commonweal* and the *Gleichheit*. Lafargue's and Deville's lectures aren't to be had here any more, and one doesn't get any reply from the authors. But I keep on drumming away at them.

You will have received the issues of *Égalité*. The Blanquists have had no luck with their *Cri du Peuple*. It was deadly boring and so they were compelled to collaborate with Guesde, Lafargue and Co. (as Vaillant wanted from the outset, but he was outvoted). In addition there are a few dissatisfied Radicals. Up to the present they are getting along well with one another — let's hope that it stays that way. Some more numbers soon.

In the last election in Paris the possibilists compromised themselves badly and worked for the opportunist Jacques. Now the workers are beginning to desert them. They have lost all their support in the provinces, which are much better than Paris. The effort, with the aid of the British trade unions and Hyndman here, their loyal ally, to convene an international congress in Paris *without* our Frenchmen, but with the Belgians, Danes, and Dutch, and, as they hoped, with the Germans, too, is failing miserably. The Germans declare they will attend *no* congress if two of them take place in Paris. And both sides are summoned to a conference at The Hague on the 28th, with Liebknecht, Bebel, and Bernstein from Germany, plus the Dutch and the Belgians. Lafargue is going there. Then they will either have to give in or else find everybody against them.

In Germany things are becoming more and more confused. Ever since old Wilhelm died and Bismarck is tottering, the philistine no longer has any confidence in the people in power. The vain young fool, the second, greater Old Fritz (*pour rire* [in jest]), wants to be Kaiser and Chancellor himself. The archreactionaries, the clergy and the Junkers at the court, are bending every effort to egg him on against Bismarck and to evoke a conflict — and in the meantime Wilhelm is pensioning all the old generals, putting his favorites in their places. Three more years of this, and the commands will all be in the hands of swaggering dandies and the army will be ripe for Jena.[1] Bismarck realizes this, and that is what might impel him to a sudden war, especially if the nincompoop Boulanger rises to the top. Then things will be pretty: an alliance between France and Russia which will *prohibit* the French from making *any revolution,* as otherwise Russia will turn against them. But I hope it will pass over.

Cordial regards to your wife.

Your

F. E.

ENGELS TO SORGE

London, May 11, 1889

Dear Sorge:

The writing and running about in connection with the damned congress leave me hardly any time for anything else. It's the devil of a nuisance—nothing but misunderstandings, squabbles, and vexation on all sides, and nothing will come of the whole thing in the end.

The participants in The Hague Conference have let the Belgians make fools of them. Instead of doing what had been decided on: immediately making a protest and calling a counter-congress after rejecting the possibilists (which the Swiss and the Belgians were to have done jointly), the Belgians did nothing, maintained stubborn silence in reply to all letters, and finally came up with the lame excuse that they had to lay the matter before their national congress —on April 21-22! Thereupon the others did even less than before (because Liebknecht was scheming with some possibilists via the Swiss, since *he* was the man for whom unification would have to succeed), and so the possibilists cornered all public opinion with their proclamations, while our people not only kept silent, but gave only noncommittal answers to the uncertain elements among the British, who were asking how things stood with the counter-congress. This smart policy ended up by making the people rebellious even in Germany, and Auer and Schippel demanded that we should attend the possibilist congress. That opened Liebknecht's eyes, and —after I and Ed Bernstein had told the Frenchmen that they were now free to call the congress for July 14th, as they originally planned —he wrote them exactly the same thing. And so the French have their way, but they are justifiably grumbling about Liebknecht's

[1] Napoleon crushed the Prussians at the battle of Jena in 1806.

delaying and scheming, for which they hold all the Germans responsible.

Over here, however, it is we who have to suffer the consequences of Liebknecht's ingenuity. Our pamphlet struck home like a thunderbolt, proving that Hyndman & Co. were liars and swindlers; everything was in our favor, and if Liebknecht had made the Belgians take rapid action, as was his confounded duty, or had let them go their own way and *dealt with the others himself,* convoking the congress for any date at all or letting the French convoke it, the masses would have flocked to us, and the Social Democratic Federation would have deserted Hyndman. In this way, however, all we got were empty promises: we should wait a while; and since the principal wrangle in the trade unions here was whether no delegates should be sent to the congress, as the leaders desired, or they should be sent against the leaders' wishes—the quality of the congress being quite unimportant, the only point at issue being entering the international movement or not—it was obvious that the rank and file would join those who knew what they wanted and not those who didn't. And so we lost a splendid position, which we had just captured, and unless a miracle occurs, not an Englishman worth mentioning will attend our congress. . . .

Yours,

F. E.

ENGELS TO SORGE

London, June 8, 1889

Dear Sorge:

. . . From the middle of March until nearly the middle of May I too was in the frame of mind about the congress in which your letter was written. Miraculously enough, everything has been saved, as the second convocation circular sent you indicates, with the signatures of almost all Europe on it (supplemented in the appendix to Bernstein, No. 2, sent you today).

The first pamphlet, signed by Bernstein, was edited by me, as is everything appearing *in English* on the affair. What you may take exception to in it was necessary from the local point of view. Especially the explanations about the possibilists, which you take as attacks. But most important of all was the publication of The Hague resolutions,[1] which the wise men in The Hague had decided to

[1] The resolutions of the preliminary conference mentioned on p. 212, not to be confused with the 1872 Congress of the First International.

keep *secret in infinitum*. Luckily, no one here or in Paris knew of this clever decision, and so we set to work, since the possibilists and their adherents over here were harping on these resolutions every day, telling the biggest lies about them, etc.

After the possibilists had been rejected, we naturally had to act fast. But the Belgians, who were supposed to call the congress together with the Swiss, didn't stir—they wanted to put the thing off until their congress at Easter time in Jolimont, and then entrench themselves behind the resolutions passed there. And among the Swiss, Scherrer was also a bit lazy, under the pretext of inducing the possibilist *masses,* with Liebknecht's approval, to come over to our side over the heads of Brousse & Co.!! Liebknecht, however, was making speeches in Switzerland, and Bebel was much too unfamiliar with the terrain to act independently in his absence.

The real battlefield was *here*. Bernstein's pamphlet No. 1[1] had struck like a thunderbolt here. The people realized that Hyndman & Co. had lied to them disgracefully. If our congress were convened at once, we would have them all, and Hyndman and Brousse would be alone. The malcontents in the trade unions here turned to us, to the Germans, the Dutch, the Belgians, the Danes. But from none of them did they get information about *our* congress: when, where, and how. Dispatching a delegation to a congress, no matter which one, was the principal consideration for them, however, by way of opposition to Broadhurst, Shipton & Co., and so they decided in favor of the Congress that had been *convoked*.

Thus we were losing ground here step by step; our foothold in the local Radical press was also becoming very shaky, and finally there came the resolution of the Belgian congress: to send one delegate to *each* congress. And even in the German party press Auer and Schippel maintained that we had to go to the possibilists if only to prove that we are not anti-French chauvinists. In short, I gave the case up as lost, at least in England.

But I wrote at once to the Frenchmen (who had insisted from the very start that the congress must be held on July 14-21 *alongside the possibilist one,* or else it wouldn't be worth the trouble) that the Belgian resolution restored their freedom of action and that they should now call the congress at once for this date. And Monsieur Liebknecht, under whose own posterior the articles by Auer and Schippel had lighted a fire, suddenly discovered that he had delayed the matter long enough and that he now had to act fast—he gave the Frenchmen the same advice. The call was issued—the effect exceeded

---

[1] The first pamphlet against the Social Democratic Federation and the possibilists issued under Bernstein's name in connection with the proposed congress.

all expectations; adherences poured in and are still coming. And even here we have more than a *succès d'estime,* and the publication of the signatures is still producing an effect. Even here we have everything outside the Social Democratic Federation (which has fallen to a very low estate), and morally a part of those still belonging to it. For John Burns, the Socialist County Councillor of London, will probably break away together with the whole Battersea Branch or has done so already. He and Parnell[1] (who signed our circular) have already been elected as delegates to the possibilist congress and will work *for us* there.

With the exception of the S. D. F., the possibilists haven't *a single socialist organization in all Europe.* They are therefore falling back on the non-socialist trade unions and would give the world if they could have even the old trade unions here, Broadhurst & Co., but the latter were fed up here in London in November. They will get one Knight of Labor from America.

The primary consideration in this connection—and this was the reason why I put my shoulders to the wheel—is that it is again the old split in the International that comes to light here, the old battle of The Hague. The adversaries are the same, with the anarchist flag merely exchanged for the possibilist one: the selling of principles to the bourgeoisie for small-scale concessions, especially in return for well-paid jobs for the leaders (city council, labor exchange, etc.). And the tactics are exactly the same. The manifesto of the S. D. F., obviously written by Brousse, is a new edition of the Sonvilliers circular.[2] And Brousse knows it too; he continues to attack *le Marxisme autoritaire* [authoritarian Marxism] with the same lies and slanders, and Hyndman is imitating him—his principal sources of information about the International and the political activity of Marx are the local malcontents of the General Council: Eccarius, Jung and Co.

The alliance of the possibilists and the S. D. F. was to constitute the nucleus of the new International that was to be founded in Paris: together with the Germans, if they fitted in as the third partner in the union, otherwise against them. Hence the many little congresses one after another, constantly growing in size; hence the exclusiveness with which the allies treated all the other French and English tendencies as nonexistent; and hence the intrigues, particularly with the small nations, which also were Bakunin's support. But

[1] A London trade unionist, not the Irish nationalist leader.
[2] Prior to The Hague Congress in 1872 the Bakuninists and Alliancists held a conference in Sonvilliers in the Jura region and issued a separatist, slanderous circular against Marx and the General Council of the First International. See also p. 111.

this activity became sinister when the Germans, with their St. Gall resolution,[1] also entered the congress movement, quite naïvely—in absolute ignorance of what was going on elsewhere. And since these little people would rather go against the Germans than with them—for the latter were considered to be too Marxified—the struggle became inevitable. But you have no idea of the Germans' naïveté. It has cost me endless effort to convince even Bebel of what it all really means, although the possibilists know it very well and proclaim it every day. And with all these mistakes I had little hope that things would end well, that immanent reason, which is gradually evolving to consciousness of itself in this affair, would win out as early as this. I am all the more pleased by the proof that affairs like 1873 and 1874 can't happen any more today. The intriguers are beaten already, and the significance of the congress—whether it draws the other one over to its side or not—lies in the fact that the concord of the socialist parties of Europe is demonstrated to all the world, with the few factionalists left out in the cold unless they submit.

The congress is of little importance otherwise. I am not going there, of course; I can't plunge into agitation over and over again. But they now *want* to play at congresses again, and it is then preferable that these congresses are not governed by Brousse and Hyndman. There was just enough time to block them.

I am curious about the effect of Bernstein No. 2.[2] Let's hope it's the last document in the affair.

As for the rest, things here are so-so. I have had to give up smoking because of my nerves; it requires remarkably little self-restraint. I smoke the contents of a third of a cigarette every two or three days, but I think I shall start smoking again next year. Sam Moore is going to the Niger region in Africa as a senior judge. He is sailing next Saturday from Liverpool, returning for half a year in eighteen months, and will translate Volume III [of *Capital*] while there.

Cordial regards to your wife.

Yours,

F. Engels

---

[1] The congress of the Social-Democratic Party of Germany in St. Gall, Switzerland.

[2] The second pamphlet against the Social Democratic Federation and the possibilists issued under Bernstein's name in connection with the proposed congress.

ENGELS TO SORGE

London, July 17, 1889

Dear Sorge:

Our congress is in session and is a brilliant success; up to the day before yesterday 358 delegates, with new ones still arriving. More than half of them foreigners, including 81 Germans from all the states and principalities and provinces with the exception of Posen. The first hall was too small the very first day, the second hall on the second day, and a third hall was sought. The sessions are entirely open to the public—sole protection against police spies—at the unanimous demand of the Germans, in spite of some French objections (they thought the possibilists would attract a bigger audience in Paris, and it would therefore be better to meet in closed sessions). The *Sozialdemokrat* will bring the attendance figures to America by the next mail. Scottish and German miners are meeting there for the first time in joint conference.

The possibilists have 80 foreigners (42 Britons, 15 of them from the Social Democratic Federation, 17 from the trade unions), seven from Austria (can't be much more than a fake, the whole actual movement there is with us), seven Spaniards, seven Italians (three representatives of Italian societies *abroad*), seven Belgians, four Americans (two of them, Bowen and Georgii, from Washington, D. C., came to see me), two Portuguese, one Swiss (*nommé par lui-même* [nominated by himself]), and one Pole. Almost all of them trade unionists. In addition, 477 Frenchmen, who represented only 136 *Chambres Syndicales* [trade-union chambers] and 77 *cercles d'études socialistes* [socialist study circles]. For each little clique can send three delegates, whereas each of our 180 Frenchmen represents a *separate* organization.

The amalgamation bubble is very powerful in both congresses, of course; the foreigners want amalgamation, while the Frenchmen are holding back in both camps. Amalgamation is quite good under rational conditions, but the fraud consists in some of our people shouting for amalgamation *à tout prix* [at any price].

I have just learned at the *S. D.* [editorial office of the *Sozialdemokrat*] that Liebknecht's amalgamation motion has actually been adopted by a large majority. What it signifies—whether it means a real amalgamation on the basis of private negotiations, or merely an abstract desire that is supposed to lead to such an amalgamation, can't be made out from the letter unfortunately. German good nature is above such details; nevertheless, the fact that the French are accepting it is sufficient guarantee for me that it involves no disgrace at the hands of the possibilists. I shall be able to learn more about it only after the mails close, probably only tomorrow.

Moreover, you are probably learning the essential facts as soon as I do, since the Avelings have made arrangements for cabling with the *New York Herald* man in Paris. Today I am sending you Saturday's *Reynolds* and the Monday *Star*—everything important that has appeared in the local press up to now. More on Saturday.

In any event, the intrigue of the possibilists and the Social Democratic Federation to obtain the position of leadership in France and England by stealth has miscarried completely, and their pretensions to international leadership even more so. If the two parallel congresses merely fulfilled the purpose of mustering forces—the possibilists and London factionalists in one hall, and the European Socialists (who figure as *Marxists,* thanks to the former) in another, thus showing the world where the true movement is concentrated and where the fraud—it suffices. Of course, the real amalgamation, if it occurs, won't prevent the continuation of the squabbles in England and France at all—quite the contrary. It will merely signify an imposing demonstration for the great bourgeois public—a workers' congress more than 900 strong, from the tamest trade unions to the most revolutionary Communists. And it will once for all block the cliques for the next congresses, for this time they have seen where the real power lies: that we are a match for them in France and more than a match for them all over on the Continent, and that their position in England is becoming very shaky. . . .

Yours,

F. E.

ENGELS TO SORGE

July 20, 1889

Dear Sorge:

. . . The reconciliation bubble in Paris has burst. How lucky that the possibilists and the S. D. F., recognizing their true position, preferred to give our people a kick, which puts an end to the fraud. The affair had been prepared *de longue main* [long ago], as is proved by a number of maneuvers and utterances of these gentlemen during the past two months, which now are more understandable. It is the old Bakuninist slander of the Hague Congress, etc.,[1] as if we had always operated with false credentials. This slander, continually rehashed by Brousse ever since 1883, had to serve them again as soon as they saw that they were being deserted by all Socialists and could

[1] See p. 215.

be saved only by the trade unions. What their credentials are like
will probably be revealed during the furious polemic that has now
broken out.

Unfortunately, this old rubbish, which didn't draw even in 1873,
doesn't draw today at all; but something had to be found to cover
up the tremendous fiasco that the gentlemen suffered. But it serves
our sentimental conciliatory brethren right, to get this stiff kick in
their tenderest spot for all their protestations of friendship. That
will probably cure them for some time to come. . . .

Yours,

F. E.

ENGELS TO SORGE

London, October 12, 1889

Dear Sorge:

The *Labour Elector* and *Commonweal* enclosed herewith as usual.
The *International Review* is said to have died already; that's how
quickly Hyndman ran it into the ground. On the other hand, Bax
is negotiating with another review; if he gets it, Aveling will probably be his associate editor. The New Yorker revolution is growing
funnier and funnier — the efforts of Rosenberg and Co. to stay at
the top *à tout prix* [at any price] are amusing but, fortunately,
useless too. Your correspondence with the Nationalists[1] in the *W.A.*
[*Workman's Advocate*] pleased me, first because one recognized old
Sorge ten miles away, and second because it is a *public* sign of life
again from you. . . .

Yours,

F. E.

---

[1] The followers of Edward Bellamy in the United States. In 1887 Bellamy had
published his social-utopian novel, *Looking Backward 2000-1887*, which won him
worldwide renown. The novel was written under the influence of Bebel's *Woman
and Socialism*, but all of Bellamy's reasoning and plans are bourgeois intellectual
fantasies. Bellamy Clubs were formed in many cities, their name being changed
to Nationalist Clubs in 1888. These clubs united to form the Nationalist Party.
Bellamy defined "nationalism" as the nationalization of industry and trade. The
Nationalist Party played only a minor part in American politics. Sorge was then
engaged in a controversy with Daniel De Leon in the columns of the Nationalist
organ.

ENGELS TO SORGE

London, December 7, 1889

Dear Sorge:

... Things won't turn out that well: to have the "Socialist Labor Party" liquidated. Rosenberg has a lot of other heirs beside Schewitsch, and the conceited doctrinaire Germans over there certainly have no desire to give up their usurped position of teachers to the "immature" Americans. Otherwise they would be nothing at all.

Over here it is being proved that a great nation simply cannot be tutored in a doctrinaire and dogmatic fashion, even if one has the best of theories, evolved out of their own conditions of life, and even if the tutors are relatively better than the S.L.P. The movement *is* under way now at last and, I believe, for good. But not directly Socialist, and those among the English who have understood our theory best remain outside it: Hyndman because he is incurably jealous and intriguing, Bax because he is a bookworm. Formally, the movement is first of all a trade-union movement, but utterly different from that of the *old* trade unions: the skilled laborers, the labor aristocracy.

The people are now putting their shoulders to the wheel in quite a different way, they are drawing far greater masses into the struggle, shaking up society far more profoundly, and putting forward much more far-reaching demands: the eight-hour day, a general federation of all organizations, and complete solidarity. Through Tussy, the Gas-Workers' and General Laborers' Union has gotten women's branches *for the first time*. Moreover, the people look on their immediate demands themselves as only provisional, although they themselves do not yet know toward what final goal they are working. But this vague idea is strongly enough rooted in them to make them elect as leaders *only* openly declared Socialists. Like everyone else, they must learn from their own experiences by drawing the conclusions from their own mistakes. But since, unlike the old trade unions, they greet every suggestion of the identity of interest between capital and labor with scornful laughter, this will not take very long. I hope that the next general elections take another three years in coming: (1) so that Gladstone, Russia's servant, does not come to the helm during the period of the worst danger of war — which would be sufficient in itself for the Tsar to provoke the war; (2) so that the anti-conservative majority will be so big that *real* Home Rule for Ireland becomes a necessity; otherwise Gladstone will bilk the Irish again, and this obstacle — the Irish question — will not be removed; and (3) so that the labor movement develops still further and possibly will mature even faster by the reaction of the depression which is certain to come after the present prosperity. Then the next Parliament may have 20-40 labor representatives, and of a different stamp than Potter, Cremer and Co.

The most repulsive thing here is the bourgeois "respectability" that has sunk deep into the bone of the workers. The division of society into innumerable strata, each recognized without question, each with its own pride but also its inborn respect for its "betters" and "superiors," is so old and firmly established that the bourgeois still find it fairly easy to have their bait accepted. I am not at all sure, for instance, that John Burns is not secretly prouder of his popularity with Cardinal Manning, the Lord Mayor, and the bourgeoisie in general than of his popularity with his own class. And Champion — an ex-lieutenant — has always intrigued with bourgeois and especially with conservative elements, preached socialism at the parsons' Church Congress, etc. And even Tom Mann, whom I regard as the best of the lot, likes to mention that he will be lunching with the Lord Mayor. If one compares this with the French, one realizes what a revolution is good for after all. However, it will not help the bourgeoisie much if they do succeed in luring some of the leaders into their toils. By that time the movement will have grown strong enough for this sort of thing to be overcome. . . .

Time has now been purchased by Bax, and I think everything has also been arranged with the Avelings. It depends, however, on what Bax turns it into. With all his talent and all his good intentions Bax is unpredictable — a bookworm who has gone into journalism and has lost his balance somewhat in doing it. Besides, there is his peculiar obsession that today women are oppressing men.

Your list of Marx's *Tribune* articles [1] is buried, no doubt, under the mountain of unsorted letters. I have the pasted and mounted *Tribune* articles, but I cannot say at present whether they are complete or not. I found them again only last autumn. . . .

Things are going splendidly in Germany. Little Wilhelm is an even better agitator than Bismarck; the Ruhr coal miners are assured to us, the Saar miners are following suit, and the Elberfeld trial is also helping with its police-spy revelations.[2] In France our

[1] In 1872 Marx got from Sorge a complete list of the articles that Marx and Engels had written for the *New York Tribune* from 1852 to 1859. The articles were sent to Marx in 1877 and later published in two books: *Germany: Revolution and Counter-Revolution* (written by Engels), and *The Eastern Question* (written by Marx).

[2] In the Elberfeld trial, which began on November 18, 1889, the defendants (including August Bebel) were accused of having organized a secret society and having distributed illegal literature. The trial lasted six weeks. Forty-three of the defendants were acquitted, including Bebel, while the rest received jail sentences ranging from fourteen days to six months.

parliamentary fraction now has eight members, *five of them delegates to the Paris Marxist Congress*. Guesde is their secretary and works out their speeches for them. There are prospects for a daily paper again. The fraction will introduce the congress resolutions as a motion. Work is going on everywhere for the First of May, 1889.[1] Things are going ahead very well in Austria, too. Adler put affairs in shape splendidly; the anarchists are dead there. . . .

Yours,

F. E.

ENGELS TO SCHLUETER

London, January 11, 1890

Dear Schlüter:

. . . The stormy tide of last summer's movement has somewhat abated. And the best of it is that the unthinking sympathy of the bourgeois gang for the workers' movement, as displayed in the dockers' strike, has also abated and is beginning to make way for the far more natural feeling of distrust and apprehension. In the South London gas strike, which was forced upon the workers by the gas company, the workers are again wholly deserted by all the philistines. This is very good, and I only hope Burns will go through this experience himself sometime, in a strike led by himself — he cherishes all sorts of illusions in that respect.

Meanwhile there is friction of all kinds, between the gas workers and the dockers, for instance, as was only to be expected. But despite all this, the masses are on the move and there is no holding them back any more. The longer the stream is dammed up, the more violent will the break be when it comes. And these unskilled are very different chaps from the fossilized brothers of the old trade unions; not a trace of the old pettifogging spirit, of the craft exclusiveness of the engineers, for instance; on the contrary, there is a general cry for the organization of *all* trade unions into one brotherhood and for a direct struggle against capital. In the dockers' strike, for instance, there were *three* engineers at the Commercial Docks who kept the steam engine going. Burns and Mann — both are engineers themselves and Burns is a member of the Executive of the Amalgamated Engineers Trades Union — were summoned to persuade these men to leave, as then none of the cranes could have worked and the dock company would have had to give in. The three engineers refused, the Engineers' Executive did not step in, and

[1] A slip of the pen; Engels meant May 1, 1890.

hence the length of the strike! Further, at the Silvertown Rubber Works — twelve-weeks' strike — the strike failed because of the engineers, who did not join in and even did laborers' work *against* their own union rules! And why? "In order to keep the supply of laborers low," these fools have a rule that *only those who have gone through a regular period of apprenticeship* are admitted to their union. By this means they have created an army of competitors, so-called blacklegs, who are just as skilled as they are themselves and who would gladly join the union, but who are forced to remain blacklegs because they are kept outside by this pedantry, which has no sense at all nowadays. And because they know that these blacklegs would have stepped into their places immediately, both in the Commercial Docks and in Silvertown, they stayed in and so became blacklegs themselves against the strikers. There you see the difference: the new unions stick together; in the present gas strike, sailors, steamer's firemen, lightermen, coal carters, etc., are all standing together, but of course not the engineers; they keep on working!

Yet these boastful old big trade unions will soon be made to look small; their chief support, the London Trades Council, is being more and more subjugated by the new ones, and in two or three years at most the Trade Union Congress will also be revolutionized. Even at the next congress the Broadhursts will get the shock of their lives.

The fact that you have got rid of Rosenberg and Co. is the main point about the revolution in your American socialist teapot. The German party over there must be smashed, *as such;* it is becoming the worst obstacle. The American workers are coming along all right, but just like the English they go their own way. One cannot drum theory into them beforehand, but their own experience and their own blunders and the resulting evil consequences will bump their noses up against theory — and then all right. Independent peoples go their own way, and the English and their offspring are surely the most independent of them all. Insular stiff-necked obstinacy annoys one often enough, but it also guarantees that what is begun will be carried out once a thing gets started. . . .

Cordial regards to your wife and yourself from Nim and your

F. Engels

ENGELS TO SORGE

London, February 8, 1890

Dear Sorge:

Your letter of the 14th and two postcards concerning H. Schlüter received.

In my opinion, we hardly lose anything worth mentioning by the defection of the official Socialists over there to the Nationalists.[1] If the whole *German* Socialist Labor Party went to pieces as a result, it would be a gain, but we can hardly expect anything as good as that. The really useful elements will finally come together again all the same, and the sooner the dross has separated itself, the sooner this will happen; when the moment comes at which events themselves drive the American proletariat farther on, there will be enough of them fitted by their superior theoretical insight and experience to take over the role of leaders, and then you will find that your years of work have not been for nothing.

The movement there, just like the one here and in the coal regions of Germany now as well, cannot be created by preaching alone. Facts must drum it into people's heads, but then it will go really fast, fastest, of course, where an organized and theoretically educated section of the proletariat already exists, as in Germany. The coal miners are ours today potentially and of necessity: in the Ruhr the process is proceeding rapidly; the Aachen and Saar basins will follow, then Saxony, then Lower Silesia, finally the Poles of Upper Silesia. With the position of our party in Germany, merely the impulse arising from the coal miners' own living conditions was sufficient to call forth an irresistible movement.

Here, things are going the same way. The movement, which I now consider irrepressible, arose from the dock strike, purely out of the absolute necessity of defense. But here too the ground had been so far prepared by the various forms of agitation in the last eight years that the people, without being Socialists themselves, still wanted to have only Socialists as their leaders. Now, without noticing it themselves, they are approaching the theoretically right track; they drift into it, and the movement is so strong that I believe it will survive the inevitable blunders and their consequences and the friction between the various trade unions and the leaders without serious damage. More of that below.

I think it will be the same with you in America, too. The Schleswig-Holsteiners and their descendants in England and America are not to be converted by lecturing; this pigheaded and conceited lot

[1] See foonote, p. 219.

must experience it in their own persons. And this they are doing more and more from year to year, but they are most conservative — just *because* America is so purely bourgeois, has no feudal past at all, and is therefore proud of its purely bourgeois organization — and so they will get rid of the old traditional mental rubbish only through practical experience. Hence it must begin with the trade unions, etc., if it is to be a mass movement, and every further step must be forced upon them by a setback. But once the first step beyond the bourgeois point of view has been taken, things will move quickly, like everything in America, where the velocity of the movement, growing with natural necessity, is setting some requisite fire underneath the Schleswig-Holstein Anglo-Saxons, ordinarily so slow; and then, too, the foreign elements in the nation will assert themselves by greater mobility. I consider the decay of the specifically German party, with its ridiculous theoretical confusion, its corresponding arrogance, and its Lassalleanism, a real piece of good fortune. Only when these separatists are out of the way, will the fruits of your work come to light again. The Socialist Law was a misfortune, not for Germany, but for America, to which it consigned the last of the louts. When I was over there, I often marveled at the many loutish faces one encountered, faces which died out in Germany, but are flourishing over there.

Well, there is another storm in a teacup over here. You will have read the squabbles in the *Labour Elector* over Parker, the associate editor of the *Star*, who in a local paper, forthrightly charged Lord Euston with pederasty in connection with the bugger scandals among the aristocracy here. The article was infamous, but it was merely personal; the matter was scarcely political. But it caused considerable scandal; the *Star* picked it up, provoked Burns directly, and Burns, instead of conferring with the committee, disavowed Champion directly in the *Star*. There was a tremendous storm in the *Labour Elector* committee, all against Champion, but each of them wants to get into Parliament and hence has separate interests. So nothing was decided, perhaps because they had no power. (Champion had told Tussy last fall that the paper belongs to the committee and he is merely a dismissable editor, but that was hardly altogether the case.) In short, Burns and Bateman resigned from the committee because of this affair, Burns, in particular, also because of the chauvinist article on the Portuguese squabble,[1] and this week the whole committee has vanished from the pages of the paper. Now

---

[1] A clash between the British and the Portuguese on the Zambesi River after Portuguese troops had been sent to Africa at the beginning of 1890.

Tussy has written off Champion also, whom she used to give international notes on France, Germany, Belgium, Holland, and Scandinavia. (The absurd stuff on Spain, Portugal, Mexico, etc., was written by Cunninghame Graham, a very honest, very courageous, but very muddled ex-ranchman.)

Now, the case proves to me that Champion actually took Tory money and then was in the embarrassing situation of having to do something for value received at the opening of Parliament. The author of the article itself is supposed to be Maltman Barry, our ex-friend of The Hague, who is considered to be a Tory agent here, and about whom Jung, Hyndman and Co. tell amazing but false cock-and-bull stories. But all these gentlemen are acting foolishly, for Champion is ruining himself completely with this, and in a meeting of his own Labor Electoral Association he was shouted down from the platform and had to be protected by two policemen. This, of course, is splendid grist for Hyndman's mill, but I think both of these gentlemen are done for. We shall see how matters go from here. But the movement will perish as little for this reason as it did because of the defeat of the gas stokers in South London. The people were too cocky, everything had been made too easy for them; a few setbacks cannot do any harm now.

In Paris our people are still trying to establish a daily. The possibilist *Parti ouvrier,* a daily subsidized by the government, has succumbed; *on n'a plus besoin de ces messieurs* [these gentlemen are not needed any more].

Bax's *Time* is quite an ordinary bourgeois affair, and he is mortally afraid of making it socialistic. Now, this won't go on like that without further ado, but there is still no place here for a *purely* socialist monthly, especially at 1 sh. per number. Whenever there is something interesting in it, I'll send it to you.

We have our Nationalists here too: the Fabians, a well-meaning lot of "eddicated" bourgeois, who have refuted Marx with the rotten vulgarized economics of Jevons, which is so vulgarized that one can make anything out of it, even socialism. As over there, their chief aim is to convert the *bourgeois* to socialism and thus introduce the thing peacefully and constitutionally. They have published a bulky book about it, written by seven authors.[1]

I hope your health is still good and that habit is making work easier for you. . . .

Yours,

F. E.

[1] *Fabian Essays in Socialism,* edited by George Bernard Shaw, London, 1889.

ENGELS TO SORGE

London, April 12, 1890

Dear Sorge:

Thanks for your letters of March 3rd-6th.

The matter of Miquel's letters [1] involves great difficulties. "Wilhelm" [Wilhelm Liebknecht] also would have liked to have them, in order to blurt them out at an inopportune time, thus permanently spoiling our means of exerting pressure on Miquel. For once the scandal is over, Miquel will snap his fingers at us. But it is of much greater value to me to have the fellow somewhat under the thumb through this means of pressure than to make a useless clamor, as a result of which he would be released and would be glad, to boot, that he had weathered it. What is more, the whole world knows that he was a member of the League.

I have had altogether too brilliant experiences with American journalism to bite at this chance. If it became known at the *Volkszeitung* that these letters were in America, those sensationalists would not rest until they had them — and I don't want to expose anyone to this temptation and torture. Moreover, what guarantee have I how long Schlüter remains with the *Volkszeitung* and whether they don't make the release of these letters the condition for his staying?

In short, it is impossible for me to enter this deal.

In Germany everything is proceeding better than one's wildest desires. Young Wilhelm is positively *crazy;* hence born, as it were, to put the old system thoroughly in disorder, to shatter the last remnant of confidence among all the possessing classes — Junkers as well as bourgeois — and to prepare the ground for us as even the liberal Friedrich III could not have. His desires for a friendly attitude to the workers — purely Bonapartist-demagogic, but mingled with confused dreams of the heaven-inspired mission of a prince — fail quite irretrievably with our people. The Socialist Law saw to that. In 1878 *something* could still have been accomplished by it, some disorder caused in our ranks, but now that is impossible.

Our people have had to feel the Prussian fist too much. A few weaklings, such as Herr Blos, and then some of the 700,000 men who have newly joined us in the last three years may be a bit shaky in this respect, but they will be quickly outvoted, and before the year is out we shall have the prettiest disappointment on Wilhelm's part regarding his power over the workers. With that love will turn

---

[1] Engels had been requested to send Johannes Miquel's letters to Marx to America for publication when the opportunity should present itself.

to rage, and caresses to persecution. Hence our policy is to avoid all clamor until the Socialist Law expires on September 30th, for it will probably not be feasible to set up a new state of emergency with the Reichstag then completely scattered. And once we have the ordinary civil liberties again, you will witness a new expansion that will even overshadow the one that came to light on February 20th.[1]

As little Wilhelm's friendliness towards the workers is complemented by hankerings for a military dictatorship (you see how the whole gang of princes becomes Bonapartist *nolens volens* [willy-nilly] nowadays), and he wants to have everyone shot down at the slightest resistance, we must see to it that he gets no opportunity to do so. We saw in the elections that our progress in the rural areas was quite enormous, especially where there are large estates and for the most part rich peasants, that is, in the East. Three runoff ballots in Mecklenburg, two in Pomerania! The 85,000 votes that were added between the first official count (1,342,000) and the second (1,427,000) were all from rural districts, where they had not expected us to get a single vote. So the prospect is that we shall soon win the agricultural proletariat of the eastern provinces, and with it the soldiers of the Prussian "élite regiments." Then the whole old order is done for, and we rule. But the Prussian generals would have to be greater jackasses than I can believe, not to know it just as well as we do, and so they *must* be burning with eagerness to put us out of action for some time to come by means of a ceremonious massacre. So there is a twofold reason to keep outwardly quiet.

A third reason is that the election victory has gone to the head of the masses, particularly the new recruits, and they think they now can force *everything* through by assault. If this is not curbed, a lot of blunders will be made. And the bourgeois — *vide* [see] the coal-mine owners — are making every effort to promote and provoke these blunders, and, besides the old reasons for doing so, they have the new ones: that they thus hope to foil little Wilhelm's "friendliness to workers."

Please do *not* communicate the passages marked in the margin above to Schlüter. He has a certain eagerness for action, and then I know the *Volkszeitung* people, who are ruthless in their journalistic wasting of everything that is usable. But these things may *not* be put in the press, neither over there nor here, at least not in the German press, and least of all as coming from me.

---

[1] Date of the Reichstag elections, when Bismarck was defeated.

So if our party apparently adopts a somewhat peaceful attitude in Germany in the near future and in respect to May First as well, you know the reasons. We know that the generals would very much like to exploit the First of May for shooting. The same intentions exist in Vienna and in Paris.

In the *Arbeiter-Zeitung* (Vienna) Bebel's correspondence from Germany is of special importance. I make no decision on any point relating to German party tactics before reading Bebel's opinion on it in the *A.Z.* or in letters. He has a marvelously keen scent. It is a pity that he knows only Germany from his own observation. This week's article "Germany without Bismarck" is also by him.

You will have received *Time* with my first article on Russian politics (sent off a week ago). . . .

Yours,

F. E.

ENGELS TO SORGE

London, April 19, 1890

Dear Sorge:

I get the *Nationalist* regularly; unfortunately there is not much in it. They are a feeble imitation of the Fabians[1] here. Superficial and shallow as the Dismal Swamp, but full of conceit regarding the lofty generosity with which they, the *"eddicated"* bourgeois, condescend to emancipate the workers, in return for which the latter must politely keep quiet and must submissively obey the orders of the "eddicated" cranks and their isms. Let them have their brief pleasures; one fine day the movement will wipe all that out. An advantage we Continentals have, who have felt the influence of the French Revolution in an altogether different fashion, is that such a thing isn't possible here.

Today I am also sending you *The People's Press*, which has taken the place of the *Labour Elector* as far as reports of the new trade unions are concerned. As you will have noticed, the latter prints nothing factual any more because the workers simply won't have anything to do with it any longer. Which doesn't prevent Burns, Mann, and others (particularly among the dockers) from still asso-

[1] The Fabian Society was founded in 1884 as a frankly opportunist organization by George Bernard Shaw, Beatrice and Sidney Webb, and other British intellectuals. Their anti-Marxist policy was based on a theory of "gradualism," the gradual evolution of society to socialism. The name "Fabian" is taken from Fabius Cunctator, dictator in Rome during the Second Punic War against Carthage, who gained successes against Hannibal by his slow, delaying tactics.

ciating closely with Champion on the sly and letting themselves be influenced by him. *The People's Press* is edited by a very young Fabian, Dell; the second in command is the priest Morris. Both are said to be decent fellows so far, and are very obliging towards the gas workers. Tussy is the leader of the gas workers (on the sly), and the union seems, at any rate, to be the best of them by far. The dockers are spoiled by philistine assistance and do not want to fall out with the bourgeois public. Moreover, their secretary, Tillett, is the mortal enemy of the gas workers, whose secretary he tried to become in vain. The dockers and gas workers really belong together; they are a single mass, dockers in summer, gas workers in winter. Hence the latter proposed a cartel to the effect that anyone who is a member of either union be not compelled to join the other upon changing his job. The dockers have rejected this up to now, demanding that the gas worker who becomes a docker in the spring also pay them an initiation fee and membership dues. Hence much unpleasantness. In general, the dockers stand for a lot from their Executive. The Gas-Workers and General Laborers accept all the unskilled, and in Ireland the agricultural day laborers are also joining — hence the discontent of Davitt, who does not go beyond Henry George and feels that his local Irish policy is threatened here, though quite without reason. Here in London the gas workers have been soundly beaten south of the Thames by the South Metropolitan Gas Co. That was very good; they were becoming too exuberant and felt they could win everything by assault. The same thing happened to them in Manchester. Now they are growing quieter; they are first consolidating the organization and filling the treasury. In the union Tussy represents the women and girls of Silvertown (India Rubber, etc. Works), whose strike she led, and she will doubtless take her seat in the London Trades Council very shortly.

In a country with such an old political and labor movement there is always a colossal heap of traditionally transmitted rubbish which has to be got rid of by degrees. There are the prejudices of the skilled unions — Engineers, Bricklayers, Carpenters and Joiners, Type Compositors, etc. — all of which have to be broken down; the petty jealousies of the various trades, which become accentuated in the hands and heads of the leaders into outright hostility and battles behind the scenes; there are the clashing ambitions and intrigues of the leaders: one wants to get into Parliament and so does someone else, another wants to get on the County Council or School Board, another wants to establish a general centralization of all the workers, another to start a paper, another a club, etc., etc. In short, there is friction upon friction. Among them the Socialist League, which looks down on everything that is not directly revolutionary (which, here in England, as with you, means: everything which does not confine itself to coining phrases and otherwise doing nothing); and the Federation, which still behaves as if everyone but itself were an ass and a bungler, although it is only the new progress of the movement that has enabled *it* itself to get some following again. In short, anyone who sees only the surface would say it was all confusion and personal squabbles. But *under* the surface the movement is going on; it is seizing ever wider sections, and for the most part precisely among the hitherto stagnant *lowest* masses; and the day is no longer far off when this mass will suddenly *find itself,* when it dawns upon it that it is this colossal moving mass; and when that day comes short work will be made of all the rascality and squabbling.

The foregoing details concerning persons and momentary dissensions are solely for your information, of course, and must not get into the *Volkszeitung* at any cost. This *once for all* — for I have already had instances here of the fact that Schlüter sometimes takes things a bit too lightly in this respect.

I am curious about the First of May. In Germany it was the duty of the Reichstag fraction to combat the exaggerated hankerings. The bourgeois, the political police (for whom it is now "a matter of jobs"), and Messrs. officers — all of them would gladly like to lay about them and to shoot, and they are seeking any pretext to prove to Young Wilhelm that he can't let them shoot quickly enough. But that would spoil our whole game. First we must be rid of the Socialist Law, that is, we must have survived the 30th of September. And then, things are moving altogether too splendidly for us in Germany to have us spoil them by pure braggadocio. Moreover, the fraction's proclamation is bad — it was written by Liebknecht — and the nonsense of a "general strike" wholly superfluous. But no matter how, the people are so elated over the 20th of February that they require a certain curb in order not to make any blunders.

In France the First of May *may* become a turning point, at least for Paris, if it helps to bring the large mass of workers who have gone over to Boulangism [1] to their senses. Our people have themselves to thank for that. They never had the courage to oppose the outcry against the Germans, as Germans, and now they are being defeated by chauvinism in Paris. Fortunately things are better in the provinces. But abroad all they see is Paris.

If the Frenchmen sent me their things, I would send them to you.

[1] A movement headed by General George Boulanger, the French "Man on Horseback," for the overthrow of the Third Republic and the establishment of a military regime.

But I think they are ashamed of them themselves. Well, it's in the French nature, they can't bear any defeats. As soon as they see a bit of success again, it will suddenly be different. . . .

Yours,

F. E.

ENGELS TO SORGE

London, November 5, 1890

Dear Sorge:

Today I have mournful tidings for you. My good faithful dear Lenchen passed away quietly yesterday afternoon after a brief and, for the most part, painful illness. We had lived seven happy years together in this house. We were the last two of the pre-1848 old guard. Now I am alone again. If Marx, for many years, and I, for the last seven years, found the quiet required for work, it was largely her doing. I don't know what will become of me now. And I shall sadly miss her wonderfully tactful advice on party affairs. Give my cordial regards to your wife and tell the Schlüters.

Yours,

F. E.

ENGELS TO SCHLUETER

London, January 29, 1891

Dear Schlüter:

. . . Unfortunately I cannot accept Sorge's invitation.[1] I am rooted with so many fibers here in Europe and have so infinitely much to do that a retreat to America can be considered only in the most extremely desperate situation. Moreover, my household is fully in order again ever since Louise Kautsky is with me.

Many thanks for the calendar.

The articles in the Cyclopedia [2] are partly by Marx and partly by me and are entirely or almost entirely on military subjects: biographies of military leaders, the articles "Artillery," "Cavalry," "Fortification," etc. Purely commercial work, nothing else; they can safely remain buried.

[1] Sorge had invited Engels to come to live with him in America after the death of Helene Demuth (Lenchen), Engels' friend and housekeeper.

[2] *The New American Cyclopedia, A Popular Dictionary of General Knowledge*, 16 vols. (New York, 1858-1863), edited by George Ripley and Charles Anderson Dana.

I see clearly enough that things are going downhill with the S.L.P. from its fraternization with the Nationalists,[1] compared to whom the Fabians here — likewise bourgeois — are radicals. I should have thought that the *Sozialist* would scarcely be able to beget extra boredom by cohabiting with the *Nationalist*. Sorge sends me the *Nationalist,* but despite all my efforts I cannot find anyone who is willing to read it.

Nor do I understand the quarrel with Gompers.[2] His Federation is, as far as I know, an association of trade unions and nothing but trade unions. Hence they have the *formal right* to reject anyone coming as the representative of a labor organization that is *not* a trade union, or to reject delegates of an association to which such organizations are admitted. I cannot judge from here, of course, whether it was *propagandistically* advisable to expose oneself to such a rejection. But it was beyond question that it had to come, and I, for one, cannot blame Gompers for it.

But when I think of next year's international congress in Brussels,[3] I should have thought it would have been well to keep on good terms with Gompers, who has more workers behind him, at any rate, than the S.L.P., and to ensure as big a delegation from America as possible there, including *his* people. They would see many things there that would disconcert them in their narrow-minded trade-union standpoint — and besides, where do you want to find a recruiting ground if not in the trade unions?

Many thanks for the silver material. If you could find something for me containing material on the *present silver production* of the U.S., I should be grateful. The European double-standard — currency — jackasses are merely dupes of the American silver producers and are quite ready to pull the latter's chestnuts out of the fire for them. To no avail, alas — nothing will come of the bubble. See my footnote on the precious metals in the fourth edition of *Capital*.[4]

Please give me fuller details of that speech by Marx on protective tariffs.[5] I recall merely that when debate grew slack in the Brussels German Workers Society, Marx and I agreed to stage a sham debate in which he defended free trade and I protective tariffs, and I still

[1] The National Citizens Alliance, a short-lived middle-class political group, collaborating with the Knights of Labor for the formation of a third political party.

[2] The A. F. of L. had refused a charter to the New York Central Labor Federation on the ground that a section of the Socialist Labor Party was affiliated to it.

[3] The second congress of the Second International was held in Brussels, August 16-22, 1891.

[4] See Karl Marx, *Capital*, Vol. I, International Publishers, pp. 119-20, *n*. 1.

[5] See footnote, p. 197.

see the astounded faces of the people when they saw the two of us suddenly attacking each other. It is possible that this speech was printed in the *Deutsche Brüsseler Zeitung.* I can't recall any other one.

You will probably be unable to come to Germany for the first year or two. Tauscher has been released, to be sure, but only because there was no evidence against him. It was disclosed, on the other hand, that the provisions of the statute of limitations have been regularly interrupted for the rest of you. . . .[1]   Your

F. Engels

ENGELS TO SORGE

London, June 10, 1891

Dear Sorge:

. . . The movement here is getting along very well. The Gas Workers and General Laborers Union is taking first place here more and more, thanks to Tussy especially. The movement is proceeding in an English fashion — systematically, step by step, but surely — and the comical phenomenon that here, as in America, the people who claim to be the orthodox Marxists, who have transformed our concept of movement into a rigid dogma to be learned by heart, appear as a *pure sect,* is very significant. What is more, that over there these people are foreigners, Germans, while over here they are true-blue Englishmen, Hyndman and his set. . . .

F. E.

ENGELS TO SORGE

Ryde, Isle of Wight, August 9-11, 1891

Dear Sorge:

. . . I am very grateful for the information regarding the *Journal of the Knights of Labor* — I have to look through such a pile of papers that it is often very hard for me to get my bearings without such reports. Likewise, regarding Gompers and Sanial;[2] very important, should I see them in London? . . .

[1] Schlüter was still under prison sentence *in contumaciam* in Germany for alleged violation of the Anti-Socialist Law.

[2] Sorge had informed Engels in a letter dated July 14, 1891, of the enmity between Sanial (delegate of the Socialist Labor Party to the Brussels Congress of the Second International) and Gompers (delegate of the American Federation of Labor). Sorge had expressed the fear that Gompers would exploit this feud at the Congress for his own political ends.

Tussy, Aveling, Thorne, and others of the Gas Workers, Sanders (John Burns's secretary), and several other Englishmen of our side are going to Brussels. I don't know as yet how matters stand with the *old* trade unions.

The dockers are on the verge of collapse. Their strike was won solely as a result of the £30,000 blindly contributed from Australia; but they think they did it themselves. Hence they are making one mistake after another — the last one was closing their lists, not accepting any more new members, and so breeding their own scabs. Then they refused to conclude a cartel with the gas workers. Many workers are dockers in summer, and gas workers in winter; the gas workers proposed that the ticket of *one* union should hold good for both with this alternating employment — rejected! Up to now the gas workers have respected the dockers' ticket nevertheless — one can't say how much longer. Then the dockers are raising an outcry against the immigration of foreign paupers (Russian Jews). Of their leaders, Tom Mann is upright but boundlessly weak, and he has been made half-crazy by his appointment as a member of the Royal Commission on Labor; Ben Tillett is an ambitious intriguer. They have no money, their members are dropping out in droves, and discipline has vanished.

They wrote me from St. Petersburg a week ago: "We are on the eve of a famine." This was confirmed yesterday by the prohibition of grain export from Russia. First of all, that assures us peace for a year; with a famine in the country the tsar will probably rattle the saber but not start an attack. BUT if Gladstone takes the helm here next year, which is likely, an effort will be made to get England and France to allow the Dardanelles to be closed to *all* fleets, even in war, which means forbidding the Sultan to get aid against the Russians. So that is the next stage of the Eastern question.

Second, however, prohibiting Russian grain exports means the *spread of the famine to rye-consuming Germany;* only Russia can cover the enormous rye deficit in Germany. That means, however, the complete collapse of the grain-tariff policy in Germany, and that involves an incalculable series of political disturbances. For example, the latifundian nobility will not relinquish its protective tariffs without causing the industrial tariffs of the bourgeoisie to totter. The protective-tariff parties will lose prestige, and the whole situation will shift. And *our party will grow enormously.* This crop failure will put us five years ahead, aside from the fact that it prevents a war, which would cost a hundred times as much.

In my opinion these two considerations will dominate European politics for the present, and if Schlüter wants to point this out in the *Volkszeitung*, it would be very useful. As soon as the Congress is over, I shall also broach it in the European press. But I cannot be responsible, of course, for what other people do with these reports. . . .

August 11th. The prohibition of grain export from Russia is not official as yet, but certain none the less; one should await the official proclamation. . . .

There were two Reichstag elections in East Prussia — an *enormous* increase in our vote. So the rural districts are opened up at last — *cela marche!* [things are on the march!] Well, with the rise in the cost of living we may live to see something by 1900, if we don't pass out before then. . . .

Your old

F. E.

ENGELS TO SORGE

Helensburgh, Scotland, September 14, 1891

Dear Sorge:

. . . The Trade Union Congress in Newcastle is also a victory. The *old* unions, headed by the textile workers, and the whole party of reaction among the workers, had exerted all their strength to over-throw the eight-hour resolution of 1890. They failed, and have won only a very small temporary concession. That is decisive. The confusion is still great, but the affair is irresistibly on the move, and the bourgeois papers recognize the defeat of the *bourgeois labor party* completely and with terror, howling, and gnashing of teeth. The Scottish Liberals especially, these most intelligent and most classic bourgeois in the kingdom, are unanimous in their outcry at the great misfortune and the hopeless perversity of the workers. . . .

Yours,

F. E.

ENGELS TO SORGE

London, October 24, 1891

Dear Sorge:

. . . For heaven's sake do me the favor of *not* sending me *any* American monthly regularly. I long for the opportunity of reading a *book* once again; though I am able to look through properly only one-third of the papers sent me, they take all my time — but the movement is gigantic by now and one must remain *au courant* [well-informed]! Send me however, . . .[1]

I can well believe that the movement over there is ebbing again. Over there everything proceeds with great ups and downs. But every up wins ground conclusively, and so one advances after all. Thus the tremendous strike wave of the Knights of Labor and the 1886-1888 strike movement has put us ahead despite all the recoils. For there is an altogether different life in the masses than before. The next time even more ground will be won. But with all that the native American workingman's standard of living is considerably higher than even that of the British, and that alone suffices to place him in the rear for still some time to come. Then there is the competition of immigration and other things. *When* the time comes, things will go ahead over there tremendously fast and energetically, but it may take some time until then. Miracles happen nowhere. And then there is the misfortune of the arrogant Germans, who want to play the schoolmaster and commander in one, and make the natives dislike learning even the best things from them . . . .

Everything went off very well in Erfurt. I shall send you the official minutes as soon as they are published. Bebel says the speeches were badly garbled in the news reports. Instead of making accusations, the opposition of the presumptuous Berliners was at once placed in the prisoner's dock itself. They behaved with miserable cowardice, and now they must work *outside* the party if they want to accomplish anything. Quite beyond doubt there are *police elements* among them, and another section consists of *concealed anarchists,* who want to do secret recruiting among our people. The rest of them are jackasses: bumptious students, unsuccessful candidates, and would-be great men of all sorts. All in all, less than two hundred strong. Herr Vollmar likewise had to submit; this fellow is much more dangerous than the former group. He is cleverer and more persistent, vain to the point of insanity, and wants to play an important part at any price. Bebel behaved very well, as did Singer, Auer, and Fischer (who was on the *Sozialdemokrat* here— a very able fellow and a very rough Bavarian into the bargain). Liebknecht had the bitter role of having to advocate Kautsky's draft program, which, supported by Bebel and myself, was taken as the *basis* of the new program's theoretical section. We have the satisfaction of seeing the Marxian critique win all along the line. Even the last trace of Lassalleanism has been removed. With the exception of a few poorly edited passages (where only the expression is

1 Blank space left by Engels.

dull and generalized) nothing can be said against the program any more, at least not after a *first* reading.

You will have seen that Lafargue is a candidate in Lille. You will get the results of tomorrow's election long before this letter. If he isn't elected, he is certain of a seat in the Nord Département in the next general elections.

The danger of war is becoming greater in spite of the Russian famine. The Russians want to exploit the new French alliance diplomatically, rapidly and thoroughly, and though I am convinced that Russian diplomacy does not want a war, and that the famine would make a war look insane, militarist and Pan-Slavic tendencies (now supported by the *very strong* industrial bourgeoisie with a view to market expansion) may get the upper hand, and blunders may likewise occur in Vienna, Berlin, or Paris which will cause war to break out. Bebel and I have been in correspondence on this point, and we are of the opinion that if the Russians start war against us, the German Socialists must fight the Russians and their allies, whoever they may be, *à outrance* [to the death]. If Germany is crushed then we shall be too, while in the most favorable case the struggle will be such a violent one that Germany will be able to maintain itself only by revolutionary means, so that very possibly we shall be forced to come into power and play the part of 1793. Bebel has made a speech on this in Berlin which has aroused a lot of comment in the French press. I shall try to make this clear to the French in their own language, which is not easy. But although I think it would be a very great misfortune if it came to war and if the latter brought us to power prematurely, still one must be armed for this eventuality and I am glad that there I have Bebel, who is by far the ablest of our people, on my side . . . .

Yours,

F. Engels

ENGELS TO SORGE

London, January 6, 1892

Dear Sorge:

. . . I have safely passed my seventy-first birthday, and all in all, I am healthier and stronger than five or six years ago. If I should live on to 1900—I don't know, to be sure, whether this would be good fortune or hard luck—I think I shall live through very much indeed. You in America have a movement that moves in ups and downs, continually gives rise to disappointments, and hence can easily lead to pessimism. Here I have the European movement right in front of my eyes, making gigantic strides on the whole, at its center the German movement, calmly progressing with irresistible natural strength, and therefore I tend to the other extreme. I have written something about this in the French calendar, which I shall send you as soon as I have a second copy.

Fortunately, war with Russia has been postponed for three or four years, if no acts of madness happen anywhere. As peaceful development in Germany promises us victory under the *most favorable* conditions, all the more surely though somewhat later, we have no reason to stake everything on one card, and we should have to stake everything on one card in such a war.

There is no place yet in America for a *third* party, I believe. The divergence of interests even in *the same* class group is so great in that tremendous area that wholly different groups and interests are represented in each of the two big parties, depending on the locality, and almost each particular section of the possessing class has its representatives in each of the two parties to a very large degree, though *today* big industry forms the core of the Republicans on the whole, just as the big landowners of the South form that of the Democrats. The apparent haphazardness of this jumbling together is what provides the splendid soil for the corruption and the plundering of the government that flourish there so beautifully. Only when the land—the public lands—is completely in the hands of the speculators, and settlement on the land thus becomes more and more difficult or falls victim to gouging—only then, I think, will the time come, with *peaceful* development, for a third party. *Land* is the basis of speculation, and the American speculative mania and speculative opportunity are the chief levers that hold the native-born worker in bondage to the bourgeoisie. Only when there is a generation of native-born workers that cannot expect *anything* from speculation *any more,* will we have a solid foothold in America. But, of course, who can count on *peaceful* development in America! There are economic jumps over there, like the political ones in France— to be sure, they produce the same momentary retrogressions.

The small farmer and the petty bourgeois will hardly ever succeed in forming a strong party; they consist of elements that change too rapidly—the farmer is often a migratory farmer, farming two, three, and four farms in succession in different states and territories, immigration and bankruptcy promote the change in personnel in each group, and economic dependence upon the creditor also hampers independence—but to make up for it they are a splendid element for politicians, who speculate on their discontent in order to sell them out to one of the big parties afterward.

The tenacity of the Yankees, who are even rehashing the Green-back humbug, is a result of their theoretical backwardness and their Anglo-Saxon contempt for all theory. They are punished for this by a superstitious belief in every philosophical and economic absurdity, by religious sectarianism, and idiotic economic experiments, out of which, however, certain bourgeois cliques profit.

Louise asks you to send her *only* the *Woman's Journal (Boston)* and even this *only until March 31st,* unless we do not write otherwise before then. She needed it for the Vienna *Arbeiterinnen-Zeitung* (she, Laura [Marx's second daughter], and Tussy are the chief contributors) and she says it could never occur to her to force the drivel of the American swell-mob-ladies[1] upon working women. What you have so kindly sent her has enabled her to become well-posted again and has convinced her that these ladies are still as supercilious and narrow-minded as ever; she merely wants to give this one magazine a couple of months' trial. In the interim she thanks you most sincerely for your kindness.

The first time Lafargue spoke in the Chamber he let himself be put out of countenance somewhat by the heckling and shouting.[2] This will iron itself out, however. The Frenchmen always improve in actual battle.

The story about Gompers is *as follows:* He wrote me and sent me detailed papers of his organization. I was out of town a great deal at the time—in summer—and tremendously busy in-between. Nor was I at all clear about the matter; I thought *Iliacos extra peccatur muros et intra* [They sin inside and outside the Trojan walls]. Then it was said that Gompers would come to Brussels or over here, and so I thought I would settle the matter orally. Afterward, when he *didn't* come, I forgot about the matter. But I shall look up the documents and write him that I decline the role[3] with thanks.

I wrote K. Kautsky a few days ago and instructed him to inquire of Dietz regarding the reprinting of your articles in a separate book; I am still waiting for a reply. Haste makes waste is the motto in Germany, especially in Stuckart[4] on the banks of the Neckar. . . .

Blatchford is out of the *Workman's Times,* which is a great gain.

---

[1] This hyphenated word is written in English.

[2] After the massacre of the workers at Fourmies during the 1891 May Day demonstration, Paul Lafargue, who had been sentenced to one year in prison, became the standard-bearer of a united front against the reactionaries and was elected to the Chamber of Deputies from the Department of the North. See p. 238.

[3] Of arbitrator between the American Federation of Labor and the Socialist Labor Party.

[4] The Swabian pronunciation of Stuttgart, where the Dietz publishing house was located.

What is more, the paper exhibits the defects that a *private* enterprise of this sort must always have as long as there is no party behind it strong enough to control it.

I now have: (1) to read proofs of the reprint of *The Condition of the Working Class in England in 1844;* (2) to look over Aveling's translation of *Socialism, Utopian and Scientific;* (3) some other minor items; and then (4) I return to Volume III [of *Capital*] where I have the hardest chapters ahead of me. But I think that, with the energetic rejection of all interludes, it will move along. What is left after that will, I think, offer merely formal difficulties. . . .

Yours,
F. Engels

ENGELS TO SORGE

London, March 5, 1892

Dear Sorge:

. . . And now Germany. Things are going ahead so splendidly there that we couldn't wish for anything better, despite the fact that hard blows will probably fall soon. From the very start little Wilhelm [II] was a splendid specimen of a "last of the breed," who is ruining the dynasty and the monarchy as no other. But now his madness has grown acute, and his megalomania doesn't let him sleep nor remain silent. Luckily the *regis voluntas* [king's will], which has become the so-called *suprema lex* [supreme law], turns against us today and against the Liberals tomorrow, and now he has even discovered that all the evil comes from the Liberals, whose progeny we are—that is what his clerics have talked into him. And now he is prosecuting the *Kölnische Zeitung* for *lèse-majesté* and he won't stop until the tame German philistine is driven into the opposition.

What more could we ask! A month ago, when Stumm delivered his speech in the Reichstag, they might have considered introducing a new Socialist bill, but now even that can't be done, for Wilhelm is angrier at the bourgeois opposition to the clerical elementary school law than at all the Social-Democrats, and they would rather leave us in peace than make a concession to the others. It is precisely the bourgeois parties that offer him the most opposition in the parliaments, not our 35 men in the Reichstag, while we haven't a single seat in the Prussian Chamber. Nevertheless there may be a few hard fights ahead of us here, too, but what could be better than having the Crown place itself on an untenable footing with the bourgeois and the workers at the same time! All the ministers are second- and third-rate persons; Caprivi is a good-natured lout, but he does not measure up to his job, while Miquel grows no smarter by eating more and more dirt every day. In short, if things go on in this way, a crisis may occur soon. A demented monarch cannot be tolerated for years on end in Prussia and in the Prussian-German Reich as could be done in Bavaria, and I should not be surprised to see them equip a private madhouse for little Wilhelm. And then a regency—that would be just what we require. . . .

Yours,

F. E.

ENGELS TO SCHLUETER

London, March 30, 1892

Dear Schlüter:

. . . The First of May will be a very decisive day for the Frenchmen this time—because of the municipal council elections throughout France, with the exception of Paris, on that day—and they are spurred on by the ambition to match the Germans.

Your great obstacle in America, it seems to me, lies in the exceptional position of the native-born workers. Up to 1848 one could speak of a permanent native-born working class only as an exception. The small beginnings of one in the cities in the East still could always hope to become farmers or bourgeois. Now such a class has developed and has also organized itself on trade-union lines to a great extent. But it still occupies an aristocratic position and wherever possible leaves the ordinary badly paid occupations to the immigrants, only a small portion of whom enter the aristocratic trade unions. But these immigrants are divided into different nationalities, which understand neither one another nor, for the most part, the language of the country. And your bourgeoisie knows much better even than the Austrian government how to play off one nationality against the other: Jews, Italians, Bohemians, etc., against Germans and Irish, and each one against the other, so that differences in workers' standards of living exist, I believe, in New York to an extent unheard of elsewhere. And added to this is the complete indifference of a society that has grown up on a purely capitalist basis, without any easygoing feudal background, toward the human lives that perish in the competitive struggle. . . .

In such a country continually renewed waves of advance, followed by equally certain setbacks, are inevitable. Only the advances always become more powerful, the setbacks less paralyzing, and on the whole the cause does move forward. But this I consider certain: the purely bourgeois foundation, with no prebourgeois swindle back of it, the corresponding colossal energy of development, which is displayed even in the mad exaggeration of the present protective tariff system, will one day bring about a change that will astound the whole world. Once the Americans get started, it will be with an energy and impetuousness compared with which we in Europe shall be mere children.

With best regards.

Yours,
F. Engels

ENGELS TO SORGE

London, December 31, 1892

Dear Sorge:

. . . Here in old Europe things are somewhat livelier than in your "youthful" country, which still doesn't quite want to get out of its hobbledehoy stage. It is remarkable, but quite natural, how firmly rooted are bourgeois prejudices even in the working class in such a young country, which has never known feudalism and has grown up on a bourgeois basis from the beginning. Out of his very opposition to the mother country—which is still clothed in its feudal disguise—the American worker also imagines that the traditionally inherited bourgeois regime is something progressive and superior by nature and for all time, a *non plus ultra* [not to be surpassed]. Just as in New England, Puritanism, the reason for the whole colony's existence, has become for this very reason a traditional heirloom and almost inseparable from local patriotism. The Americans may strain and struggle as much as they like, but they cannot discount their future—colossally great as it is—all at once like a bill of exchange; they must wait for the date on which it falls due; and just *because* their future is so great, their present must occupy itself mainly with preparatory work for the future, and this work, as in every young country, is of a predominantly material nature and involves a certain backwardness of thought, a clinging to the traditions connected with the foundation of the new nationality. The Anglo-Saxon race—these damned Schleswig-Holsteiners, as Marx always called them—is slow-witted anyhow, and its history, both in Europe and America (economic success and predominantly peaceful political development), has encouraged this still more. Only great events can be of assistance here, and if, added to the more or less completed transfer of the public lands to private ownership, there now comes the expansion of industry under a less insane tariff policy and the conquest of foreign markets, it may go well with you, too. The class struggles here in England, too, were more turbulent during the *period of development* of large-scale industry and died down just in the period of England's undisputed industrial domination of the world. In Germany, too, the development of large-scale industry since 1850 coincides with the rise of the Socialist movement, and it will be no different, probably, in America. It is the revolutionizing of all established conditions by industry *as it develops* that also revolutionizes people's minds.

Moreover, the Americans have for a long time been providing the European world with the proof that the bourgeois republic is the republic of capitalist businessmen, in which politics are a business deal like any other; and the French, whose ruling bourgeois politicians have long known this and practiced it in secret, are now at last, through the Panama scandal, also learning this truth on a national scale. But to keep the constitutional monarchies from putting on virtuous airs, every one of them has its little Panama: England, the building societies' scandals, one of which, the Liberator, has thoroughly "liberated" a mass of small depositors from some £8,000,000; Germany, the Baare scandals and Löwe's guns (which prove that the Prussian officer steals as he always did, but very, very little—the one thing in which he is modest); Italy, the Banca Romana, which is already nearly a Panama, having bought up about 150 deputies and senators; I am informed that documents about this are to be published in Switzerland shortly — Schlüter should watch for everything that appears in the papers about the Banca Romana. And in Holy Russia the Old-Russian Prince Meshchersky is outraged by the indifference with which the Panama disclosures are received in Russia and can explain it to himself only by the fact that Russian virtue has been corrupted by French examples, and "we ourselves have more than one Panama at home."

But, all the same, the Panama affair is the beginning of the end of the bourgeois republic and may soon put us in a very responsible position. The *whole* of the opportunist gang and the majority of the Radicals are disgracefully compromised; the government is trying to hush it up, but that is no longer possible; the documentary evidence is in the hands of people who *want* to overthrow the present rulers: (1) the Orleanists; (2) the fallen minister Constans, whose career has been ended by revelations about his scandalous past; (3) Rochefort and the Boulangists; (4) Cornelius Herz, who, himself deeply involved in all sorts of fraud, has evidently fled to London only to buy himself out by putting the others into a hole. All these have more than enough evidence against the gang of thieves, but are holding back, first, in order not to use up all their ammunition at once, and, second, in order to give both the government and *the courts* time to compromise themselves beyond hope of rescue. This can only suit us; enough stuff is coming to light by degrees to keep up the excitement and to compromise the *dirigeants* [leaders] more and more, while it also gives time for the scandal and the revelations to make their effect felt in the most remote corner of the country before the inevitable dissolution of the Chamber and new elections, which however ought *not* to come *too soon.*

It is clear that this affair brings the moment considerably nearer when our people will become the only possible leaders of the state in France. Only things should not move too quickly; our people in France are not ripe for power by a long shot. But as things stand at present it is absolutely impossible to say what intermediate stages will fill out this interval. The old Republican parties are compromised to the last man, and the Royalists and Clericals sold Panama lottery tickets on a large scale and identified themselves with them —if the ass Boulanger had not shot himself, he would now be master of the situation. I'm curious to know whether the old unconscious logic of French history will again hold good this time. There will be plenty of surprises. If only some general or other does not swing himself to the top during the intervals of clarification and start war—that is the one danger.

In Germany the steady irresistible progress of the party goes quietly on. Minor successes everywhere, which prove the advance. If the essential part of the military bill is passed, new masses of the discontented will stream to us; if it is rejected, the Reichstag dissolved, and new elections held, we shall get at least 50 seats in the Reichstag, which in cases of conflict may often give us the decisive vote. At any rate, the struggle will be fought out only in Germany, even if, as is possible, it first breaks out in France. But it is good that Volume III will now at last be finished—when? I cannot say, to be sure; the times are growing stormy and the waves are beginning to rise high.

Happy New Year to you and your wife, from Frau Kautsky, too.

Yours,
F. Engels

ENGELS TO SORGE

Sunday, January 18, 1893

Dear Sorge:

. . . Here there has been a conference in Bradford of the Independent Labor Party,[1], which you know from the *Workman's Times*. The S.D.F. on the one hand and the Fabians on the other have not been able, with their sectarian attitude, to absorb the rush towards socialism in the provinces, so the foundation of a third party was quite good. But the rush has now become so great, especially in the industrial districts of the north, that this new party makes its appearance at this very first congress already stronger than the S.D.F. or the Fabians, if not stronger than both of them together. And as the *mass* of the membership is definitely very good, as the center of gravity lies in the provinces and not in London, the home of cliques, and as the program is ours in the main points, Aveling was right in joining and in accepting a seat on the Executive. If the petty private ambitions and intrigues of the London would-be great men are now held in check somewhat, and the tactics do not turn out too wrongheaded, the Independent Labor Party may succeed in detaching the masses from the Social-Democratic Federation, and in the provinces from the Fabians, too, and thus force unity.

Hyndman has pushed the S.D.F. completely into the background. It has done so badly under his policy of intrigue that H. has fallen into complete disrepute with his own people, under the pressure of the provincial delegates. An attempt to restore his popularity in the Unemployed Committee (to which others also belong) by r-r-revolutionary boasting (though his personal cowardice is common knowledge among his best friends!) merely resulted in Tussy and Aveling obtaining greater influence in that committee. By now, S.D.F. relies solely on its seniority as the *oldest* socialist organization here, but otherwise it has become much more tolerant of others. It has ceased its abuse, and in general it feels much more like what it is, viz., much smaller than it pretended to be.

The Fabians[2] here in London are a band of careerists who have understanding enough to realize the inevitability of the social revolution, but who could not possibly entrust this tremendous job to the crude proletariat alone and are therefore kind enough to set themselves at the head. Fear of the revolution is their fundamental principle. They are the "eddicated" *par excellence.* Their socialism is municipal socialism; the *community,* not the nation, should be-

[1] The independent Labor Party was founded at the Bradford Conference on January 13-14, 1893.

[2] See footnote, p. 229.

come the owner of the means of production, at least temporarily. This socialism of theirs is then represented as an extreme but inevitable consequence of bourgeois liberalism, and from this follow their tactics, not to fight the Liberals decisively as opponents, but to push them on to socialist conclusions: therefore to intrigue with them, to *permeate* liberalism with socialism — not to put up Socialist candidates against Liberals, but to palm them off and force them upon the Liberals, or to deceive the latter into taking them. They naturally do not realize that in doing this they are either betrayed and deceived themselves or else are betraying socialism.

With great industry they have produced, among all sorts of rubbish, some good propaganda writing as well, in fact the best that the English have turned out in this respect. But as soon as they come to their specific tactic: hushing up the class struggle, it gets rotten. Hence, too, their fanatical hatred of Marx and of all of us— because of the class struggle.

These people have, of course, a considerable bourgeois following and hence money, and have many able workers in the provinces who would have nothing to do with the S.D.F. But five-sixths of the provincial members agree more or less with our point of view and will certainly fall away at the critical moment. In Bradford, where they were represented, several times they declared themselves decisively against the London Executive of the Fabians.

You see, it is a critical point for the movement here, and something may come of the new organization. For a moment it was close to falling into the clutches of Champion — who consciously or unconsciously is working for the Tories just as the Fabians are for the Liberals — and of his ally Maltman Barry, whom you got to know at The Hague (Barry is now an acknowledged and permanent paid Tory agent and manager of the socialistic wing of the Conservatives!) — see the *Workman's Times* for November and December. But in the end Champion preferred to start publishing his *Labour Elector* again and has thus placed himself in opposition to the *Workman's Times* and the new party.

Keir Hardie executed a clever stroke by putting himself at the head of this new party, and John Burns, whose complete inactivity outside his constituency has already done him a lot of harm, committed a fresh piece of stupidity by keeping aloof here, too. I am afraid he is stuck fast in an untenable position.

That here, too, people like Keir Hardie, Shaw, Maxwell, and others are pursuing all sorts of secondary aims of personal ambition is a matter of course. But the danger arising from this diminishes in the degree that the party itself becomes stronger and more of a mass party, and it is already diminished by the necessity for exposing the competing sects. Socialism has penetrated the masses in the industrial districts enormously in the past few years, and I am counting on these masses to keep the leaders in order. Of course, there will be blunders enough, and cliques of all kinds too; if they only succeed in keeping them within tolerable limits.

At worst, the foundation of the new organization has the advantage that unity is more easily achieved with *three* competing sects than with two that are diametrically opposed to each other.

As for what you write on December 23rd regarding the Poles: Ever since Kronstadt the Prussians have been expecting a war with Russia, and hence they have been *friendly* towards the Poles (and they have given us proof of that). The Poles in question will have tried to make use of this *in order to provoke war, which is to liberate them with Germany's aid.* But in Berlin they don't want this *at all,* and if the coup should come off, Caprivi will decidedly leave them in the lurch. At the present time we have no use for a war; we have more certain means of making headway, which would only be disturbed by war. . . .

Yours,

F. E.

ENGELS TO SORGE

London, March 18, 1893

Dear Sorge:

. . . The Brussels Conference regarding the Zurich Congress [1] takes place next Sunday (a week from tomorrow), so Bebel will drop in for a few days on his way back, and the Lafargues will come at about the same time. I am glad to have that youngster here again in order to talk over French affairs thoroughly with him. Still, enough time is left me to finish Volume III, as the chief difficulties are now behind me.

The matter of the *Socialiste* has been settled.

The silver business in America does not seem to be able to settle down otherwise than through a crash. Nor does Cleveland seem to have the power and courage to break the necks of this bribery ring. And it would be really good if things came to a head. A nation—a *young* nation — so conceited about its "practice" and so frightfully dense theoretically as the Americans are gets thoroughly rid of so

[1] The third congress of the Second International was held in Zurich in August 1893. This was the only congress of the International that Engels attended.

deep-rooted a fixed idea only through its own sufferings. The plausible idea of imagining that there isn't enough money in the world because one hasn't any when one needs it — this childish idea common to the paper-currency swindle *à la* Kellogg and to the silver swindle is most surely cured by experiment and bankruptcy, which may also take a course that is very favorable for us. If only some sort of tariff reform is effected this fall, you may be quite satisfied. The rest will follow; the main thing is that American industry is enabled to compete in the world market.

Here things are going *very well.* The masses are unmistakably in motion; you are getting the details from Aveling's somewhat long-winded reports in the *Volkszeitung.* The best evidence is that the *old sects* are losing ground and must fall into line. The Social-Democratic Federation has actually deposed Mr. Hyndman; he is allowed to grumble and complain a bit about international politics here and there in *Justice,* but he is finished — his own people have found him out. The man provoked me personally and politically wherever he could for ten years; I never did him the honor of answering him, in the conviction that he was man enough to ruin himself, and in the end I have been justified. After all the ten years' persecution, they have recently asked Tussy to write reports on the international movement for *Justice,* which she refused to do, of course, as long as the infamous slanders that *Justice* has heaped on Aveling and her for years are not publicly withdrawn.

The same thing is happening to the Fabians. Their own branches in the provinces are outgrowing these people as well as the S.D.F. Lancashire and Yorkshire are again taking the lead in this movement, too, as in the Chartist movement. People like Sidney Webb, Bernard Shaw, and the like, who wanted to permeate the Liberals with socialism, must now allow themselves to be permeated by the spirit of the workingmen members of their own society. They are resisting with might and main, but it's no use; either they remain alone, officers without soldiers, or they must go along. The former is more likely and also more desirable.

The Independent Labor Party — as the most recent arrival — has brought with it fewer fixed prejudices; it has good elements — the workers of the North in particular — and so far is the most genuine expression of the present movement. To be sure, there are all sorts of funny people among the leaders, and most of the best of them, even, have the annoying clique habits of the parliamentary regime, just as with you in America, but the masses are behind them and will either teach them manners or throw them overboard. There are still blunders enough, but the main danger has been weathered, and I now expect rapid progress, which will also react upon America.

In Germany the situation is coming to a crisis. A compromise is hardly possible after the recent reports of the [Reichstag] military commission's sessions; the government is making it impossible for the gentlemen of the Center and the Liberals to change sides, and without forty to fifty of them no majority is feasible. Hence dissolution and new elections. I expect 2,500,000 votes for us, *if things go well,* as we have grown at an amazing rate. Bebel expects fifty to sixty seats, for we have the election-district gerrymander against us and all the others are combining against us, so that we cannot convert even big minorities into majorities on the runoff ballots. I should prefer the thing to proceed peacefully until 1895, when we should create an altogether different effect, but whatever happens, everything must help us along, from the judge to Little Wilhelm.

F. Wiesen, a young man of Baird, Texas, has asked me for a statement against the putting up of candidates "for President," for we want to abolish the Presidency and that is a denial of revolutionary principle. I have sent him the enclosed reply; if it should be published *in curtailed form,* please have it printed in the *Volkszeitung....*

Your
F. Engels

ENCLOSURE

London, March 14, 1893

Mr. F. Wiesen
Baird, Texas, U.S.A.
Dear comrade:

Accumulated work prevented me from answering your lines of January 29th any earlier.

I do not see what violation of the social-democratic principle is necessarily involved in putting up candidates for any elective political office or in voting for these candidates, even if we are aiming at the abolition of this office itself.

One may be of the opinion that the best way to abolish the Presidency and the Senate in America is to elect men to these offices who are pledged to effect their abolition, and then one will consistently act accordingly. Others may think that this method is inappropriate; that's a matter of opinion. There may be circumstances under which the former mode of action would also involve a violation of revolutionary principle; I fail to see why that should always and everywhere be the case.

For the immediate goal of the labor movement is the conquest of political power for and by the working class. If we agree on that, the difference of opinion regarding the ways and means of struggle to be employed therein can scarcely lead to differences of principle among sincere people who have their wits about them. In my opinion those tactics are the best in each country that leads to the goal most certainly and in the shortest time. But we are yet very far from this goal precisely in America, and I believe I am not making a mistake in explaining the importance still attributed to such academic questions over there by this very circumstance. I leave it to your discretion to publish these remarks — unabridged.

Yours very sincerely,

F. Engels

ENGELS TO LLOYD[1]

[London, March 1893]

Dear Sir:

I have duly received your two favors of February 3rd and March 9th with enclosures. I very much regret that I shall not be able either to assist personally at your congresses or to supply the papers you ask me for. I should send them to you with the greatest pleasure, were it not that all my time is at present taken up with the manuscript of the third book of my late friend Karl Marx's great work on *Capital*, which I am preparing for publication. This third book ought to have been out years ago; but never until now could I secure that continued freedom from interruption which alone will enable me to finish my task. I have been compelled to decline all outside work, though ever so tempting, unless absolutely necessary. By the time your congress meets, the MS. ought to go to press, but this could not be, were I to accede to your request. For the work you ask me to do ought not to be journalistic commonplace; it ought to be the very best I can furnish; it would require mature study and thought, and that means a considerable amount of time, which for the reasons given I am not in a position to sacrifice.

I have, however, forwarded you per bookpost a copy of the Eng-

---

[1] This letter was written in English. Henry Demarest Lloyd, as Secretary of the Committee on Program and Correspondence of the World's Congress Auxiliary of the 1893 Columbian Exposition in Chicago, had asked Engels to read a paper on international labor congresses before the Labor Congress to be held at the exposition.

lish edition of the *Communist Manifesto* of 1848 (by K. Marx and myself) and another of my *Socialism, Utopian and Scientific,* published a few months ago, as a small tribute which I hope may prove of interest to some members of your Labor Congress.

F. Engels

ENGELS TO SORGE

London, May 17, 1893

Dear Sorge:

The Lincoln affair occurred while I was still in Manchester — at the end of 1864 — but I remember it only vaguely, nor have I ever come upon Lincoln's reply among my papers or those of Marx.[1] It is possible that it will come to light somewhere when I find time to classify and work over the enormous mass, but it is unthinkable without three or four weeks of work. All I can find is the following in Eichhoff's pamphlet on the International, Berlin 1868, p. 53 (based on Marx's notes and material):

"The re-election of Lincoln, assured by the election of November 8, 1864, furnished the General Council with an opportunity to send an address of congratulations. At the same time it called mass meetings in support of the Union's cause. That is why Lincoln expressly acknowledged the services of the International Workingmen's Association to the good cause."

In general I can only say that my materials on the I.W.A. *before 1870* are very incomplete — part of the minutes of the General Council, Marx's and Lessner's collections of newspaper clippings, as well as part of Becker's, and finally Marx's letters to me. I haven't even a complete file of the official documents of the General Council, proclamations, and the like, not to mention the correspondence of the secretaries, which nearly all of them kept for themselves. There are no official minutes of the Congresses in existence. None the less it is much better than anything anybody else has, and it will be worked up as soon as I can. But when? . . .

The atmosphere in Germany has changed greatly; the bourgeois

1 Sorge had been asked to obtain the text of Abraham Lincoln's letter thanking the General Council of the I.W.A. in London for its aid to the Union cause. Through publication of this letter it was hoped to obtain the pardon of the defendants in the Chicago Haymarket trial still in prison. See pp. 65-66 for the text of the General Council's address to Lincoln; the letter from the American Minister to Great Britain conveying Lincoln's reply is printed in Karl Marx and Frederick Engels, *The Civil War in the United States* (International Publishers, New York, 1937) , pp. 282-83.

press may still shriek in the old tone, but the respect that our people have gained for themselves in the Reichstag has won them an altogether different position. In addition, one can't close one's eyes to the steadily growing might of the party. If we again display considerable growth in the next elections, respect will increase on the one hand, as will fear on the other. And the later will then drive Messrs. Philistines unanimously into the arms of the government.

The May First demonstration here was very nice; but it is already becoming somewhat of an everyday or rather an annual matter; the first fresh bloom is gone. The narrow-mindedness of the Trades Council and of the socialist sects — Fabians and the S.D.F. — again compelled us to hold two demonstrations, but everything went off as we desired and we — the Eight-Hour Committee — had many more people than the united opposition. In particular, our international platform had a very good audience. I figure that there was a total of 240,000 in the park, of which we had 140,000 and the opposition at most 100,000. . . .

If we get a large increase in votes in Germany, it will have a good effect on the autumn elections in France as well. If our people there put a dozen men in the Chamber (they are counting on four seats in the Département du Nord alone), they'll have a nucleus that is strong enough to force the Blanquists and Allemanists to join them. . . .

F. Engels

ENGELS TO HOURWICH[1]

London, May 27, 1893

Dr. Isaac A. Hourwich,

Dear Sir:

Many thanks for your interesting study on the *Economics of the Russian Village* which I read, I hope, not without profit.

As to the burning questions of the Russian revolutionary movement, the part which the peasantry may be expected to take in it, these are subjects on which I could not conscientiously state an opinion for publication without previously studying over again the

[1] This letter was written in English. Hourwich had sent Engels a copy of his monograph, *The Economics of the Russian Village*, New York, 1892, with a request that Engels comment on Hourwich's views of the peasant problem in tsarist Russia.

whole subject and completing my very imperfect knowledge of the facts of the case by bringing it up to date. But for that, I am sorry to say, I have not at present the time. And then, I have every reason to doubt whether such a public statement by me would have the effect you expect of it. I know from my own experience (1849-1852) how unavoidably a political emigration splits itself up into a number of divergent factions so long as the mother-country remains quiet. The burning desire to act, face to face with the impossibility of doing anything effective, causes in many intelligent and energetic heads an overactive mental speculation, an attempt at discovering or inventing new and almost miraculous means of action. The word of an outsider would have but a trifling, and at best a passing, effect. If you have followed the Russian emigration literature of the last decade, you will yourself know how, for instance, passages from Marx's writings and correspondence have been interpreted in the most contradictory ways, exactly as if they had been texts from the classics or from the New Testament, by various sections of Russian emigrants. Whatever I might say on the subject you mention would probably share the same fate, if any attention was paid to it. And so for all these various reasons, I think it best for all whom it may concern, including myself, to abstain.

Yours very truly,
F. Engels

ENGELS TO SORGE

London, October 7, 1893

Dear Sorge:

We got back here on Friday, September 29th, and soon after received your letter of the 22nd. I was away for two months; I went to Cologne with Louise Kautsky, where we met Bebel and his wife; then we all traveled together *via* Mainz and Strasbourg to Zurich, whence I sneaked away for a week to Grisons, where I met a brother of mine. But I had had to promise that I would be back for the close of the Congress, and there *malgré moi* [in spite of me] they put on the closing scene, with me, that you have read about.[1] But that set the note for the whole trip, and my intention of traveling purely as a private individual was totally foiled. I stayed in Switzerland two weeks more and then left with Bebel for Vienna *via* Munich and Salzburg. There the parade began all over again. First I had to

[1] As honorary president of the Zurich Congress, Engels made the closing speech of the Congress.

attend a banquet, but there was room for only about six hundred, and the others also wanted to see me, so there was a mass meeting the evening before I left, where I also had to say a few words. From there *via* Prague to Berlin, and there, after an energetic protest against a planned mass meeting, I got off with a banquet, at which there were 3,000 to 4,000 people. All that was very nice of the people, but it's not for me. I am glad it's all over, and next time I shall demand a written agreement that I do not have to parade before the public, but am traveling as a private individual on private affairs. I was and am astonished at the grandeur of the reception I was given everywhere, but I prefer to leave that to the parliamentarians and popular speakers; that is part of *their* job, but hardly of mine.

But, otherwise, I found Germany completely revolutionized after seventeen years' absence — industry enormously developed, agriculture, big and small, *very much* improved, and as a result our movement progressing excellently. Our people themselves have had to win the bit of freedom they have — especially win it from the police and the *Landräte* [district administrators] *after* the respective laws had already been proclaimed on paper. And so you find a confident, firm demeanor, such as has never been found among the German bourgeois. Of course, there is much to be criticized in minor details — the party press, for instance, is not up to the level of the party, especially in Berlin — but the masses are excellent and usually better than the leaders or at least than many who have assumed the role of leaders. One can do everything with these people; they feel really happy only in the struggle, they live only for the struggle and are bored when their opponents don't give them any work to do. It is positively a fact that most of them would greet a new Socialist Law with scornful laughter, if not with actual rejoicing — for then they would have something new to do every day!

But alongside our Germans in the Reich the Austrians should not be forgotten either. They are not so far advanced on the whole as the Germans, but they are livelier, more French, more easily stirred to great deeds, but also to blunders. I prefer the average Austrian, as an individual, to the average German, the average Viennese worker to the Berliner, and as for the women, I prefer the Viennese working women by far. They possess such naïve originality, compared with which the reflected precociousness of the Berliners is insufferable. If Messrs. Frenchmen don't look out and return to their old tradition of revolutionary initiative soon, it may come to pass that the Austrians will take the wind out of their sails and strike the first blow at the next opportunity.

Moreover, Berlin and Vienna have become the most beautiful cities in the world, alongside Paris. London and New York are dirty holes in comparison, London in particular, which seems quite strange to us ever since our return.

Messieurs les Français [Messrs. Frenchmen] will have to prove their mettle in November. Twelve Marxists and four Blanquists, five Allemanists and two Broussists, besides a few independents and some twenty-four *Socialistes-radicaux* [Radical-Socialists] *à la* Millerand, are a sizable lump of yeast in the Chamber and they ought to produce a pretty fermentation *if* they stick together. I wonder whether they will? Most of the twelve Marxists are wholly unknown persons; Lafargue is missing, while Guesde, who is a much better speaker but also a much more credulous optimist, has a seat. I am very curious. Our Marxists had already concluded a sort of alliance with Millerand and Co. before the elections, which the Blanquists, and Vaillant in particular, now seem to have joined through their collaboration with Millerand's *Petite République Française.* The Blanquists are also now coming out very decidedly against the Russian alliance. But I have no direct news of the present status of the various parties, probably because they are not yet clear about it themselves.

I hope that you and your wife are in good health. Cordial regards to both of you from   Your

F. Engels

I saw De Leon and Sanial in Zurich. They did not impress me.

ENGELS TO SORGE

London, November 11, 1893

Dear Sorge:

. . . Read the article by Autolycus (Burgess) on the manifesto of the Fabians on the front page of today's *Workman's Times.* After having said for years that the emancipation of the working class can only be accomplished through the Great Liberal Party, and after having denounced all independent election activity, even against Liberal candidates, as concealed Toryism and proclaimed the permeation of the Liberal Party by socialist principles as the sole task of the socialists, these gentlemen now declare that the Liberals are traitors, that they will have nothing to do with them, and that the workers should put up candidates of their own at the next election without regard for Liberals or Tories, with the aid of £30,000 to be raised by the trade unions — if the latter do the

Fabians this favor, which certainly won't be the case. This is a complete *pater peccavi* [Father, I have sinned] of these arrogant bourgeois, who are graciously willing to condescend to emancipate the proletariat from above if it will only be sensible enough to realize that so raw and uneducated a mass cannot free itself and can achieve nothing except through the grace of these smart lawyers, literati, and sentimental females. And now the first effort of these gentlemen, announced with drums and trumpets as world-shaking, has failed so brilliantly that they must admit it themselves. That is the humorous aspect of the story. . . .

Yours,

F. E.

ENGELS TO SORGE

London, December 2, 1893

Dear Sorge:

. . . The repeal of the silver-purchase law has saved America from a severe money crisis and will promote industrial prosperity. But I don't know whether it wouldn't have been better for this crash to have actually occurred. The phrase "cheap money" seems to be bred deep in the bone of your Western farmers. First, they imagine that if there are lots of means of circulation in the country, the interest rate must drop, whereby they confuse means of circulation and available money capital, concerning which very enlightening things will be brought out in Volume III. Second, it suits all debtors to contract debts in good currency and to pay them off later in depreciated currency. That is why the debt-ridden Prussian Junkers also clamor for a double currency, which would provide them with a veiled Solonic riddance of their debts. Now if they had been able to wait with the silver reform in the United States until the consequences of the nonsense had also reacted upon the farmers, that would have opened many of their dense heads.

The tariff reform, slow as it is in getting started, does seem to have caused a sort of panic among the manufacturers in New England already. I hear — privately and from the papers — of the layoff of numerous workers. But that will calm down as soon as the law is pased and the uncertainty is over; I am convinced that America can boldly enter into competition with England in all the great branches of industry.

The German socialists in America are an annoying business. The people you get over there from Germany are usually not the best

— they stay here — and in any event they are not at all a fair sample of the German party. And as is the case everywhere, each new arrival feels himself called upon to turn everything he finds upside down, turning it into something *new,* so that a new epoch may date from himself. Moreover, most of these greenhorns remain stuck in New York for a long time or for life, continually reinforced by new additions and relieved of the necessity of learning the language of the country or of getting to know American conditions properly. All of that certainly causes much harm, but, on the other hand, it is not to be denied that American conditions involve very great and peculiar difficulties for a steady development of a workers' party.

First, the Constitution, based as in England upon party government, which causes every vote for any candidate not put up by one of the two governing parties to appear to be *lost.* And the American, like the Englishman, wants to influence his state; he does not throw his vote away.

Then, and more especially, immigration, which divides the workers into two groups: the native-born and the foreigners, and the latter in turn into (1) the Irish, (2) the Germans, (3) the many small groups, each of which understands only itself: Czechs, Poles, Italians, Scandinavians, etc. And then the Negroes. To form a single party out of these requires quite unusually powerful incentives. Often there is a sudden violent *élan,* but the bourgeois need only wait passively, and the dissimilar elements of the working class fall apart again.

Third, through the protective tariff system and the steadily growing domestic market the workers must have been exposed to a prosperity no trace of which has been seen here in Europe for years now (except in Russia, where, however, the bourgeois profit by it and not the workers).

A country like America, when it is really ripe for a socialist workers' party, certainly cannot be hindered from having one by the couple of German socialist doctrinaires.

Part I of Volume III (246 pages of ms., dating from about 1850) is ready for the printer. *This is between us*. It will now go ahead rapidly, I hope. . . .

Your
F. Engels

ENGELS TO SCHLUETER

[London] December 2, 1893

Dear Schlüter:

. . . Now you are at last on the road to getting rid of bimetallism and of the McKinley tariff; that will do much to promote developments over there, though a good silver crash would have been very good to enlighten the marvelously stupid American farmer and his cheap money. . . .

Yours,

F. E.

ENGELS TO SORGE

Eastbourne, February 23, 1894

Dear Sorge:

I am here again for a few weeks because of a temporary lameness; I shall be back in London in six days or so.

You will have received the announcement of Louise's marriage. Her husband, Dr. Freyberger, is a young Viennese physician who gave up his career at the University of Vienna because he wasn't allowed to tell the workers the *social* causes of their diseases, and who has now established himself here. He has already shown the British that they learn more medicine on the Continent than they do here! For the present all of us are staying in Regent's Park Road. . . .

Our singular socialist group in the French Chamber is still somewhat mysterious. Neither its numbers nor its tendency is very clear as yet. Guesde is introducing a whole stack of bills, none of which will be passed, of course. Jaurès' initial sensational victories will hardly be repeated, as the anarchists' bomb-throwing has quickly succeeded in providing a stable majority for the Cabinet and the cause of law and order.

Complete disorganization prevails here among the official politicians, both among the Liberals and the Conservatives. The Liberals can maintain their position only through new political and social concessions to the workers, but they lack the courage to do so. Hence they are trying an election cry against the House of Lords, proposing a second ballot and payment of election expenses by the government instead of payment of members. That is, they merely want to give the bourgeoisie more power against the lords instead of offering the workers more power against the bourgeoisie *and* the lords, and the workers aren't being taken in by this any more. In any event we shall have general elections here next summer, and if the Liberals don't pluck up a great deal of courage and make *real* concessions to the workers, they will be defeated and will fall apart. They are being kept together now by Gladstone alone, who may give up the ghost any day. Then there will be a bourgeois-democratic party with pro-labor tendencies, and the rest of the Liberals will go over to Chamberlain. And all of this is taking place under the pressure of the working class, still disunited and half-unconscious. If the latter gradually becomes conscious things will take an altogether different turn.

Something violent may happen any day in Italy. The bourgeois have maintained all the horrors of decaying feudalism, grafting on it their own infamies and oppression. The country is at the end of its resources; a change must take place, but the Socialist Party is still *very* weak and *very* confused, although there are some rather able Marxists in it.

Something is also to be expected in Austria. Down there we have the comical sight of the Socialists having the support of the Emperor, who, by approving the Taaffe election reform plan, has come out for an approximation to universal suffrage, and actually believes that this is a necessary complement to universal military service. The coalition Cabinet won't accomplish anything, or if it does succeed in having an election law passed, that will be taken solely as a payment on account, and the movement will continue calmly, with the tacit approval of the Emperor, until at least Taaffe's reform is effected. And then our people will take care of the rest.

In short, things are moving merrily everywhere, and the *fin de siècle* [end of the century] is being prepared for more and more prettily.

The *Workman's Times* seems to be in its death throes. Nor is the Independent Labor Party much more alive; it is remarkable how slowly and in what zigzag fashion everything moves here.

Many regards to you and your wife from the two Freybergers and
Your

F. Engels

ENGELS TO SORGE

London, March 21, 1894

Dear Sorge:

. . . Over here things are moving full speed ahead toward dissolution of Parliament. There will be more worker candidates put up in the elections than ever before, but far from enough, and I am not sure but that a whole lot of them will be put up with Tory money. Both the Liberals and the Tories hold fast to the indirect eligibility qualification that is implied in burdening the candidates with all the costs of election — from £100 as a minimum to £400-£600 and even more for the *official* costs alone: polling places, and the like. So when the workers fall into the clutches of Champion, who offers them £100 per constituency (he got the money from the soap manufacturer Hudson), the Liberals have no cause to complain. In general, they are approaching the elections with a remarkably obstinate misunderstanding of the situation. They act as if they want to abolish the *House of Lords,* but they refuse to change the *House of Commons* in such a way (by strengthening the power of the workers) as to enable it to do something by itself. On the other hand, the Tories are more stupid than ever before, and that's saying a good deal. For two years they have been actually playing hob with the Liberal government in both Houses. The Liberals have stood for it quietly, and the philistine, who has grown conservative en masse, has liked it because it was done under the pretext of over-throwing the treasonable anti-Empire Home Rule Bill and Home Rule government. But now they are continuing the game with serious English measures, and that might become a bit too out-rageous for the pacific philistine. So the matter is very uncertain, and the elections will at any rate yield surprising results: strengthening of the workers in any event, with the Liberals under the necessity of making further concessions to the workers.

Electoral reform is likewise the order of the day in Austria, Belgium, and Holland; soon there won't be a parliament in Europe without workers' representatives. The cause is going very well in Austria: Adler is leading the movement with quite excellent skill, and Sunday's party convention will help along.

After the tariff business is put in order somewhat over there and the import duty on raw materials is abolished, the crisis will prob-ably subside and the superiority of American over European industry will have a telling effect. Only then will things grow serious here in England; but then they'll do so rapidly. . . .

Yours,

F. Engels

ENGELS TO SORGE

London, May 12, 1894

Dear Sorge:

. . . For the past fifteen years, off and on, I have had trouble with my eyes. I have followed medical advice and have reached the point where they don't bother me at all so long as I don't write too much by artificial light.

I had a cold during the past few days which convinces me that I am an old man at last. What I used to be able to treat as a trifle laid me rather low for a week and kept me for fully two weeks more under medical police-supervision. Even now I am supposed to be careful for another two weeks. It was a mild bronchitis, and among the elderly that can never be taken lightly, particularly when they have tippled as freely and merrily as I have. Taking care is hard enough for me, but after all Freyberger is right when he orders me to do so, and then, as far as carrying it out is concerned, Louise sees to that, watching over me with double and triple Argus eyes. I think I wrote you already that we have left our domestic establishment as much unchanged as possible by taking the young husband in as a boarder. That is very nice and cheerful, but alas, only as long as one is well. I have never been so badgered medically in all my life, and, I must end up by consoling myself with the thought that it's all being done for my own good. . . .

Things here are as always. No possibility of obtaining any unity among the labor leaders. But none the less the *masses* are moving forward, slowly, to be sure, and just wrestling for consciousness, but yet unmistakably. Things will develop here as they are doing in France and as they did in Germany: unity will be forced as soon as a number of independent workers (especially those not elected with Liberal aid) are in Parliament. The Liberals are doing their best to prevent this. (1) They don't even extend the franchise to those who already possess it *on paper;* (2) on the contrary, they are making the voters' lists more expensive *for the candidates* than before, since they are to be drawn up twice a year and the costs of drawing them up *correctly* are borne by the candidates or the representatives of the political *parties,* and not by the state; and they expressly refuse (3) the transfer of election costs to the state or the municipality, as well as (4) members' salaries, and (5) runoff elections. All these retentions of old abuses are a forthright prohibition of eligibility for worker candidates in three-quarters of the constituencies. Parliament is to remain a *rich men's club.* And this at a time when the rich are all turning Conservative because they are satisfied with the *status quo,* and the Liberal Party is *dying out* and growing more and more dependent upon workers' votes. But the Liberals insist that the workers should elect *only* bourgeois, no workers and certainly no independent workers.

This will ruin the Liberals. Their lack of courage is losing workers' votes for them throughout the country, is dissolving their small majority in Parliament, and if they don't take *very bold* steps at the eleventh hour, they are most likely lost. Then the Tories take over and *carry out* what the Liberals were really supposed to do — and not merely to promise. And then an independent workers' party is fairly certain.

The Social-Democratic Federation here shares with your German-American Socialists the distinction of being the only parties that have managed to reduce the Marxian theory of development to a rigid orthodoxy, which the workers are not to reach themselves by their own class feeling, but which they have to gulp down as an article of faith at once and without development. That is why both of them remain mere sects and come, as Hegel says, from nothing through nothing to nothing. I haven't had time as yet to read Schlüter's polemic with your Germans, but shall look through it tomorrow. From former articles in the *Volkszeitung* the right tone seems to have been struck. . . .

Cordial regards,

Yours,

F. E.

ENGELS TO SORGE

London, November 10, 1894

Dear Sorge:

. . . The movement over here still resembles the American movement, save that it is *somewhat* ahead of you. The mass instinct that the workers must form a party of their own against the two official parties is getting stronger and stronger; it again showed itself more than ever in the municipal elections on November 1st. But the various old traditional memories, and the lack of people able to turn this instinct into conscious action and to organize it all over the country, encourage the persistence, in this early stage, of haziness of thought and local isolation of action. Anglo-Saxon sectarianism prevails in the labor movement, too. The Social-Democratic Federation, just like your German Socialist Labor Party, has managed to transform our theory into the rigid dogma of an orthodox sect; it is narrow-mindedly exclusive and, thanks to Hyndman, it has a thoroughly rotten tradition in international politics, which is shaken from time to time, to be sure, but which hasn't been broken with as yet. The Independent Labor Party is extremely indefinite in its tactics, and its leader Keir Hardie is a supercunning Scot, whose demagogic tricks can't be trusted for a minute. Although he's a poor devil of a Scottish coal miner, he has founded a big weekly, *The Labour Leader,* which couldn't have been established without considerable money, and he is getting this money from Tory or Liberal-Unionist, that is, anti-Gladstone and anti-Home Rule, sources. There can be no doubt about it, and his notorious literary connections in London as well as direct reports and his political attitude confirm it. Consequently, owing to the desertion of the Irish and Radical voters, he may very easily lose his seat in Parliament at the 1895 general elections and that would be a stroke of luck — the man is the greatest obstacle at present. He appears in Parliament only on demagogic occasions, in order to cut a figure with phrases about the unemployed without accomplishing anything, or to address imbecilities to the Queen on the occasion of the birth of a prince, which is infinitely hackneyed and cheap in this country, and so forth. Otherwise there are very good elements both in the S.D.F. and in the I.L.P., especially in the provinces, but they are scattered, although they have at least managed to foil all the efforts of the leaders to incite the two organizations against each other. John Burns stands pretty much alone politically; he is being viciously attacked both by Hyndman and by Keir Hardie and acts as if he despairs of the political organization of the workers and sets his hopes solely on the trade unions. To be sure, he has had bad experiences with the former and might starve if the Engineers' Union didn't pay him his Parliamentary salary. He is vain and has allowed himself to be rather thoroughly ensnared by the Liberals, that is, by the "social wing" of the Radicals. He attaches altogether too much importance to the many single concessions that he has forced through, but with all that he is the only really honest fellow in the whole movement, that is, among the leaders, and he has a thoroughly proletarian instinct which will, I believe, guide him more correctly at the decisive moment than cunning and not disinterested calculation will the others.

On the Continent success is developing the appetite for more success, and catching the peasant, in the literal sense of the word, is becoming the fashion. First the French, in Nantes, declare through Lafargue not only (what I had written to them) that it is not our business to hasten by our direct interference the ruin of the small peasants, which capitalism is effecting for us, but they add that we must *protect* the small peasant directly against taxation, usury, and big landowners. But we cannot join in this, first because it is stupid, and second because it is impossible. And now Vollmar comes along in Frankfurt, wanting to bribe the *peasantry as a whole,* though the peasant he has to deal with in Upper Bavaria is not the debt-ridden small peasant of the Rhineland, but the middle and even the big peasant, who exploits male and female farmhands and sells cattle and grain in quantity. And that cannot be done without giving up the whole principle. We can win the Alpine peasants and the Lower Saxon and Schleswig-Holstein rich peasants only if we sacrifice the fieldhands and day laborers to them, and in doing that we lose even more politically than we gain. The Frankfurt Party Convention did not take a stand on the question, and that is to the good in so far as the matter will now be studied thoroughly; the people who were there knew far too little about the peasantry and rural conditions, which vary so fundamentally in different provinces, to have been able to do anything but make decisions in the air. But the matter has to be decided some time all the same. . . .

After the Belgian election victories the Belgians and the French are preparing for regular contact between the Socialist parliamentarians of the various countries, with periodic conferences. It is questionable whether anything will come of it. For the present the fifty French parliamentarians (of whom about twenty-six are converted Radicals of doubtful quality) are talking very big, but there's a hitch in the affair: among the twenty-four original Socialists the Marxists are privately wrangling in capital style with the Blanquists on the one hand and with the Allemanists (possibilists) on the other. Whether it will come to an open break is uncertain.

In addition to the other socialist papers I now get the Rumanian (*Muncaz*) and the Bulgarian (formerly the *Rabotnik,* now the *Socialist*), and I am gradually familiarizing myself with the languages. The Rumanians are going to get out a daily paper in Bucharest.

Of the other world events the death of the Russian Tsar will probably bring about a change, either through inner movement or through the financial difficulties and the impossibility of getting money abroad. I cannot imagine that the present system will outlast the change of sovereigns, which brings an idiot, physically and mentally deranged by masturbation, to the helm. (This fact is notorious in all the medical faculties; Professor Krause of Dorpat, who had Nicholas under observation, told Tsar Alexander straight to his face, at the latter's request, that this, the masturbation, was the cause of the illness. Thereupon he got a slap in the face from the Tsar, resigned, returned the Order of St. Vladimir that had been sent after him, and went back to Germany, where he is now telling the story.) If things start in Russia, however, Young Wilhelm will also notice something in Germany. Then a liberal wind will blow through all Europe, which can only be helpful to us *now*.

The war in China has given the old China a deathblow. Isolation has become impossible; the introduction of railways, steam engines, electricity, and large-scale industry has become a necessity if only for reasons of military defense. But with it the old economic system of small peasant agriculture, where the family also made its industrial products itself, falls to pieces too, and with it the whole old social system which made relatively dense population possible. Millions will be turned out and forced to emigrate; and the millions will find their way to Europe, en masse. But as soon as Chinese competition sets in on a mass scale, it will rapidly bring things to a head in your country and over here, and thus the conquest of China by capitalism will at the same time furnish the impulse for the overthrow of capitalism in Europe and America. . . .

Yours,

F. Engels

ENGELS TO SORGE

London, December 4, 1894

Dear Sorge:

Thanks for your and your wife's birthday greetings! Between us, the 75th isn't starting off as sturdily as its predecessors. I am still fresh and quick on my feet, fond of my work too and comparatively able-bodied, but I find that stomach upsets and colds, which I used to be able to treat with sovereign disdain, now require very respectful treatment. But that's nothing, if there's nothing else. . . .

The Bavarians, who have become very, very opportunistic and are *almost* an ordinary populist party by now (that is to say, most of the leaders and many of those who have recently joined the party), had voted for the budget as a whole in the Bavarian Diet. Vollmar, in particular, had started agitation among the peasantry in order to win over, *not the farm hands,* but the well-to-do peasants of Upper Bavaria—people who own 25 to 80 acres of land (10 to 30 hectares), who therefore *cannot manage at all without wage laborers.* They didn't expect anything good to come of the Frankfurt party convention. They therefore organized a special Bavarian party convention *a week before* the former, and there they established a downright separatist federation by agreeing that the Bavarian delegates at

Frankfurt should vote *in a bloc* on all Bavarian questions in accordance with the Bavarian resolutions already agreed upon. They came to Frankfurt, declared that they had to vote for the over-all budget in Bavaria, it couldn't be avoided, and that, furthermore, this was a purely Bavarian question that did not concern anyone else. In other words: if you vote anything that we Bavarians find unwelcome, if you reject our ultimatum, then you are to blame if a split occurs!

They appeared before the other delegates, who were unprepared for all this, with these demands, hitherto unheard of in the party. And since the cry for unity had been pushed to the utmost during the past few years, no wonder that this viewpoint (under which the party cannot exist) slipped through, in view of the many new adherents won in recent years, and no decision was reached on the budget question.

Now imagine that the Prussians, who are in the majority at the convention, also should want to hold a preliminary convention and adopt resolutions on the position of the Bavarians or other matters that would be binding on all Prussian delegates, so that all the delegates, the majority as well as the minority, voted en bloc for these resolutions—what would then be the use of general party conventions altogether? And what would the Bavarians say if the Prussians were to do exactly what they have just done?

In short, the matter could not be allowed to remain as it was, and so Bebel sprang into the breach. He has just placed the question on the agenda again, and it is now being debated. Bebel is by far the clearest and most farseeing head of them all; I have been in regular correspondence with him for some fifteen years, and we nearly always are in agreement. Liebknecht, on the other hand, has dried up in his ideas considerably; the old South German-federalistic-particularistic democrat still breaks out in him; and, what is worst of all, he cannot stand having Bebel (who outgrew him long ago) gladly allow him to be at his side but no longer let him manage him. Moreover, he has organized the central organ *Vorwärts* so badly—mostly because of jealousy of his leadership (with him wanting to manage everything and actually managing nothing, so that he hampers everything)—that the paper, which could be the biggest one in Berlin, is only fit to yield the party a surplus of 50,000 marks, but no political influence. Liebknecht, of course, now wants to play the conciliator by main force and is scolding Bebel, but I think the latter will gain his point. In Berlin the party executive and our people are already on his side, and I am convinced that he will get a large majority if he appeals to the party membership. For the present we'll have to wait. I would send you the Vollmariades, etc., too, but I have only one copy for my own use. . . .

Your old
F. E.

ENGELS TO SCHLUETER

London, January 1, 1895

Dear Schlüter:

Your letter of August 11 is still unanswered, and I still owe you my thanks for the Census Compendium, which I received in good order. But I have been overburdened with all sorts of work, and the urgent party and business correspondence has made it almost impossible for me to carry on any private correspondence; Sorge has also had to suffer this fate. You will have heard from him that Louise Kautsky is now married to Dr. Freyberger and the mother of a strong and healthy little girl, and that we have all moved together to 41, Regent's Park Road.

As Sorge will have told you, I have sent you a copy of Volume III of *Capital,* addressed to the *Volkszeitung* because I don't know whether your Hoboken address is still good. In any event, the *Volkszeitung* seemed safer to me. I couldn't carry out your commission concerning Ede, as the latter had been engaged for *Die Neue Zeit* in the same capacity long ago.[1] I should have written you this; please excuse me.

Over here things are going about as they are over there. The socialist instinct is becoming ever stronger among the *masses,* but whenever the instinctive drives have to be converted into clear demands and ideas, the people fall asunder. Some join the Social-Democratic Federation, others the Independent Labour Party, still others stay in the Trades Union Organization, etc., etc. In short, a lot of sects and no party. Almost all the leaders are unreliable, the candidates for the top leadership are very numerous but far from outstandingly fitted for the job, and the two big bourgeois parties stand ready, money bag in hand, to buy up whomever they can. For the so-called "democracy" over here is largely limited by *indirect* restrictions. A periodical costs a tremendous amount of money, as does a candidacy for Parliament and living as a member of Parliament — if only because of the enormous correspondence it

---

[1] Schlüter had apparently asked that Engels secure Eduard Bernstein as the London correspondent of the *New-Yorker Volkszeitung.*

entails. Revision of the miserably kept voters' lists likewise costs lots of money, and up to now only the two official parties can defray the costs. Hence, anyone who does not sell himself to one of these parties finds it hard to become a candidate. In all these matters people over here are far behind the Continent, and they are beginning to realize it. Then there is no second ballot, the relative majority or, as you Americans say, a plurality being sufficient for election. Everything is arranged with *only two* parties in mind; a third party can at most tip the balance one way or the other until it is as strong as the other two.

Nor are the local trade unions able to bring off anything like the Berlin beer boycott — an arbitration court like the one achieved there is still something unattainable over here.

On the other hand (as is the case with you in America), once the workers know what they want, then the state, the land, the industries, everything will belong to them.

All this is for you, not for the *Volkszeitung*.

Louise sends you her best regards, and both of us wish you a Happy New Year!

Yours,

F. Engels

ENGELS TO SORGE

London, January 16, 1895

Dear Sorge:

. . . The temporary decline of the movement in America has attracted my attention for some time now, and the German socialists won't stop it. America is the *youngest,* but also the *oldest* country in the world. Over there you have old-fashioned furniture styles alongside those you have invented all yourselves, cabs in Boston such I last saw in 1838 in London, and in the mountains stagecoaches dating from the seventeenth century alongside the Pullman cars. and in the same way you keep all the intellectual old clothes discarded in Europe. Anything that is out of date over here can survive in America for one or two generations. Karl Heinzen, for instance, not to mention religious and spiritualist superstition. Thus the old Lassalleans still survive among you, and men like Sanial, who would be superannuated in France today, can still play a role over there. That is due, on the one hand, to the fact that America is only now beginning to have time, beyond concern for material production and enrichment, for free intellectual labor and the preparatory education that this requires; and, on the other hand, to the duality of American development, which is still engaged in the *primary* task — clearing the tremendous virgin area—but is already compelled to enter the competition for first place in industrial production. Hence the ups and downs of the movement, depending upon whether the mind of the industrial worker or that of the pioneering farmer gains predominance in the average man's head. Things will be different in a couple of years, and then great progress will be observed. For the development of the Anglo-Saxon race with its old Germanic freedom is quite peculiar, slow, zigzag in form (here in England small zigzags, in your country colossal ones), a tacking against the wind, but it advances none the less.

Things will be very complicated here in Europe during the new year. The peasant problem in Germany has been pushed to the background by the Sedition Bill, and this has been accomplished by Young Wilhelm (his song to Angir, the ruler of the waves, is merely the result of the seasickness he always gets, and that is why he always sails with his fleet to the calm Norwegian fjords). The young man has thrown everything in Germany into disorder; no one knows where he stands or what will happen tomorrow. The confusion in the governing groups, as in the ruling classes in general, is increasing day by day, so that the only ones with smiling faces in the debate on the Sedition Bill were our people. It is too good: the antirevolutionists are headed by the man who can't abstain from revolutionizing for five minutes. And now this Young Wilhelm has fallen into the hands of the Junkers, who, in order to keep him in the mood in which he is ready to give them augmented state aid for their bankrupt estates, are now enticing him with the prospect of new taxes and new soldiers and warships through their haughty advocacy of the *regis voluntas suprema lex* [the king's will is the supreme law], and are forcing him to dissolution of the Reichstag and a *coup d'état*. Yet these Messrs. Köller and Co., who are so overbearing in their phrases, have so little courage that they are already feeling all sorts of uneasiness, and it is still doubtful whether they won't grow afraid at the moment for action.

And then France! There, as in Italy, the bourgeoisie has plunged head over heels into corruption in a way that would put America to shame. For three years everything in both of these countries has turned on finding a bourgeois cabinet that is — not free of corruption — yet so little compromised *directly* in scandals that have come to *public notice,* as to be capable of support by Parliament without outraging the commonest decency too violently.

In Italy Crispi is holding on for a little while only because the

King and the Crown Prince are as deeply involved in the bank scandals as he is himself. In France our forty-five to fifty Socialist deputies have now effected the fall of a Cabinet for the third time, because of direct corruption, and Casimir-Périer tumbled after it. Presumably he wants to have himself re-elected by an immense majority as the sole savior of society, thus obtaining a stronger position. But that is a hazardous game. In any event everything is shaky in France, too, and we may have new elections this year in Germany and France in addition to Britain, this time of *decisive* importance. What is more, a crisis of the first rank in Italy, and an unavoidable reform of the suffrage in Austria; in short, things are becoming critical throughout Europe. . . .

Your

F. E.

APPENDICES

I

PREFACE TO THE RUSSIAN TRANSLATION OF *LETTERS FROM J. F. BECKER, J. DIETZGEN, F. ENGELS, K. MARX, AND OTHERS TO F. A. SORGE AND OTHERS*

By V. I. Lenin

The collection of letters by Marx, Engels, Dietzgen, Becker, and other leaders of the international labor movement of the past century here presented to the Russian public is a needed addition to our foremost Marxist literature.

We will not dwell in detail here on the importance of these letters for the history of socialism and for a comprehensive treatment of the activities of Marx and Engels. This aspect of the matter requires no explanation. We shall only note that an understanding of the published letters necessitates an acquaintance with the principal works on the history of the International (see Jaeckh, *The International*, Russian translation in the *Znaniye* edition), on the history of the German and American labor movements (see Franz Mehring, *History of German Social-Democracy*, and Morris Hillquit, *History of Socialism in the United States*), etc.

Neither do we intend here to attempt a general outline of the contents of this correspondence or to appraise the importance of the various historical periods with which it deals. Mehring has done this extremely well in his article, *"Der Sorgesche Briefwechsel"*[1]. . . .

The lessons that the militant proletariat must draw from an acquaintance with the intimate sides of Marx's and Engels' activities over the course of nearly thirty years (1867-1895) are of particular interest to Russian Socialists in the present revolutionary period. It is, therefore, not surprising that in our Social-Democratic literature the first endeavors to acquaint the readers with Marx's and Engels' letters to Sorge were made in connection with the "burning" issues of Social-Democratic tactics in the Russian revolution (Plekhanov's *Sovremennaya Zhizn* and the Menshevik *Otkliki*). And it is to an appreciation of those passages in the published correspondence that are especially important from the standpoint of the contemporary tasks of the workers' party in Russia that we intend to draw the attention of our readers.

Marx and Engels deal most frequently in their letters with the burning questions of the British, American, and German labor movements. This is natural, because they were Germans who at that time lived in England and corresponded with their American comrades. Marx expressed himself

[1] "The Sorge Correspondence," *Die Neue Zeit*, Vol. 25, Nos. 1 and 2.

much more frequently and in much greater detail on the French labor movement, and particularly on the Paris Commune, in the letters he wrote to the German Social-Democrat, Kugelmann.[1]

A comparison of the comments by Marx and Engels on the Anglo-American and German labor movements is highly instructive. This comparison acquires all the greater importance when we remember that Germany on the one hand, and England and America on the other, represent different stages of capitalist development and different forms of domination by the bourgeoisie, as a class, of the entire political life of these countries. From the scientific standpoint, what we observe here is a sample of materialist dialectics, of the ability to bring out and stress the different points and different sides of a question in accordance with the specific peculiarities of various political and economic conditions. From the standpoint of the practical policy and tactics of the workers' party, what we see here is a sample of the way in which the creators of the *Communist Manifesto* defined the tasks of the militant proletariat in accordance with the different stages of the national labor movement in various countries.

What Marx and Engels most of all criticize in British and American socialism is its isolation from the labor movement. The burden of all their numerous comments on the Social Democratic Federation in England and on the American Socialists is the accusation that they have reduced Marxism to a dogma, to a "rigid (*starre*) orthodoxy," that they consider it "a *credo* and not a *guide* to action,"[2] that they are incapable of adapting themselves to the theoretically helpless, but living, powerful, mass labor movement marching past them.

"Had we from 1864 to 1873 insisted on working together only with those who openly adopted our platform," Engels exclaims in his letter of January 27, 1887, "where should we be today?"[3] And in an earlier letter (December 28, 1886), in reference to the influence of the ideas of Henry George on the American working class, he writes:

"A million or two of workingmen's votes next November for a *bona fide* workingmen's party is worth infinitely more at present than a hundred thousand votes for a doctrinally perfect platform."[4]

These are very interesting passages. There are Social-Democrats in our country who hastened to make use of them in defense of the idea of a "labor congress" or something along the lines of Larin's "broad labor party." Why not in defense of a "Left bloc," we would ask these precipitate "utilizers" of Engels. The letters from which the quotations are taken relate to a time when the American workers voted at the elections for Henry George. Mrs. [Florence Kelley] Wischnewetzky—an American who married a Russian and who translated Engels' works—asked him, as may be seen from Engels' reply, to make a thorough criticism of Henry George. Engels writes (December 28, 1886) *that the time has not yet come* for that,

---

[1] Karl Marx, *Letters to Kugelmann*, International Publishers, 1934.
[2] See p. 163.
[3] See p. 168.
[4] See p. 167.

for it is better to let the workers' party begin to consolidate itself, even if on a not altogether immaculate program. Later on the workers will themselves come to understand what is at stake, will "learn from their own mistakes," but "anything that might delay or prevent that national consolidation of the workingmen's party—on no matter what platform— I should consider a great mistake. . . ." [1]

Engels, of course, perfectly understood and frequently pointed out all the absurdity and *reactionary character* of the ideas of Henry George from the *Socialist* standpoint. In the Sorge correspondence there is a most interesting letter from Karl Marx dated June 20, 1881, in which he characterizes Henry George as an ideologist of the *radical bourgeoisie*. "Theoretically the man [Henry George] is utterly backward (*total arrière*)," wrote Marx.[2] Yet Engels was not afraid to join with this veritable *social reactionary* in the elections, provided there were people who could warn the masses of "the consequences of their own mistakes" (Engels, in the letter dated November 29, 1886).[3]

Regarding the Knights of Labor, an organization of American workers existing at that time, Engels wrote in the same letter:

"The weakest (literally: rottenest, *faulste*) side of the K. of L. was their *political neutrality*. . . . The first great step of importance for every country newly entering into the movement is always the constitution of the workers as an independent political party, no matter how, so long as it is a distinct workers' party." [4]

It is obvious that absolutely nothing in defense of a leap *from* Social-Democracy to a non-party labor congress, etc., can be deduced from this. But whoever wants to escape Engels' accusation of degrading Marxism to a "dogma," "orthodoxy," "sectarianism," etc., must conclude from this that a joint election campaign with radical "social-reactionaries" is sometimes permissible.

But what is more interesting, of course, is to dwell not so much on these American-Russian parallels (we had to touch on them to answer our opponents), as on the *fundamental* characteristics of the British and American labor movement. These characteristics are: the absence of any big, nationwide, *democratic* problems whatever facing the proletariat; the complete subjection of the proletariat to bourgeois politics; the sectarian isolation of groups, handfuls of Socialists from the proletariat; not the slightest success of the Socialists in the elections among the working masses, etc. Whoever forgets these fundamental conditions and sets out to draw broad conclusions from "American-Russian parallels" displays extreme superficiality.

If Engels lays so much stress on the economic organizations of the workers in such circumstances, it is because he is dealing with the most firmly established democratic systems, which confront the proletariat with purely socialist tasks.

If Engels stresses the importance of an independent workers' party, even though with a bad program, it is because he is dealing with countries

[1] See p. 167.
[2] See p. 128.
[3] See p. 164.
[4] See p. 163.

where hitherto there had not been even a hint of political independence of the workers, where, in politics above all, the workers trailed, and still trail, after the bourgeoisie.

It would be making a mockery of Marx's historical method to attempt to apply the conclusions drawn from such considerations to countries or historical situations where the proletariat had established its party before the bourgeois liberals, where the proletariat does not have even the ghost of a tradition of voting for bourgeois politicians, and where it is not socialist, but bourgeois-democratic tasks that are up for immediate decision.

Our thought will become even clearer to the reader if we compare Engels' opinions of the British and American movements with his opinions of the German movement.

There is an abundance of such opinions in the published correspondence, and extremely interesting ones. And what runs like a red thread through all these opinions is something quite different, namely, a warning against the "right wing" of the workers' party, a merciless (sometimes—as with Marx in 1877-79—a *furious*) war upon *opportunism* in Social-Democracy.

Let us first confirm this by quotations from the letters, and then make an evaluation of this phenomenon.

First of all, we must here note the opinions expressed by Marx on Höchberg and Co. Franz Mehring, in his article *"Der Sorgesche Briefwechsel,"* endeavors to tone down Marx's attacks, as well as Engels' subsequent attacks on the opportunists—excessively so in our opinion. As regards Höchberg and Co. in particular, Mehring insists on his view that Marx's judgment of Lassalle and the Lassalleans was incorrect.[1] But, we repeat, what interests us here is not an historical appraisal of whether Marx's attacks on particular Socialists were correct or exaggerated, but appraisal *in principle* of definite *currents* in socialism on the whole.

While complaining about the compromises of the German Social-Democrats with the Lassalleans and with Dühring (letter of October 19, 1877), Marx also condemns the compromise "with a whole gang of half-mature students and super-wise doctors" ("doctor" in German is a scientific degree corresponding to our "candidate" or "university graduate, class I"), "who want to give socialism a 'higher, ideal' turn, that is to say, to replace its materialist basis (which calls for serious, objective study by anyone) by modern mythology, with its goddessess of Justice, Freedom, Equality, and Fraternity. Dr. Höchberg, who publishes the *Zukunft,* is a representative of this tendency and has 'bought his way' into the party—with the 'noblest' intentions, I assume, but I do not give a damn for 'intentions.' Anything more miserable than his program or the *Zukunft* has seldom seen the light of day with more 'modest' presumption.' " [2]

In another letter, written almost two years later (September 19, 1879). Marx rebuts the gossip that Engels and he were behind J. [*Johann*] *Most,*

---

[1] Documents discovered in Berlin in 1924, revealing relations between Lassalle and Bismarck, proved that Marx was right and Mehring wrong.—*Ed.*

[2] See pp. 116-17.

and he gives Sorge a detailed account of his attitude towards the opportunists in the German Social-Democratic Party. The *Zukunft* was run by Höchberg, Schramm, and Ed. Bernstein. Marx and Engels *refused* to participate in such a publication, and when the question was raised of establishing a new party organ with the participation of this same Höchberg and with his financial assistance, Marx and Engels first demanded the acceptance of their nominee, Hirsch, as responsible editor to exercise control over this "crew of doctors, students and professorial socialists" and then directly addressed a circular letter to Bebel, Liebknecht, and other leaders of the Social-Democratic Party, warning them that they would openly combat "such dissipation *(Verluderung—an even stronger* word in German) of the party and its theory," unless the tendency of Höchberg, Schramm, and Bernstein changed.

This was the period in the German Social-Democratic Party that Mehring described in his *History* as "a year of confusion" *(Ein Jahr der Verwirrung)*. After the Anti-Socialist Law, the party did not at once find the right path, first swinging over to the anarchism of Most and the opportunism of Höchberg and Co.

"These fellows," Marx writes of the latter, "zeros theoretically, incompetent practically — want to take the teeth out of socialism (which they have trimmed up according to university recipes) and out of the Social-Democratic Party in particular, to enlighten the workers or, as they put it, feed them 'the elements of education' through their confused half-knowledge, and, above all, to make the party respectable in the eyes of the philistine. They are poor counter-revolutionary windbags." The result of Marx's "furious" attack was that the opportunists retreated and disappeared from sight. In a letter of November 19, 1879, Marx announces that Höchberg has been removed from the editorial board and that all the influential leaders of the party—Bebel, Liebknecht, Bracke, etc.—have *repudiated* his ideas. The Social-Democratic Party organ, the *Sozialdemokrat*, began to appear under the editorship of Vollmar, who at that time belonged to the revolutionary wing of the party. A year later (November 5, 1880), Marx relates that he and Engels were constantly combating the "miserable" way in which the *Sozialdemokrat* was being managed and often clashed *sharply (wobei's oft scharf hergeht.)*[1] Liebknecht visited Marx in 1880 and promised an "improvement" in *all respects.*

Peace was restored, and the war never came out into the open. Höchberg retired, and Bernstein became a revolutionary Social-Democrat—at least until Engels' death in 1895.

On June 20, 1882, Engels writes to Sorge and speaks of this struggle as already a thing of the past:

"In Germany things are going ahead excellently on the whole. To be sure, Messrs. Literati of the party have tried to turn it toward reactionary, tame-bourgeois education, but this failed utterly. The infamies to which the Social-Democratic workers are everywhere subjected have made them everywhere much more revolutionary than they were even three years ago. . . . These people (the party literati) would like to beg off the

[1] See p. 123.

Socialist Law at any price by mildness, meekness, toadying, and tameness, because it makes short work of their literary earnings. As soon as the law is abolished . . . the split will probably become an open one, and the Vierecks, Höchbergs, etc., will form a separate Right wing, where we can negotiate with them from case to case until they finally collapse. We said this immediately after the passage of the Socialist Law, when Höchberg and Schramm published in the *Jahrbuch* what was under the circumstances a quite infamous estimate of the party's activity up to that time and demanded of the party more 'eddicated' (*jebildetes* instead of *gebildetes*— Engels is alluding to the Berlin accent of the German literati), respectable, Sunday-best manners." [1]

This forecast of a Bernsteiniad made in 1882 was strikingly confirmed in 1898 and subsequent years. And from that time on, particularly after Marx's death, Engels, it may be said without exaggeration, was untiring in his efforts to straighten out what the German opportunists had distorted.

The end of 1884. The "petty-bourgeois prejudices" of the German Social-Democratic Reichstag deputies, who voted for the steamship subsidy (*Dampfersubvention,* see Mehring's *History*) are condemned. Engels informs Sorge that he has to carry on a great deal of correspondence on this subject (letter of December 31, 1884).[2]

1885. Assessing the whole *Dampfersubvention* affair, Engels writes (June 3) that "it almost resulted in a split." The "philistinism" of the Social-Democratic deputies was *"colossal."* "A petty-bourgeois Socialist fraction is unavoidable in a country like Germany," Engels says.[3]

1887. Engels replies to Sorge, who had written that the party was disgracing itself by electing such deputies as Viereck (a Social-Democrat of the Höchberg type). That can't be helped—Engels excuses himself—the workers' party cannot find good deputies for the Reichstag.

"The gentlemen of the right wing know that they are being tolerated merely because of the Socialist Law, and will be thrown out at once the day the party regains freedom of action."

And, in general, it is preferable for "the party to be better than its parliamentary heroes — rather than the other way round" (March 3, 1887). Liebknecht is a conciliator — Engels complains — he always glosses over differences by phrases. But when it comes to a split, he will be with us at the decisive moment.[4]

1889. Two International Social-Democratic congresses in Paris. The opportunists (headed by the French possibilists) split away from the revolutionary Social-Democrats. Engels (he was then sixty-eight years old) flings himself into the battle like a young man. A number of letters (from January 12 to July 20, 1889), are devoted to the fight against the opportunists. Not only they, but also the Germans—Liebknecht, Bebel, and others — are castigated for their attitude of compromise.

The possibilists have sold out to the government, writes Engels on January 12, 1889. And he accuses the members of the British Social-Democratic Federation of having allied themselves with the possibilists.[5]

"The writing and running about in connection with this damned congress leave me hardly any time for anything else." (May 11, 1889.)[6]

[1] See p. 132.   [4] See p. 176.
[2] See p. 144.   [5] See pp. 208-09.
[3] See p. 147.   [6] See p. 212.

The possibilists are busy, but our people are asleep, Engels writes angrily. Now even Auer and Schippel are demanding that we attend the possibilist congress. But this "at last" opened Liebknecht's eyes. Engels, together with Bernstein, writes pamphlets (signed by Bernstein—Engels calls them "our pamphlets") against the opportunists.

"With the exception of the S.D.F., the possibilists haven't a single socialist organisation in all Europe. [June 8, 1889.] They are therefore falling back on the non-socialist trade unions [let our advocates of a broad labor party, of a labor congress, etc., take note!] They will get one *Knight of Labor* from America."

The adversary is the same as in the fight against the Bakuninists:

"With the anarchist flag merely exchanged for the possibilist one: the selling of principles to the bourgeoisie for small-scale concessions, especially in return for well-paid jobs for the leaders (city council, labor exchange, etc.)."

Brousse (the leader of the possibilists) and Hyndman (the leader of the S.D.F., united with the possibilists) attack "authoritarian Marxism" and want to form the "nucleus of a new International."

"You have no idea of the Germans' naïveté. It has cost me tremendous effort to convince even Bebel of what it really means." (June 8, 1889.)[1] And when the two congresses met, when the revolutionary Social-Democrats numerically exceeded the possibilists (*united with the trade unionists,* the S.D.F., part of the Austrians, etc.), Engels was jubilant (July 17, 1889).[2] He was glad that the conciliatory plans and proposals of Liebknecht and others had failed (July 20, 1889).

"It serves our sentimental conciliatory brethren right, to get this stiff kick in their tenderest spot for all their protestations of friendship. That will probably cure them for some time to come."[3]

. . . Mehring was right when he said (*"Der Sorgesche Briefwechsel"*) that Marx and Engels knew little about "good form":

"If they did not think long over every blow they dealt, neither did they whimper over every blow they received. 'If they think their needlepricks can pierce my old well-tanned and pachydermatous hide, they are mistaken,' Engels once wrote."

And this insensibility they had acquired, says Mehring of Marx and Engels, they took for granted in others as well.

1893. The settling of accounts with the "Fabians," which obviously suggests itself . . . for judging the Bernsteinians (was it not among the "Fabians" in England that Bernstein "learned" his opportunism?).

"The Fabians here in London are a band of careerists who have understanding enough to realize the inevitability of the social revolution, but who could not possibly entrust this tremendous job to the crude proletariat alone and are therefore kind enough to set themselves at the head. Fear of the revolution is their fundamental principle. They are the 'eddicated' *par excellence.* Their socialism is municipal socialism; the *community,* not the nation, should become the owner of the means of production, at least temporarily. This socialism of theirs is then represented as an extreme but inevitable consequence of bourgeois liberalism, and from this follow

---

[1] See pp. 215-16.   [3] See p. 219.

[2] See p. 217.

their tactics, not to fight the Liberals decisively as opponents, but to push them on to socialist conclusions: therefore to intrigue with them, to *permeate* Liberalism with socialism—not to put up Socialist candidates against Liberals, but to palm them off and force them upon the Liberals, or to deceive the latter into taking them. They naturally do not realize that in doing this they are either betrayed and deceived themselves or else are betraying socialism.

"With great industry they have produced, among all sorts of rubbish, some good propaganda writing as well, in fact, the best that the English have turned out in this respect. But as soon as they come to their specific tactic: hushing up the class struggle, it gets rotten. Hence, too, their fanatical hatred of Marx and of all of us—because of the class struggle.

"These people have, of course, a considerable bourgeois following and hence money. . . ."[1]

A CLASSICAL APPRAISAL OF THE OPPORTUNISM OF THE INTELLECTUALS IN SOCIAL-DEMOCRACY

1894. The Peasant Question. "On the Continent," Engels writes on November 10, 1894, "success is developing the appetite for more success, and catching the peasant, in the literal sense of the word, is becoming the fashion. First the French, in Nantes, declare through Lafargue not only . . . that it is not our business to hasten . . . the ruin of the small peasants, which capitalism is effecting for us, but they add that we must *protect* the small peasant directly against taxation, usury, and big landowners. But we cannot join in this, first because it is stupid and second because it is impossible. And now Vollmar comes along in Frankfort, wanting to bribe the *peasantry as a whole,* though the peasant he has to deal with in Upper Bavaria is not the debt-ridden small peasant of the Rhineland, but the middle and even the big peasant, who exploits his male and female farmhands and sells cattle and grain in quantity. And that cannot be done without giving up the whole principle."[2]

1894, December 4.

" . . . The Bavarians, who have become very, very opportunistic and are *almost* an ordinary populist party by now (that is to say, most of the leaders and many of those who have recently joined the party), had voted in the Bavarian Diet for the budget as a whole. Vollmar, in particular, had started agitation among the peasantry in order to win over, *not the farm hands,* but the well-to-do peasants of Upper Bavaria— people who own 25 to 80 acres of land (10 to 30 hectares), who therefore *cannot manage at all without wage laborers.*"[3]

We thus see that for more than ten years Marx and Engels systematically and unswervingly fought opportunism in the German Social-Democratic Party and attacked intellectual philistinism and petty-bourgeois narrow-mindedness in socialism. This is an extremely important fact. The general public knows that German Social-Democracy is regarded as a model of the

[1] See p. 247.   [3] See p. 266.
[2] See pp. 264-65.

Marxist policy and tactics of the proletariat, but it does not know what a constant war the founders of Marxism had to wage against the "right wing" (Engels' expression) of that party. And it is no accident that soon after Engels' death this war turned from a concealed into an open war. This was the inevitable result of the decades of historical development of German Social-Democracy.

And now we very clearly perceive the two lines of Engels' (and Marx's) recommendations, directives, corrections, threats, and exhortations. They most insistently called upon the British and American Socialists to merge with the labor movement and to eradicate the narrow and hidebound sectarian spirit from their organizations. They most insistently taught the German Social-Democrats: do not succumb to philistinism, to "parliamentary idiocy" (Marx's expression in the letter of September 19, 1879),[1] to petty-bourgeois intellectual opportunism.

Is it not characteristic that our Social-Democratic gossips have noisily proclaimed the recommendations of the first kind and have pursed their lips, remained silent about the recommendations of the second kind? Is not *such* one-sidedness in appraising Marx's and Engels' letters the best indication, in a sense, of our, Russian, Social-Democratic "one-sidedness"?

At the present time, when the international labor movement is displaying symptoms of profound ferment and wavering, when extremes of opportunism, "parliamentary idiocy," and philistine reformism have evoked opposite extremes of revolutionary syndicalism, the general line of Marx's and Engels' "corrections" to British, American, and German socialism acquires exceptional importance.

In countries where there are *no* Social-Democratic workers' parties, *no* Social-Democratic members of parliament, *no* systematic and consistent Social-Democratic policy either at elections or in the press, etc., Marx and Engels taught the Socialists *at all costs* to rid themselves of narrow sectarianism and *join* the labor movement so as to rouse the proletariat *politically, for* in the last third of the nineteenth century the proletariat displayed *almost no* political independence either in England or America. In these countries — where bourgeois-democratic historical tasks were almost entirely absent — the political arena was *wholly* filled by the triumphant and self-complacent bourgeoisie, which has no equal anywhere in the world in the art of deceiving, corrupting, and bribing the workers.

To think that these recommendations of Marx and Engels to the British and American labor movement can be simply and directly applied to Russian conditions is to use Marxism not in order to elucidate its *method*, not in order to *study* the concrete historical peculiarities of the labor movement in certain countries, but in order to settle petty factional, intellectual accounts.

On the other hand, in a country where the bourgeois-democratic revolution was still incomplete, where "military despotism, embellished with parliamentary forms" (Marx's expression in his *Critique of the Gotha Programme*) prevailed, and still prevails, where the proletariat had long ago been drawn into politics and was pursuing a Social-Democratic policy, what Marx and Engels feared most of all in such a country was parliamen-

[1] See p. 121.

tary vulgarization and the philistine compromising of the tasks and scope of the labor movement.

It is all the more our duty to emphasize and advance this side of Marxism in the period of the bourgeois-democratic revolution in Russia because in our country an extensive, "brilliant," and rich bourgeois-liberal press is vociferously trumpeting to the proletariat the "exemplary" loyalty, the parliamentary legalism, the modesty, and the moderation of the neighboring German labor movement.

This mercenary lie of the bourgeois betrayers of the Russian revolution is not due to accident or to the personal depravity of certain past or future ministers in the Cadet[1] camp. It is motivated by profound economic interests of the Russian liberal landowners and bourgeois liberals. And in combating this lie, this "stupefying the masses" (*Massenverdummung* — Engels' expression in his letter of November 29, 1886),[2] the letters of Marx and Engels should serve as an indispensable weapon for all Russian Socialists.

The mercenary lie of the bourgeois liberals holds up to the people the exemplary "modesty" of the German Social-Democrats. The leaders of these Social-Democrats, the founders of the theory of Marxism, tell us:

"The revolutionary language and action of the Frenchmen made the whining of the Vierecks and Co. (the opportunist Social-Democrats in the German Reichstag Social-Democratic fraction) appear feebler than ever (the reference is to the formation of a labor party in the French Chamber and to the Decazeville strike, which split the French Radicals from the French proletariat), and thus only Bebel and Liebknecht spoke in the last debate . . . both of them very good. With this debate we can show our faces in respectable society again, which was by no means the case with all of them. In general, it is good for the Germans to have their leadership (of the international socialist movement) disputed somewhat, especially since they have elected so many philistine elements (which was unavoidable, to be sure). *In Germany everything becomes philistine in quiet periods;* the spur of French competition then becomes *absolutely necessary* [Lenin's emphasis]. . . ." (Letter of April 29, 1886.)[3]

Such are the lessons which must be drawn most firmly of all by the R.S.D.L.P.[3] which is ideologically dominated by the influence of German Social-Democracy.[4]

These lessons are taught us not by any particular passage in the correspondence of the greatest men of the nineteenth century, but by the whole spirit and substance of their comradely and frank criticism, free from diplomacy and petty considerations, of the international experience of the proletariat.

How far all the letters of Marx and Engels were indeed imbued with this spirit may also be seen from the following passages, which are, to

[1] Constitutional Democrats, bourgeois-monarchist party in tsarist Russia.—*Ed.*
[2] See p. 164.   [3] See p. 155.
[4] Russian Social-Democratic Labor Party, renamed Communist Party in 1917. —*Ed.*
[5] The Mensheviks were still members of the Russian Social-Democratic Party at the time of the writing of this preface.—*Ed.*

be sure, comparatively fragmentary, but, on the other hand, are highly characteristic.

In 1889 a young, fresh movement of untrained, unskilled, ordinary laborers (gasworkers, dockers, etc.) began in England, a movement full of a new and revolutionary spirit. Engels was delighted with it. He refers exultingly to the part played by Tussy, Marx's daughter, who agitated among these workers.

"The most repulsive thing here," he says, writing from London on December 7, 1889, "is the bourgeois 'respectability' that has sunk deep into the bone of the workers. The division of society into innumerable strata, each recognized without question, each with its own pride but also its inborn respect for its 'betters' and 'superiors,' is so old and firmly established that the bourgeois still find it fairly easy to have their bait accepted. I am not at all sure, for instance, that John Burns is not secretly prouder of his popularity with Cardinal Manning, the Lord Mayor, and the bourgeoisie in general than of his popularity with his own class. And Champion—an ex-lieutenant—has always intrigued with bourgeois and, especially, with conservative elements, preached socialism at the parsons' Church Congress, etc. And even Tom Mann, whom I regard as the best of the lot, likes to mention that he will be lunching with the Lord Mayor. If one compares this with the French, one realizes what a revolution is good for after all." [1]

Comment is superfluous.

Another example. In 1891 there was danger of a European war. Engels corresponded on the subject with Bebel, and they agreed that in the event of Russia attacking Germany, the German Socialists must desperately fight the Russians and any allies of the Russians.

"If Germany is crushed, then we shall be too, while in the most favorable case the struggle will be such a violent one that Germany will be able to maintain itself only by revolutionary means, so that very possibly we shall be forced to come into power and play the part of 1793." (Letter of October 24, 1891.) [2]

Let this be noted by those opportunists who cried from the housetops that "Jacobin" prospects for the Russian workers' party in 1905 were un-Social-Democratic! Engels squarely suggests to Bebel the possibility of the Social-Democrats having to participate in a provisional government.

Holding such views on the tasks of Social-Democratic workers' parties, Marx and Engels were filled with the most fervent faith in the Russian revolution and its great worldwide significance. We see this ardent expectation of a revolution in Russia in this correspondence over a period of nearly twenty years.

Here is Marx's letter of September 27, 1877. The Eastern crisis arouses Marx's enthusiasm:

"Russia . . . has long been standing on the threshold of an upheaval; all the elements for it are prepared. The gallant Turks have hastened the explosion by years through the blows they have dealt. . . . The upheaval

[1] See p. 221.
[2] See p. 238.

will begin *secundum artem* (according to the rules of the art) with some *playing at constitutionalism* [Lenin's emphasis], and then there will be a fine row *(il y aura un beau tapage)*. If Mother Nature is not particularly hard on us we shall still live to see the fun!"[1] Marx was then fifty-one years old.)

Mother Nature did not—and could not very well—permit Marx to live "to see the fun." But he *foretold* the "playing at constitutionalism," and it is as though his words were written yesterday about the First and Second Russian Dumas.[2] And we know that the warning to the people against "playing at constitutionalism" was the "living soul" of the boycott tactics so detested by the liberals and opportunists. . . .

Here is Marx's letter of November 5, 1880. He is delighted with the success of *Capital* in Russia, and takes the part of the Populists against the newly arisen Black Redistribution group. Marx correctly perceives the anarchistic elements in the latter's views, and, not knowing and at the time having no opportunity of knowing the future evolution of the Black Redistribution Populists into Social-Democrats, Marx attacks the Black Redistribution group with all the power of his trenchant sarcasm:

"These gentlemen are against all political-revolutionary action. Russia is to leap into the anarchist-communist-atheist millennium in one breakneck jump! In the meantime, they are preparing for this leap by a tiresome doctrinairism, whose so-called principles have been commonplaces ever since the late Bakunin." [3]

We can gather from this how Marx would have appraised the importance of the "political-revolutionary action" of *Social-Democracy* for Russia of 1905 and the following years.[4]

Here is a letter by Engels dated April 6, 1887:

"On the other hand, the crisis in Russia seems to be impending. The recent assassinations have fairly capped the climax. . . . "

A letter of April 9, 1887, says the same thing.

"The army is full of discontented, conspiring officers. [Engels at that time was influenced by the revolutionary struggle of the People's Will party, setting his hopes on the officers and not yet seeing the revolutionary *élan* of the Russian soldier and sailor disclosed so magnificently eighteen years later (Note by Lenin)]. . . . I do not believe it will last out this year. . . . And if it but starts *(losgeht)* in Russia, then hurrah!" [5]

A letter of April 23, 1887:

"In Germany one persecution (of the Socialists) after another. It seems

[1] See p. 115.

[2] Following the Revolution of 1905, a Duma (parliament) based on limited suffrage and exercising limited powers was established. The First Duma was elected in 1906 and its second in 1907. Both Dumas were prorogued by the Tsarist government.—*Ed.*

[3] See p. 126.

[4] By the way, if my memory does not deceive me, Plekhanov or V. I. Zasulich told me in 1900-03 about the existence of a letter of Engels to Plekhanov on *Our Differences* and on the character of the impending revolution in Russia. It would be interesting to know precisely—is there such a letter, does it still exist, and is it not time to publish it?—*Note by Lenin.* See letter in Marx-Engels, *Selected Correspondence,* International Publishers, 1935, pp. 436-38.—*Ed.*

[5] See p. 182.

that Bismarck wants to have everything ready, so that when the revolution breaks out in Russia, which is probably only a question of months, it can immediately be started (*losgeschlagen werden*) in Germany too." [1]

The months proved to be very long ones. Doubtless, philistines will be found who, knitting their brows and wrinkling their foreheads, will sternly condemn Engels' "revolutionism" or indulgently laugh at the old utopias of the old revolutionary exile.

Yes, Marx and Engels erred much and erred often in determining the closeness of the revolution, in their hopes in the victory of the revolution (*e.g.*, in 1848 in Germany), in their faith in the imminence of a German "republic" ("to die for the republic," wrote Engels of that period, recalling his sentiments as a participant in the military campaign for an imperial constitution in 1848-49). They erred in 1871 when they were engaged in "raising revolt in Southern France, for which" they (Becker writes "we," referring to himself and his closest friends: Letter No. 14 [from Johann Philipp Becker to Sorge] of July 21, 1871) "worked, sacrificed, and risked all that was humanly possible. . . . " The same letter says: "If we had had more funds in March and April, we would have roused the whole of Southern France to revolt and would have saved the Commune in Paris."

But *such* errors of titans of revolutionary thought, who tried to raise and did raise the proletariat of the whole world above the level of petty, commonplace, and trifling tasks, are a thousand times nobler, more sublime, and *historically truer and more valuable* than the trivial wisdom of official liberalism, which sings, shouts, appeals, and jabbers about the vanity of revolutionary vanities, the futility of revolutionary struggle, and the charms of counter-revolutionary "constitutional" rot. . . .

The Russian working class will win its freedom and give a fillip to Europe by its revolutionary action, full though it may be of mistakes—and let the vulgarians pride themselves on the infallibility of their revolutionary inaction.

April 6, 1907

II

THE LABOR MOVEMENT IN THE UNITED STATES

Ten months have elapsed since, at the translator's wish, I wrote the Appendix to this book; [2] and during these ten months, a revolution has been accomplished in American society such as, in any other country,

[1] See p. 184.

[2] The American edition of *The Conditions of the Working Class in England in 1844*. Published in New York in 1887, this was the first edition of the book in English language, the original German edition having been issued in Germany in 1845. The book did not appear in England until 1892. The translation for the American edition was done by Florence Kelley Wischnewetzky, and it was edited and revised by Engels. His special preface for the American edition is reproduced here. (See pp. 145-200 *passim*.)

would have taken at least ten years. In February 1885, American public opinion was almost unanimous on this one point; that there was no working class, in the European sense of the word, in America; that consequently no class struggle between workmen and capitalists, such as tore European society to pieces, was possible in the American Republic; and that, therefore, socialism was a thing of foreign importation which could never take root on American soil. And yet, at that moment, the coming class struggle was casting its gigantic shadow before it in the strikes of the Pennsylvania coal miners, and of many other trades, and especially in the preparations, all over the country, for the great eight hours' movement which was to come off and did come off in the May following. That I then duly appreciated these symptoms, that I anticipated a working class movement on a national scale, my "Appendix" shows; but no one could then foresee that in such a short time the movement would burst out with such irresistible force, would spread with the rapidity of a prairie fire, would shake American society to its very foundations.

The fact is there, stubborn and indisputable. To what an extent it had struck with terror the American ruling classes, was revealed to me, in an amusing way, by American journalists who did me the honor of calling on me last summer; the "new departure" had put them into a state of helpless fright and perplexity. But at that time the movement was only just on the start; there was but a series of confused and apparently disconnected upheavals of that class which, by the suppression of Negro slavery and the rapid development of manufactures, had become the lowest stratum of American society. Before the year closed, these bewildering social convulsions began to take a definite direction. The spontaneous, instinctive movements of these vast masses of working people, over a vast extent of country, the simultaneous outburst of their common discontent with a miserable social condition, the same everywhere and due to the same causes, made them conscious of the fact, that they formed a new and distinct class of American society: a class of—practically speaking—more or less hereditary wage-workers, proletarians. And with true American instinct this consciousness led them at once to take the next step towards their deliverance: the formation of a political workingmen's party, with a platform of its own, and with the conquest of the Capitol and the White House for its goal. In May the struggle for the eight hours' working-day, the troubles in Chicago, Milwaukee, etc., the attempts of the ruling class to crush the nascent uprising of labor by brute force and brutal class justice; in November the new Labor Party organized in all great centers, and the New York, Chicago and Milwaukee elections. May and November have hitherto reminded the American bourgeoisie only of the payment of coupons of U. S. bonds; henceforth May and November will remind them too, of the dates on which the American working class presented *their* coupons for payment.

In European countries, it took the working class years and years before they fully realized the fact that they formed a distinct and, under the existing social conditions, a permanent class of modern society; and it took years again until this class-consciousness led them to form themselves into a distinct political party, independent of, and opposed to, all the old political parties, formed by the various sections of the ruling classes. On the more favored soil of America, where no medieval ruins bar the way, where history begins with the elements of the modern bourgeois society as evolved in the seventeenth century, the working class passed through these two stages of its development within ten months.

Still, all this is but a beginning. That the laboring masses should feel their community of grievances and of interests, their solidarity as a class in opposition to all other classes; that in order to give expression and effect to this feeling, they should set in motion the political machinery provided for that purpose in every free country—that is the first step only. The next step is to find the common remedy for these common grievances, and to embody it in the platform of the new Labor Party. And this—the most important and the most difficult step in the movement—has yet to be taken in America.

A new party must have a distinct positive platform, a platform which may vary in details as circumstances vary and as the party itself develops, but still one upon which the party, for the time being, is agreed. So long as such a platform has not been worked out, or exists but in a rudimentary form, so long the new party, too, will have but a rudimentary existence; it may exist locally but not yet nationally; it will be a party potentially but not actually.

That platform, whatever may be its first initial shape, must develop in a direction which may be determined beforehand. The causes that brought into existence the abyss between the working class and the capitalist class are the same in America as in Europe; the means of filling up that abyss are equally the same everywhere. Consequently, the platform of the American proletariat will in the long run coincide as to the ultimate end to be attained, with the one which, after sixty years of dissensions and discussions, has become the adopted platform of the great mass of the European militant proletariat. It will proclaim, as the ultimate end, the conquest of political supremacy by the working class, in order to effect the direct appropriation of all means of production—land, railways, mines, machinery, etc.—by society at large, to be worked in common by all for the account and benefit of all.

But if the new American party, like all political parties everywhere, by the very fact of its formation aspires to the conquest of political power, it is as yet far from agreed upon what to do with that power when once attained. In New York and the other great cities of the East, the organization of the working class has proceeded upon the lines of trades' societies, forming in each city a powerful Central Labor Union. In New York the Central Labor Union, last November, chose for its standard bearer Henry George, and consequently its temporary electoral platform has been largely imbued with his principles. In the great cities of the Northwest, the electoral battle was fought upon a rather indefinite labor platform, and the influence of Henry George's theories was scarcely, if at all, visible. And while in these great centers of population and of industry the new class movement came to a political head, we find all over the country two widespread labor organizations: the Knights of Labor and the Socialist Labor

Party, of which only the latter has a platform in harmony with the modern European standpoint as summarized above.

Of the three more or less definite forms under which the American labor movement thus presents itself, the first, the Henry George movement in New York, is for the moment of a chiefly local significance. No doubt New York is by far the most important city of the States; but New York is not Paris and the United States are not France. And it seems to me that the Henry George platform, in its present shape, is too narrow to form the basis for anything but a local movement, or at least for a short-lived phase of the general movement. To Henry George, the expropriation of the mass of the people from the land is the great and universal cause of the splitting up of the people into rich and poor. Now this is not quite correct historically. In Asiatic and classical antiquity, the predominant form of class oppression was slavery, that is to say, not so much the expropriation of the masses from the land as the appropriation of their persons. When, in the decline of the Roman Republic, the free Italian peasants were expropriated from their farms, they formed a class of "poor whites" similar to that of the Southern slave states before 1861; and between slaves and poor whites, two classes equally unfit for self-emancipation, the old world went to pieces.

In the Middle Ages, it was not the expropriation of the people *from,* but on the contrary, their appropriation *to* the land which became the source of feudal oppression. The peasant retained his land, but was attached to it as a serf or villein, and made liable to tribute to the lord in labor and in produce. It was only at the dawn of modern times, towards the end of the fifteenth century, that the expropriation of the peasantry on a large scale laid the foundation for the modern class of wage-workers who possess nothing but their labor power and can live only by the selling of that labor power to others. But if the expropriation from the land brought this class into existence, it was the development of capitalist production, of modern industry and agriculture on a large scale which perpetuated it, increased it, and shaped it into a distinct class with distinct interests and a distinct historical mission. All this has been fully expounded by Marx (*Capital,* Part VIII: "The So-called Primitive Accumulation"). According to Marx, the cause of the present antagonism of the classes and of the social degradation of the working class is their expropriation from *all* means of production, in which the land is of course included.

If Henry George declares land monopolization to be the sole cause of poverty and misery, he naturally finds the remedy in the resumption of the land by society at large. Now, the Socialists of the school of Marx, too, demand the resumption, by society, of the land, and not only of the land but of all other means of production likewise. But even if we leave these out of the question, there is another difference. What is to be done with the land? Modern Socialists, as represented by Marx, demand that it should be held and worked in common and for common account, and the same with all other means of social production, mines, railways, factories, etc.; Henry George would confine himself to letting it out to individuals as at present, merely regulating its distribution and applying the rents for public, instead of, as at present, for private purposes. What the Socialists demand, implies a total revolution of the whole system of social production; what Henry George demands, leaves the present mode of social production untouched, and has, in fact, been anticipated by the extreme section of Ricardian bourgeois economists who, too, demanded the confiscation of the rent of land by the state.

It would of course be unfair to suppose that Henry George has said his last word once for all. But I am bound to take his theory as I find it.

The second great section of the American movement is formed by the Knights of Labor. And that seems to be the section most typical of the present state of the movement, as it is undoubtedly by far the strongest. An immense association spread over an immense extent of country in innumerable "assemblies," representing all shades of individual and local opinion within the working class; the whole of them sheltered under a platform of corresponding indistinctness and held together much less by their impracticable constitution than by the instinctive feeling that the very fact of their clubbing together for their common aspiration makes them a great power in the country; a truly American paradox clothing the most modern tendencies in the most medieval mummeries, and hiding the most democratic and even rebellious spirit behind an apparent, but really powerless despotism—such is the picture the Knights of Labor offer to a European observer. But if we are not arrested by mere outside whimsicalities, we cannot help seeing in this vast agglomeration an immense amount of potential energy evolving slowly but surely into actual force. The Knights of Labor are the first national organization created by the American working class as a whole; whatever be their origin and history, whatever their shortcomings and little absurdities, whatever their platform and their constitution, here they are, the work of practically the whole class of American wage workers, the only national bond that holds them together, that makes their strength felt to themselves not less than to their enemies, and that fills them with the proud hope of future victories. For it would not be exact to say that the Knights of Labor are liable to development. They are constantly in full process of development and revolution; a heaving, fermenting mass of plastic material seeking the shape and form appropriate to its inherent nature. That form will be attained as surely as historical evolution has, like natural evolution, its own immanent laws. Whether the Knights of Labor will then retain their present name or not, makes no difference, but to an outsider it appears evident that here is the raw material out of which the future of the American working-class movement, and along with it, the future of American society at large, has to be shaped.

The third section consists of the Socialist Labor Party. This section is a party but in name, for nowhere in America has it, up to now, been able actually to take its stand as a political party. It is, moreover, to a certain extent foreign to America, having until lately been made up almost exclusively by German immigrants, using their own language and, for the most part, little conversant with the common language of the country. But if it came from a foreign stock, it came, at the same time, armed with the experience earned during long years of class struggle in Europe, and with an insight into the general conditions of working-class emancipation, far superior to that hitherto gained by American workingmen. This is a fortunate circumstance for the American proletarians who thus are enabled to appropriate, and to take advantage of the intellectual and moral fruits of the forty years' struggle of their European classmates, and thus to hasten on the time of their own victory. For, as I said before, there cannot be any doubt that the ultimate platform of the American working class must and will be essentially the same as that now adopted by the whole militant working class of Europe, the same as that of the German-American Socialist Labor Party. In so far as this party is called upon to play a very important part in the movement. But in order to do so they will have to doff every remnant of their foreign garb. They will have to become out and out American. They cannot expect the Americans to come to them; they, the minority and the immigrants, must go to the Americans, who are the vast majority and the natives. And to do that, they must above all things learn English.

The process of fusing together these various elements of the vast moving mass—elements not really discordant, but indeed mutually isolated by their various starting-points—will take some time and will not come off without a deal of friction, such as is visible at different points even now. The Knights of Labor, for instance, are here and there, in the Eastern cities, locally at war with the organized trades unions. But then this same friction exists within the Knights of Labor themselves, where there is anything but peace and harmony. These are not symptoms of decay, for capitalists to crow over. They are merely signs that the innumerable hosts of workers, for the first time set in motion in a common direction, have as yet found out neither the adequate expression for their common interests, nor the form of organization best adapted to the struggle, nor the discipline required to insure victory. They are as yet the first *levées en masse* of the great revolutionary war, raised and equipped locally and independently, all converging to form one common army, but as yet without regular organization and common plan of campain. The converging columns cross each other here and there; confusion, angry disputes, even threats of conflict arise. But the community of ultimate purpose in the end overcomes all minor troubles; ere long the struggling and squabbling battalions will be formed in a long line of battle array, presenting to the enemy a well-ordered front, ominously silent under their glittering arms, supported by bold skirmishers in front and by unshakable reserves in the rear.

To bring about this result, the unification of the various independent bodies into one national labor army, with no matter how inadequate a provisional platform, provided it be a truly working-class platform—that is the next great step to be accomplished in America. To effect this, and to make that platform worthy of the cause, the Socialist Labor Party can contribute a great deal, if they will only act in the same way as the European Socialists have acted at the time when they were but a small minority of the working class. That line of action was first laid down in the *Communist Manifesto* of 1848 in the following words:

"The Communists [that was the name we took at the time and which even now we are far from repudiating] do not form a separate party opposed to other working-class parties.

"They have no interests separate and apart from those of the proletariat as a whole.

"They do not set up any sectarian principles of their own, by which to shape and mould the proletarian movement.

"The Communists are distinguished from the other working-class parties by this only: 1. In the national struggles of the proletarians of the different countries, they point out and bring to the front the common interests of the entire proletariat, independently of all nationality; 2. In the various stages of development which the struggle of the working class against the bourgeoisie has to pass through, they always and everywhere represent the interests of the movement as a whole.

"The Communists, therefore, are on the one hand, practically, the most advanced and resolute section of the working-class parties of every country, that section which pushes forward all others; on the other hand, theoretically, they have over the great mass of the proletariat the advantage of clearly understanding the line of march, the conditions, and the ultimate general results of the proletarian movement. . . .

"The Communists fight for the attainment of the immediate aims, for the enforcement of the momentary interests of the working class; but in the movement of the present, they also represent and take care of the future of that movement." [1]

That is the line of action which the great founder of modern socialism, Karl Marx, and with him, I and the Socialists of all nations who worked along with us, have followed for more than forty years, with the result that it has led to victory everywhere, and that at this moment the mass of European Socialists, in Germany and in France, in Belgium, Holland and Switzerland, in Denmark and Sweden, as well as in Spain and Portugal, are fighting as one common army under one and the same flag.

Frederick Engels

London, January 26, 1887

III

AMERICAN TRAVEL NOTES [2]

September 1888

We usually think of America as a New World, new not merely because of when it was discovered, but new in all its institutions—a world far ahead of us old-fashioned, sleepy Europeans with its disdain for everything traditional, handed down from the past, a world built entirely anew

[1] *The Communist Manifesto,* New York, 1948, pp. 22, 43.—*Ed.*

[2] This fragment was written by Engels on the letterhead of the steamship company while aboard the *City of New York* en route to Europe. He intended to use it later for an article for *Die Neue Zeit;* the article was never written.

on virgin soil by modern people and founded on modern, practical, rational principles. For their part, the Americans strive to confirm us in this opinion. They look down upon us with scorn, considering us to be sluggish, impractical people, with hidebound, antiquated prejudices, dreading everything new, while they, the most progressive nation, boisterously developing, instantly try out any plan for improvement simply from the standpoint of its practical advantages and, if the plan is found to be good, put it into effect immediately, almost the very next day. Everything in America has to be new, everything has to be rational, everything has to be practical, consequently, everything is different from what it is with us.

On the steamship *City of Berlin* I encountered a fairly large group of Americans for the first time. Most of them were very nice people, both men and women, more social than the English, occasionally too outspoken. but otherwise pretty much like more or less well-dressed people everywhere. What set them apart, in any case, was their singular petty-bourgeois bearing: not the bearing that is characteristic of the timid, diffident German philistine or the English bourgeois, but a bearing that seems to be the inherent trait of its possessor, as the result of the unconstrained, most matter-of-course, fullest self-confidence. The young ladies, in particular, gave the impression of a certain naïveté, such as could be encountered in Europe only in the smaller towns. When they walk along the deck energetically and almost impetuously, arm in arm or on the arm of a man, they have such a light, dancing stride, and—like our simple village belles—they hold their skirts demurely if a gust of wind threatens. In their health and stature they reminded me most of all of the Swedes, and it seemed to me that they were just about to make curtsies, as Swedish women do. My American fellow-travelers have inherited a bit of the physical and mental awkwardness that is the universal congenital trait of the Germanic race, nor have they overcome it at all. In short, my first impressions of Americans by no means indicated their national superiority to Europeans or that I had met with a new, young, national type. On the contrary, I came to the conclusion that these were a people stubbornly holding on to inherited petty-bourgeois customs that were considered old-fashioned in Europe, and that in this respect Europeans are, compared to Americans, what Parisians are compared to people from the provinces.

In New York, when I first entered my bedroom, I found furniture of the most antediluvian style one could imagine: chests of drawers with brass rings or bows as drawer handles, the kind that were in fashion at the beginning of this century and are still found in villages; nearby there shone objects in a later style, English or French, but they, too, were old-fashioned enough and, moreover, not in their right place. The latest thing is a tremendous rocking-chair, describing an arc of 240° and likewise out of fashion. And the picture is the same everywhere. Tables, chairs, and wardrobes look for the most part as if they had been inherited from bygone generations. The vehicles in the streets of New York look so old-fashioned that at first glance it seems that carts of this make can't be found in a single farmyard in Europe. When one looks at them more closely, to be sure, one notices that these vehicles are considerably improved, very comfortable, fitted with excellent springs, extremely light, and made of extremely strong wood, but with all these improvements the old-fashioned model has remained inviolate. London still had cabs at the beginning of the forties, which the passengers entered from the rear, sitting opposite one another at the right and left, as in an omnibus; these cabs disappeared after 1850. These boxes on wheels still flourish today in Boston—the only American city, so far as I know, where they actually use droshkies. [Russian horse-drawn cab.]

Modern American hotels, with their luxurious equipment and hundreds of rooms, owe their purely American type of arrangement to the circumstance that they grew out of farmhouses located far from the colonies in sparsely settled areas, where even today board and lodgings for the night are offered the casual wayfarer (I shall return to this topic later) in return for payment. Hence their characteristic features, which to us seem to be not only peculiar, but also downright old-fashioned. And there is much along the same lines everywhere.

Anyone desiring to enjoy a trip that could have been made in Europe at the time of the Thirty Years' War should set out for any American mountain district, travel to the end of the railroad line, and then—by stagecoach—into the forests. The four of us made an excursion of this sort to the Adirondacks, and never did we laugh as uproariously as on the top of that stagecoach. An old wreck defying description, compared to which the celebrated Prussian carts of the days of yore would have been de luxe carriages, with seats in the same style for six or nine persons on the roof and on the coachboxes—that was what the structure was like. And then the road. I beg your pardon, that wasn't a road; one could hardly have called it a path: two deep ruts cut into the sandy clay soil, uphill and down. . . .

[The manuscript breaks off here]

BIOGRAPHICAL NOTES AND INDEX

tee of Communist League; later Lord Mayor of Mainz. 15

WALTHER, OTTO, German-American socialist; on Executive of Socialist Labor Party in New York after 1875; editor of New York labor papers, *Sozialdemokrat* and *Arbeiterstimme*. 172

WEBB, SIDNEY JAMES *(1859-1947)*, English sociologist, a founder of the Fabian Society; took a stand for the U.S.S.R. in his book, *Soviet Communism* (in collaboration with his wife, Beatrice Webb). 249

WEERTH, GEORG LUDWIG *(1822-1856)*, German poet and journalist; member of Communist League, feuilleton editor of *Neue Rheinische Zeitung;* called by Engels "the first and most important poet of the German proletariat." 25, 29-30, 32-33, 47, 60

WEITLING, WILHELM *(1808-1871)*, German-American Utopian communist, tailor by trade; joined League of the Just (1837); propagandized communist ideas in Paris and Switzerland (1835-41); published *Republik der Arbeiter* in New York (1850-55). 30, 117-18

WELLINGTON, ARTHUR WELLESLEY, DUKE OF *(1769-1852)*, British field marshal, commander-in-chief during Napoleonic wars; diehard Tory, Prime Minister (1827-29, 1834). 40, 67

WESTPHALEN, EDGAR VON *(1819-1890)*, brother of Jenny Marx and schoolmate of Karl Marx; joined Communist League in 1846; lived in U.S. for a long time. 47

WEYDEMEYER, JOSEPH *(1818-1866)*, German-American communist, editor, and soldier; pioneer American Marxist; emigrated to U.S. in 1851; published *Die Revolution* (1852) and on staff of *Die Reform,* both in New York; founded *Stimme des Volkes* in Chicago (1860); served in Union army, retiring as brigadier general; edited *Die Neue Zeit* in St. Louis after the war. 3-5, 9-11, 16-18, 20, 22-23, 25, 27-28, 30-33, 36-37, 40, 42, 46-48, 53, 60, 63, 65, 67

WHALEY, J. C. C., president of Washington Trades' Assembly and member of First International; first president of National Labor Union (1866). 74

WILLICH, AUGUST VON *(1810-1878)*, Prussian ex-officer, commanded a volunteer corps in Baden 1849 uprising; member of Central Committee of Communist League (1849-50); emigrated to U.S. (1853); fought in Union army, rising to brigadier general; later held high civil service post in Cincinnati. 16-17, 24, 57, 60, 64

WISCHNEWETZKY, MRS. *See* Florence Kelley.

WOLFF, FERDINAND ["RED WOLFF"] *(1812-ca. 1893)*, German democratic publicist, nicknamed "Red" because of his red beard and radical views; member of Communist League and of editorial staff of *Neue Rheinische Zeitung;* emigrated to England; broke with Marx in 1850's. 30-32

WOLFF, WILHELM ["LUPUS"] *(1809-1864)*, member of Central Committee of Communist League; an editor of *Neue Rheinische Zeitung* (1848-49); fought in Revolution of 1848; emigrated to England in 1851; a close friend of Marx and Engels, Vol. I of *Capital* is dedicated to him. 23, 25, 28-33, 38-39, 43, 48, 50-52, 60

WOODHULL, VICTORIA CLAFLIN *(1838-1927)*, American feminist and "social freedom" advocate; leader of Section No. 12 of First International in New York; with her sister, Tennessee Claflin, founded *Woodhull and Claflin's Weekly* (1870); nominated for President of the U.S. by Equal Rights Party (1872). 85

ZASULICH, VERA *(1851-1919)*, together with Plekhanov, a founder of Emancipation of Labor (1883), the first Marxist group in Russia; translated a number of Marx's works into Russian; became a Menshevik after split in Russian Social-Democratic Party (1903). 126 *n.*, 284